DEEP SELLING

DEEP SELLING

How to Engage Buyers and Drive Growth in the Age of AI

GRAHAM HAWKINS
MARK MICALLEF

WILEY

First published 2025 by John Wiley & Sons Australia, Ltd

ISBN: 978-1-394-30306-9

A catalogue record for this book is available from the National Library of Australia

Registered Office
John Wiley & Sons Australia, Ltd. Level 4, 600 Bourke Street, Melbourne, VIC 3000, Australia

For details of our global editorial offices, customer services, and more information about Wiley products visit us at www.wiley.com.

Wiley also publishes its books in a variety of electronic formats and by print-on-demand. Some content that appears in standard print versions of this book may not be available in other formats.

Cover design by Wiley

Set in Utopia 10.5pt/15pt by Straive, Chennai, India

SKY2178108F-2F20-4614-9389-6C351750E5DE_111524

CONTENTS

FOREWORD BY BRENT ADAMSON

The world of sales is constantly evolving. But it's evolving far too slowly.

Yes, we're using new tools, deploying new tactics and employing new technology, but the speed of change in B2B sales today is far too slow relative to the speed of change in everything else. Today's go-to-market models look completely different. Customer buying behavior has shifted dramatically. Technological and digital innovation threatens to cut out sales altogether. And generative AI is rapidly rewriting the rule book for ... everything.

Yet, inside the eye of this swirling storm of dramatic change, it's not uncommon to hear sales executives call for a return to the 'basic blocking and tackling of sales' that drove *their* success as sellers 10–20 years earlier. Indeed, if there were a single, common thread across most sales leaders' strategy for performance improvement, it would be an almost nostalgic call to 'get back to basics'. To return to a set of skills that worked at a time and in a commercial environment that no longer exists.

To be fair, many sales leaders seeking a 'return to the brass tacks of selling' are referring less to a set of specific skills or tactics and more to a sense of discipline and process they believe to be lacking across their team. They often express a desire for their team to work with 'a greater sense of urgency,' 'greater purpose', and 'a higher degree of precision' without fully articulating exactly what that might mean in terms of specific or concrete behaviors. Instead, they'll speak in terms of outcomes, rather than inputs: 'We need to have better customer conversations'; 'We need to help our customers see our value'; 'We need to create Raving Fans'. After all, those are the results they're looking to (re)capture with far greater consistency.

But if we step back for a moment, take our selling hat off, and look at B2B commerce through the lens of B2B buying, we begin to appreciate just how insufficient an individual seller strategy may be, no matter how disciplined, to drive sales success going forward.

Today's B2B buying is a world of complex solutions purchased by large, diverse buying groups, engaging across an increasingly broad range of digital and human-led channels, supported by a vast array of technology, data and AI. It is informed by an unfathomably deep library of online content, information and research, all supported by a diverse cast of third-party consultants, advisory services and independent advocates. Relying on individual sellers to effectively navigate this kind of complex, team-based buying environment through a simple upgrade to individual skills is like sharpening a knife to win a gun fight. It's not necessarily a bad idea, but it's likely to prove desperately insufficient nonetheless.

Today's world of B2B buying is emphatically a team-sport activity, spanning sometimes well over 10 different customer stakeholders each representing different functions, geographies, business units, organisational priorities and even performance metrics. To ask an individual seller to corral that kind of complexity on their own, no matter how skilled, is not only unfair, but far more importantly, unwise.

But you don't need to take my word for it. In *Deep Selling* Graham Hawkins and Mark Micallef break down, step by step, the range of challenges facing today's sales professionals — and sales organisations — supported by an extensive survey of recent B2B sales research and the synthesis of mountains of data. And the conclusion is pretty clear: The path forward for sales success is less an individual one than an organisational one. Effective selling is Deep Selling. And Deep Selling is a team sport.

What exactly is 'Deep Selling?' I'll let Graham and Mark unpack the concept in detail but, at a high level, Deep Selling represents a broad organisational strategy for winning, retaining and expanding customers through the entire customer lifecycle. It is not only an acknowledgement of the radically different commercial environment in which sales operates today, but both a tactical and strategic framework for adapting to that new reality.

At the heart of Deep Selling lies a deliberate, systemic shift to customer-centric selling, aligning the entire commercial organisation—sales, marketing, customer success, support, even partners—to engage customers on their terms, through their preferred channels, around their specific challenges.

In many ways, *Deep Selling* serves as the one-stop textbook for any senior executive looking to re-orient their entire organisation around the customer. Irrespective of role, function or level, *Deep Selling* provides tactical frameworks for assessing current performance, identifying the gaps in greatest need of upgrade, and prioritising practical next steps for rewiring the entire commercial enterprise.

Deep Selling isn't about individual upgrade, but organizational improvement. Effectively, it's a roadmap for building the go-to-market engine for today and tomorrow.

How do we win in a very different world of B2B buying? By building a completely new engine for B2B selling. *Deep Selling* is that engine.

Happy reading,
Brent Adamson

ABOUT THE AUTHORS

Graham Hawkins

Graham Hawkins is a globally recognised sales leader and international keynote speaker, having been voted one of the top 25 global sales leaders by CrunchBase and top 50 global sales experts and influencers by Thompson Reuters, along with receiving the 2018 LinkedIn Top Voice award.

He holds an MBA (Distinction) from RMIT University where he is an adjunct lecturer and is the author of two bestselling books: *The future of the sales profession* and *Sales transformation*. The founder and CEO of SalesTribe and Transform Sales International and founding member of The Sales Enablement Society, he has dedicated his career to figuring out what works in sales and how business-to-business (B2B) sales professionals and vendor organisations can adapt to the modern, buyer-led environment.

His most recent venture is co-founding Qoos.ai, an AI-Guided Selling platform for sales professionals, with Brent Adamson, co-author of bestselling books *The challenger sale* and *The challenger customer.*

Dr Mark Micallef

Dr Mark Micallef is a digital transformation expert with extensive experience in designing, building and deploying multi-year transformation programs in various industries. He holds a PhD in digital transformation and innovation management from RMIT University, where he is also an adjunct lecturer in strategic and network marketing.

Mark is a respected academic, having authored several publications in leading international journals including the *Journal of personal selling & sales management* and *Industrial marketing management*. His work has won several prestigious awards including *Industrial Marketing Management*'s Best thesis in B2B marketing for 2024.

He is also an experienced sales director, sales manager and salesperson, with more than 20 years of practical experience and a further eight years' experience consulting in sales, transformation, leadership and buyer success.

INTRODUCTION

Today's sales leaders find themselves in an almost impossible situation, caught in a vortex of competing pressures. They must meet the rising expectations of senior management and the board, adapt to the changing reality of the sales and buying landscapes, and find a way to boost falling sales team performance and reduce attrition rates. At the same time, new technologies promise to solve these challenges, and yet when vendor organisations attempt to innovate, these projects fail more often than they succeed.

How did we get here?

Simply, the rise of globalisation, digitalisation and servitisation have irrevocably transformed the sales and buying landscape.

From a buyer perspective, these trends mean buyers are more informed, have more choice and are therefore more powerful than ever before. However, this power has led to greater responsibility, and between 40 and 60 per cent of purchasing decisions now end in a 'no decision' outcome due to buyer fear of messing up.[1] Increased risk averseness means that buyers are less likely to take chances on unproven vendors than in the past, and they are rationalising the vendors they do have.

Meanwhile, globalisation and market maturity have led to higher competition across every industry, with lower barriers to entry than ever before. Previously niche products are becoming increasingly commoditised, forcing vendors to compete on price and squeezing vendor margins and profits. The combination of risk-averse buyers, higher competition and increased commoditisation often means the only way for vendor organisations to expand is within their existing buyer base.

Yet, despite these changes taking place, many vendor organisations continue to operate the same way they always have. Among many sales teams, and even at the executive level, there is a mistaken belief that sales is the way it's always been: just follow the script, follow the formula. One-hundred calls equals 30 interested parties. Thirty interested parties equals 10 meetings. Ten meetings equals three sales. Keep working the numbers and always be closing. This was what worked when your executives were in the field, and if it worked for them, why shouldn't it work for today's sales professionals?

While this might be the executive point of view, any switched-on sales leader knows that the old-world, push-selling, product-centric approach is no longer working. B2B sales cycles are longer than ever before, typically ranging from six to twelve months for complex, high-value solutions. Meanwhile, the time required to bring a new hire to full productivity is longer than ever, with 65.2 per cent of organisations saying it takes at least seven months to bring new hires up to speed, and 28.8 per cent of organisations saying it takes at least one year.[2] Average tenure among salespeople has also dropped to just 1.4 years (or 16.8 months), with the median annual turnover among sales professionals sitting at 50 per cent in 2022![3]

If you do the maths, this means the average salesperson only has time to complete one to two sales cycles before moving on to their next role, and many will not successfully close those sales, with only 22 per cent of salespeople hitting their quota in the fourth quarter of 2022.[4]

In tandem, we have experienced an explosion of digital technologies over the past 15 years, with the latest trend being the rise of generative artificial intelligence (AI). In the face of falling profits and opportunities, many vendor organisations are eager to jump on the technology bandwagon. Whether the push comes from leaders who are keen to remain on the bleeding edge, or tech-savvy junior employees who want to make an impact, each new tool is treated as a magic pill that might solve their struggles.

This leaves sales leaders stuck like flies in a metaphorical web.

They are caught between the pressure to drive strategic change while managing the day-to-day operations of their sales team. On one hand, they are charged with innovating, yet they don't know where to start. Some might even lack clarity around what exactly should change. They know they are getting left behind, but don't know how to catch up. At the same time, when they are buried in day-to-day pressures it is impossible for them to get a broader perspective. In some cases, they might *intentionally* blinker themselves to reduce the noise so they can focus on just getting the job done.

These leaders are also caught between innovation and risk reduction. In a typical vendor organisation, where costs are climbing and revenue is falling, sales leaders likely have the CEO on one shoulder and the CFO on the other, with the CEO pushing for innovation and transformation, while the CFO wants to reduce risk and focus on reliable revenue drivers (like quotas and commissions).

Ultimately, sales leaders are facing challenges from all directions, and attempting to address any of them only results in an even more tangled web.

The sales innovation paradox

We know things can't continue as they are. Yet, in cases where sales leaders attempt to innovate, or even attempt to implement a change forced on them by another part of the organisation, this rarely ends well.

Many changes being implemented by vendor organisations are those driven by technology. These changes might start with the vague direction of 'let's leverage AI' (or any other trending tool), and leaders quickly find themselves overwhelmed by the hundreds of tools available in any category without the knowledge and resources to choose appropriately. Or they might start with a specific tool (or selection of tools) in mind, yet even in this case many vendor organisations lack an understanding of how to use these technologies to create value.

These changes rarely deliver the promised results. The first outcome is where the implementation doesn't get off the ground because the process of managing the change becomes too complex and too costly. The second outcome is that the new technology is implemented, but it only makes existing processes and structures more difficult to manage. This leads to end users finding workarounds, and often doing manual work that takes more time than the way they were managing things before.

These outcomes leave leaders biased against new ideas and technology because they believe these implementations will fail. Every time there is a failure, vendor organisations become even more risk averse and less willing to take chances on wide-scale technology transformations.

Even worse for sales leaders is that if these implementations fail, it is seen as the sales leader's responsibility (even if the original drive for the change came from outside the team).

What is going wrong?

First, the leadership at many vendor organisations doesn't see the need to change, which means there is an immediate barrier to doing anything differently. This is particularly common in organisations where the executive team and board are made up of former field sales professionals who have a mindset of knuckling down and getting on with it. They don't recognise that the old ways of working are no longer effective in the modern sales and buying environment.

In cases where organisations *do* see a need to change, they see technology as being the answer—the magic pill we mentioned earlier. This puts organisations in a position of doubling down on what doesn't work. Generally, new tools don't change the way an organisation is doing things—they allow the organisation to do those things more efficiently. If an organisation is focusing on the wrong things (or things that don't work in today's sales and buying landscape), new technology will simply accelerate poor behaviour.

Howard Dover coined the term 'the sales innovation paradox' to describe this. Organisations have high expectations for growth and they invest in training, technology and enablement, but they experience failing sales performance as a result. In short, they don't see the expected return after implementation.

As software engineer Grady Booch said, 'A fool with a tool is still a fool'.

It is clear that something needs to change, but vendor organisations keep focusing on the wrong things.

The way forward: Deep Selling

The world has changed, and it is time for vendor organisations to change with it. Vendor organisations must shift from the old-world, product-centric approach of push selling to the new-world, buyer-centric, data-driven approach of *Deep Selling*.

The old-world approach to sales was Shallow: vendor salespeople would play the numbers game, going a mile wide and an inch deep, knowing that the more prospects they pitched, the more deals they would eventually close. In the past, this worked: vendor organisations had proprietary solutions, buyers had limited access to solutions and information, and buyers treated salespeople as trusted advisers who could help them solve business problems.

Today, with changing buyer dynamics, new technology and more competitive markets, everyone is fishing in the Shallows. To borrow the term 'blue ocean' from Renée Mauborgne and W Chan Kim's book *Blue ocean strategy*, going Deep is your blue ocean. The Deep water is where the big fish are. Yes, it is harder to get to, but there's less competition there.

What do we mean by Deep Selling?

- Going Deep is all about the quality of relationships over quantity. Say goodbye to spray and pray and hello to competitive differentiation.
- Going Deep necessitates fewer buyer engagements. This is more sustainable over the long term and is critical for today's business models, which rely on net retention.
- Going Deep requires vendors to strategically use technology to uncover data and derive actionable insights about their buyers, which can then be leveraged to deliver the expected buyer experience. You can't meet expectations if you don't go Deep.
- Going Deep means creating value for buyers and improving buyer outcomes over internal vendor outcomes, like revenue and profit.
- Going Deep on the upfront research (pre-approach and approach) allows the vendor salesperson to quickly hit the key buyer requirement 'show me you know me'.
- Going Deep is about highlighting how products can meet individual buyer needs.

While Shallow sales approaches tend to promote the use of technology to accelerate behaviours that annoy, interrupt or even badger potential buyers, Deep Selling approaches encourage vendor organisations to spend more time understanding the buyer before engaging with them. This meets the needs and preferences of the modern buyer, including building trust and developing a truly consultative relationship. At the same time, going Deep has a real impact on an organisation's financial metrics and internal engagement.

Deep Selling is a buyer-centric approach for vendor organisations, and being buyer centric has a range of benefits. Buyer-centric organisations are 25 per cent more profitable and have 5.1 times higher revenue growth than their product-centric counterparts.[5,6] These organisations have 25 per cent higher loyalty and, when it comes to employee satisfaction and retention, 83 per cent of those who work for companies that prioritise buyer satisfaction are at least pretty sure that they'll still be there in two years.[7,8]

Ultimately, going Deep means more opportunity with less competition and more value. And this approach addresses many of the issues facing today's sales leaders.

How to achieve Deep-Selling excellence

Every sales leader we've spoken to in every industry, bar none, knows there needs to be a shift in thinking. We call it the mindset, skill set and toolset.

Mindset includes elements like vision, values and culture—it's who you are and what you believe. Skill set spans structure, processes and incentives—how you get things done. And toolset comprises the tools that will support these changes, namely the technology and systems you implement. To achieve Deep-Selling excellence, there must be a shift in your organisation's mindset, skill set and toolset towards Deep Selling.

While every sales leader we've spoken to agrees with this in principle, most of them don't know where to start. This book is your starting point.

In this book, we will show you how to evolve your organisation and sales team for the buyer-led era.

In part 1, you will discover the current trends facing the sales and buying landscape, and why these trends mean it is essential for vendor organisations to change if they want to survive. These include:

- the role digitalisation has played in the evolution of sales and buying models
- how buyers have changed, and why they expect more from their vendors than ever before
- why traditional, field sales teams are struggling, and the real cost this is having on sales teams and vendor organisations
- why Deep Selling is the way forward.

We will then share the four elements of Deep Selling as well as the Deep-Selling maturity model, giving you the ability to assess where your organisation currently sits on the maturity model and to develop a clear roadmap for moving from Shallow to Deep. Figure 1 summarises the four elements.

In part 2, this roadmap is broken down into three phases (Shallow to Emerging; Emerging to Exploring; and Exploring to Deep) and encompasses the following activities:

1. *Audit your organisation's current state:* After performing a current-state analysis, you will perform a guided audit on your organisation's level of buyer centricity and digital readiness as well as conducting an audit of your current sales tech stack. These results will combine to indicate your organisation's level on the Deep-Selling maturity model.

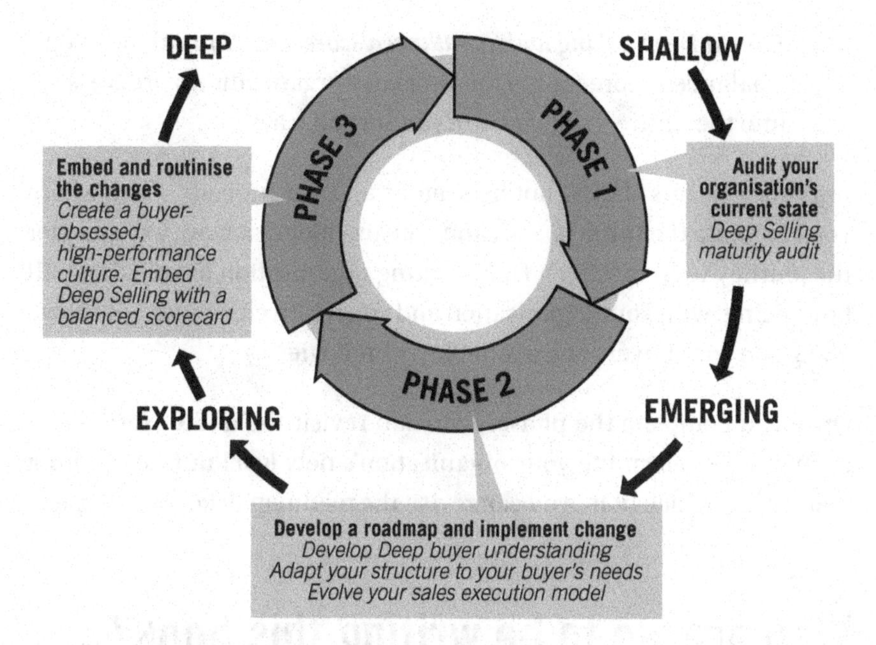

Figure 1: moving from Shallow to Deep Selling

2 *Develop Deep buyer understanding:* You will understand your current buyers, leverage AI to create ideal and minimum buyer personas and map out the ideal buyer journey.

3 *Adapt your structure to your buyers' needs:* With the ideal buyer journey mapped out, you will reorganise teams into functional buckets that align with this buyer journey.

4 *Evolve your sales execution model:* We will explore the main sales execution models for different buyer and product types, diving into a deeper, consultative approach. You will also develop a one-page sales playbook that can be shared throughout the organisation.

5 *Create a buyer-obsessed, high-performance culture:* You will redefine what success means to your organisation and measure and reward performance based on those metrics. Within the sales team, you will assess current team composition and performance to set the benchmark for ongoing improvement.

6 *Embed Deep Selling with a balanced scorecard:* You will develop a balanced scorecard to monitor your organisation's progress into the future and to ensure you stay on track.

Importantly, this should not be seen as a linear process — one where you complete the three phases and you are done. Instead, we consider the journey to becoming a Deep-Selling organisation as one that will be ongoing, with your organisation and your team continuing to evolve alongside your buyers and available technologies.

Once you complete the phases, you can revisit the audit exercises in chapter 6 to determine your organisation's new level of Deep-Selling maturity, at which point you can revisit the roadmap to go even *deeper.*

Who are we to be writing this book?

As you will have read in the section 'About the authors' at the beginning of the book, we (Mark Micallef and Graham Hawkins) are both B2B sales professionals with a combined 55 years of experience in the profession.

Between the two of us, we have worked with hundreds of vendor organisations and thousands of sales professionals. We have seen what works and what doesn't when it comes to sales success in the modern, buyer-led era, and how to effectively leverage digital technology to drive that success.

The Deep-Selling roadmap shares what we have learned and how you can redesign your sales organisation.

After reading this book, you will understand what isn't working in your organisation and what can be done about it. You will have the proof points you need to effectively communicate your organisation's current state both upstream and downstream, and you will have a guide for achieving Deep-Selling excellence.

When you face resistance and objections to the change (because every change encounters resistance), you will have a defendable position. This book is based on extensive study of what works, drawn from our personal experience, organisations we've consulted with, hundreds of interviews with sales professionals and vendor organisations, and two decades of academic literature on sales. This will give you more effective levers to pull when making your case across the organisation.

You will also have more awareness about your organisation's competitive advantage and gain the ability to create further competitive advantage through Deep Selling. You will have a deeper understanding of what your buyers expect, which takes out the guesswork, empowering you and your team to deliver to those expectations. This will propel you and your team towards better results, meaning that not only are your executive team and board satisfied, but the people on the ground are happy as well.

Simply, until now, you have been a passenger in a car that has been driven by the board, executives, the market and your buyers. After reading this book, you will be the one in the driver's seat.

Before we get started

This book is designed as a complete 'how-to' to guide for managers who want to transform their sales organisation and capture greater value from the latest digital technologies and tools.

For more information, and access to the tools, processes and frameworks contained in this book, visit www.deepselling.com, or scan the QR code.

Before we get started

PART I

HOW THE WORLD HAS CHANGED

CHAPTER 1
THE DIGITALISATION ARMS RACE

Over the past three decades, there has been an explosion of digital connectivity. Of the eight billion people on the planet, 5.35 billion use the internet and there are more than 15 billion connected devices globally.[9,10] Sixty-nine per cent, or 5.6 billion, subscribe to a mobile service, and this is expected to hit 74 per cent by 2030.[11] Active social media identities are also approaching the five billion mark.[12]

The adoption of digital technologies, including personal computers, mobile phones, the internet, social media, AI and digital platforms, has radically changed and evolved the requirements for effective selling and buying. Consider social selling—a common approach used by salespeople to find and interact with potential buyers—which wouldn't be possible without social media technology.

In a similar vein, vendors and suppliers are being forced to adapt their approaches to match each other. In this digitalisation arms race, the use of new technologies on one side necessitates adaptations on the other. For instance, as vendors use Google and other search engines to find solutions, suppliers must develop websites, advertise their products online, create content and develop e-commerce solutions so they are able to be found in the new environment.[13]

These changes come with a range of benefits such as automating and speeding up tasks, increasing communication efficiency, and giving both buyers and sellers greater access to information and the ability to disseminate that information.[14,15] However, challenges have also arisen from the adoption of these technologies.

In traditionally relationship-based professions like sales, one of the clearest implications is the reduction of face-to-face interaction. Seventy-five per cent of B2B buyers use social media to research vendors, with 50 per cent naming LinkedIn as a trusted source.[16] Digital technologies are able to replace human salespeople for up to 47 per cent of the sales process, with multiple predictions over the years reporting that the need for salespeople will continue to decline.[17] In fact, as of 2019, buyers already completed *87 per cent* of their purchasing journey before contacting a vendor salesperson.[18]

And this is the way modern buyers *prefer* to engage—nearly 75 per cent of B2B buyers would prefer to buy from a website than a human salesperson, with 93 per cent preferring to buy online once they have decided what to purchase.[19] When sellers and buyers *do* interact, it is often through digital channels.

This is why increasing numbers of sales and buying organisations are investing in new technologies to support, supplement and replace human workforces, with digital technology being used in buying to autonomously process orders and replenish inventory, or in selling for content creation and identifying prospects.[20,21,22]

Activities that were previously conducted exclusively by humans are now completed more efficiently and effectively through digital technology, demonstrating an unmistakable trend in selling and buying away from human-to-human interaction and towards digitalisation and automation. This has reduced the importance of humans in selling and buying approaches and has significant implications for the future.

A timeline of sales digitalisation

In Graham's 2017 book, *The future of the sales profession*, he gave an overview of the evolution of modern sales from the birth of James H Patterson's National Cash Register Company (NCR) in 1884 up to the mid 2010s.[23] In this discussion, we will focus on the role technology has played in driving the evolution of buying and selling approaches.

This starts with the pre-digital technology era: before 1980.

The pre-digital technology era: before 1980

The pre-digital technology era was one where a salesperson would try to influence a buyer to purchase during sales encounters. The sales and buying process was typically completed in a single meeting and between an individual buyer and seller.[24] During these encounters, the salesperson would follow a formalised sales process that focused on explaining the proposition of their offering, demonstrating the offering and then persuading the buyer to buy.[25]

We can see this approach dating all the way back to Patterson and the NCR, where he developed a four-step sales process following an audit of the company's most successful salesmen:[26]

1. *Approach:* In the approach, the salesman did not mention the cash register. Instead, he explained that he wanted to help the businessman find ways to increase his profit.

2. *Proposition:* The proposition was when the salesman first described the register, explaining how it would prevent theft and give an accurate account of the day's receipts.
3. *Demonstration:* In this stage, the salesman would demonstrate the machine at the local NCR office, or at a nearby hotel where he had set up a display.
4. *Close:* Salesmen were not to ask for an order, but to take for granted that the buyer would buy by asking questions like, 'What colour should I make it?' or 'How soon do you want delivery?' They were then instructed to fill out their order form with the buyer's details and hand it to him to sign.

Over the next century, there was an explosion of sales methodologies. In the 1930s, this included mood selling, brand-based selling, psychological selling and barrier selling, alongside the 1936 release of Dale Carnegie's seminal book *How to win friends and influence people.*

The trend of sales methodologies continued through the next few decades, with SELL, ADAPT, ARC and AIDA in the 1940s and 1950s, the Xerox Corporation's 'needs satisfaction selling' system in the 1960s and SPIN selling in the 1980s.

Throughout this era, buying approaches were situational and recognised that different buying situations carried different levels of risk.[27] Buyers focused on each transaction independently and would invest different levels of effort based on the risk inherent in each buying situation. For example, when purchasing a solution for the first time, buyers would spend a significant amount of time and effort at each stage of the buying process, while they would put less time and effort into repeat purchases due to the lower level of risk.[28,29]

Not surprisingly, the persuasive approaches of vendor salespeople often clashed with the situational, risk-avoiding approaches of buyers, which resulted in an adversarial relationship between buyers and sellers.[30] Unfortunately, this relationship dynamic persists in many buying and selling relationships today, particularly when vendor organisations and their sales teams cling to outdated approaches.

The information technology era: 1980–1995

After 1980, digital technology started to play a more significant role in selling and buying practice as personal computers and other information technologies were heavily adopted by both selling and buying organisations.

The introduction of information technologies enabled buyers to access more information and to consider how their decisions impacted the organisation's performance.[31] This meant that buyers began to take a more strategic and holistic approach to buying, rather than making purchases in isolation.[32,33] Buyers began to recognise that involving vendors in buying decisions improved buying outcomes and they subsequently put more effort into managing their vendor relationships.[34,35]

Meanwhile, vendors began to identify that the one-size-fits-all sales approaches of the previous era were becoming less effective because buyers had different processes, buying rationality and relationship approaches, depending on their personal characteristics or roles.

In response, vendor salespeople began to practise adaptive selling behaviours and made efforts to understand and respond to each buyer differently.[36] This had the effect of salespeople focusing on problem-solving over persuasion and required them to invest in developing long-term and mutually beneficial relationships with buyers. This period saw the selling centre become more strategic as vendor organisations moved away from product-based strategies and instead focused on customer relationship management (CRM) strategies that allocated sales resources to buyers based on their ability to achieve an organisation's strategic goals.[37]

Selling and buying transitioned from transactional processes with adversarial buyer-seller relationships to a more cooperative process whereby sales and buying centres worked together to solve problems for mutual benefit. Sales approaches focused on concepts like value creation, relationship management, commitment-trust and adaptive selling, and vendor organisations spoke to strategic alignment and competitive advantage to appeal to buying rationality.[38,39]

Information technologies enhanced these capabilities by providing the means for buyers and sellers to manage their relationships more strategically and effectively. For example, personal computers, which gained widespread uptake during this era, made information more accessible and provided new ways to store, analyse and use data, which had previously been decentralised across sales and buying centres.[40,41] Likewise, mobile phones provided salespeople with a new level of freedom and mobility, enabling them to visit more customers while staying connected when they were on the road.

The internet era: 1995–2010

The period between 1995 and 2010 saw a significant increase in the use of digital technologies to support and transform selling and buying approaches.

Increased competition saw buyers start sourcing solutions and services rather than products — especially for complex buying tasks — to relieve growing commoditisation pressures.[42] The buying of services and solutions required more collaborative buying approaches and — unlike previous buying approaches, which could be completed independently — solutions buying required buyers to establish and define needs with vendor organisations, as these needs were not always known or clearly defined.[43] This period therefore saw the evolution of more collaborative purchasing approaches.

The product-to-solutions transition also required corresponding changes to sales approaches, as the approaches of previous eras had become less effective.[44] Sellers responded by seeking more collaborative relationships with buyers, which enabled them to offer customised solutions that better aligned with the buyers' needs.[45] The selling of solutions required new skills, including the ability to diagnose fuzzy, ill-defined, and/or latent buyer needs and to reach out to and access multiple stakeholders in both the buyer and vendor organisations. This transition from product to solutions resulted in buyer interactions that were more complex and strategic in nature and required resources and collaboration with multiple actors across not only the selling and buying organisations, but also the wider business network or ecosystem.[46,47]

Key technologies introduced during the internet era included:

- the internet and e-commerce
- mobile technology
- social media
- CRM technologies.

Let's look at each of these.

The internet and e-commerce

The internet transformed selling and buying practice by providing buyers with the ability to easily access global supply networks and conduct independent research.[48,49]

Access to the internet enabled buyers to search for information independently and revolutionised the relationship between buyers and vendor salespeople, as buyers no longer had to rely on salespeople for information — a theme that grew more prevalent as this era progressed and the technology continued to evolve.

Organisational buyers began to divide their buying activities across multiple channels and were engaging with digital channels more often for buying tasks that had previously involved human salespeople.[50]

The availability of internet-based technologies like email and video conferencing meant that when buyers did consult salespeople, they were more likely to do so via electronic communication.[51]

On the sales side, vendor organisations began to harness emerging internet technologies such as e-commerce and other forms of digital platforms to reach and interact with buyers digitally.[52,53,54] The availability of digital platforms enabled buyers to engage with supplier firms without the need for a salesperson, leading to questions around the future need for the sales profession altogether.[55]

Mobile technology

Mobile technologies were also heavily adopted by salespeople during this period.[56] Mobile devices provided salespeople with more mobility and, with the assistance of wi-fi networks and the internet, allowed sales activities to be conducted remotely, requiring less physical office time.[57] The introduction of the iPhone in 2007 led to an acceleration in the adoption and use of mobile phones in B2B applications.

Social media

The emergence of social media platforms during this phase enabled salespeople to find and interact with more buyers more effectively than ever before.[58,59] The launch of Facebook in 2004 also enabled a previously unseen level of global interconnection.

LinkedIn was introduced in 2003 as the world's first social network for business and had grown to more than one billion users worldwide in 2024.[60] Social media platforms like WhatsApp, YouTube, TikTok, X and Instagram are now also regularly used by businesses for content distribution and advertising, while networks like WeChat and Kakao have huge followings in international markets.

Since this era, social media has been used across the entire sales and buying process as a way to distribute and consume content, gather reviews, look for references, and contact and interact with buyers and vendors.

CRM technologies

CRM technologies were also born during this phase. While vendor organisations had previously used crude databases, or even rolodexes, to store their buyer data, CRM systems like Salesforce gave vendor organisations a way to centrally store buyer data and enabled large sales teams to manage their interactions with buyers more strategically. These technologies grew in importance across this era, with additional capabilities like enterprise resource planning integration and advanced analytical capabilities adding to their appeal and adoption. Leveraging these advanced features, CRM systems helped vendor organisations enhance knowledge management and relationship management and automate many sales activities.[61,62,63,64,65,66]

Overall, this period saw both buyers and sellers leverage digital technology to collaborate more effectively in the pursuit of mutual value creation.[67,68,69]

The digital era: 2010–2020

After 2010, more advanced digital technologies were adopted into B2B sales and buying practice, including next-generation digital technologies like AI and advanced analytical, cloud and embedded technologies.[70,71]

Digital technologies became more integrated into selling and buying practice as organisations began to link and synergise their digital technologies into common platforms that unlocked even more of their potential.[72,73] This integration enabled sales and buying organisations to use digital technologies to complete activities more effectively, including segmenting and targeting buyers, developing pricing strategies, predicting buyer behaviours, analysing vendor offerings, and providing negotiation support and supplier selection recommendations.[74,75,76]

The increased use of digital technologies during this era had the effect of changing the buying process, as many stages were now completed electronically and across multiple actors, channels and time frames. While digital technologies had previously been used to complete purchasing tasks, enhancing the capabilities and efficiency of human buyers and sellers, the digital era saw these technologies become more integrated into the buying process. Digital technologies enabled sales and buying tasks to be performed without human involvement, with buyers simultaneously using multiple channels and completing multiple stages of the process at once.[77,78] These multi-channel buying approaches increased both the amount and speed of information that could be accessed for decision making.[79,80] Additionally, the use of digital technologies for decision support meant that there was less manual effort involved in some process stages.[81,82,83]

Key technologies introduced during the digital era are discussed below. They included:

- artificial intelligence
- embedded technologies
- digital marketplaces.

Artificial intelligence (AI)

In this era, AI capabilities grew to the point where organisations were able to analyse data and complete simple or repetitive tasks far more efficiently than was possible previously.[84,85,86] As a result, many organisations began to digitalise parts of their sales and buying operations to improve efficiency and reduce overheads.[87,88] However, despite its potential, the application of AI-powered digital technologies during this era was mostly limited to statistical analysis, decision support and simple process optimisation, as significant investment was required to build and train customised AI models.[89]

Embedded technologies

Technology became more integrated into products and services during this era as vendor firms began to embed sensors into products to track and monitor usage, wear and tear and other statistics important to the performance of their solutions. Combined with digital platforms and AI, these technologies — commonly referred to as the Internet of Things (IoT) — facilitated interconnection and information transparency, which in turn enabled vendor firms to deliver more value to buying organisations.[90]

Digital marketplaces

Digital marketplaces, otherwise known as digital multi-sided platforms, became more embedded in buying and selling practice at this time. While leading global digital marketplaces such as Amazon and eBay launched in the mid 1990s, they were generally considered digital extensions of traditional two-sided marketplaces, and a resource, rather than a threat, to traditional businesses.

Newer digital platforms such as Uber and Airbnb began to enter and disrupt traditional markets around 2010. These platforms are different because although they don't own any cars or hotels, they have managed to completely change their respective industries by offering new and more efficient ways for buyers and sellers to interact by cutting out the middleman. Clearly these platforms represent a threat for traditional vendor organisations, as they reroute traditional relationships between firms in business networks.

Organisational buyers began to leverage self-service tools and platforms during this era to help find solutions, seek independent product reviews and complete transactions independently.[91,92]

Overall, this era saw a significant increase in the use and integration of digital technologies into selling and buying practices as organisations divided their resources across multiple channels. Organisations began to consider how multiple digital technologies could be effectively integrated across the buying journey rather than used in isolation.

The generative AI era: post 2020

After 2020, two major transformational events accelerated the digitalisation of selling and buying approaches, namely the COVID-19 pandemic and the introduction of generative AI technology.

While digitalisation was already an important part of the sales and buying processes, the pandemic—and the lockdowns imposed by many governments during this period—led to a significant acceleration of the digitalisation processes for many sales and buying organisations.[93,94] Because of the lockdowns, salespeople were unable to meet with buyers face to face and buyers were forced to interact with salespeople virtually, or revert to online digital platforms for information and to complete transactions.[95] This meant organisational buyers became even more independent in their buying processes and more comfortable buying large, complicated, high-risk items online, without interacting with salespeople.[96] This further reduced the importance of face-to-face buyer-seller interactions, which had once been the cornerstone of selling and buying practice.

Generative AI technologies were introduced to the world in November 2022 through OpenAI's ChatGPT, immediately leading to questions about the future role of salespeople and organisational buyers.[97]

First-generation AI was based on machine learning technology that automated simple and repetitive tasks, and it was thought that these technologies would only replace humans for operational or transactional activities. The current generation of AI, however, is based on generative technologies, meaning they can generate new content based on training data. This technology can be easily adopted into selling and buying practice and can be used for far more complex tasks than the previous generation.

While human interaction has always been considered necessary to both selling and buying practice, generative AI provides the means to effectively cut humans from involvement in many selling and buying tasks altogether. Generative AI technologies are already being deployed by sales organisations as autonomous agents that interact with human buyers for online enquiries, and it seems inevitable that more advanced versions of these technologies will evolve to take on more complex tasks.[98]

We will discuss the implications of generative AI in more depth in the next chapter, including future implications of this technology. For now, just keep in mind that the AI era promises to be even more disruptive and transformational to B2B selling and buying than any other era.

The dark side of digitalisation

When looking at each new wave of technology, it is clear that digitalisation has led to changes to buying approaches, with vendor organisations needing to adapt selling approaches to remain relevant. Additionally, when one vendor adapts, similar organisations are forced to follow suit or get left behind, creating a digitalisation arms race.

However, the implementation of new technologies rarely goes to plan, with McKinsey finding that large IT projects run 45 per cent over budget and 7 per cent over schedule, while delivering 56 per cent less value than predicted.[99]

Why are so many organisations failing to see the benefits of these new technologies? We've found issues arise from three primary areas. The first is not considering the needs of the organisation or end users. The second is using tools to substitute existing processes, instead of taking advantage of the larger opportunities they provide. And the third is not understanding and addressing the internal tensions that arise from technology implementation, even when the implementation is successful.

The technology/needs mismatch

CRM is a well-established tool in the business landscape, yet CRM implementation projects still fail anywhere between 18 and 69 per cent of the time.[100]

One famous example is the General Motors Acceptance Corp Commercial Mortgage (GMACCP) 1999 CRM initiative project, which would implement a voice recording system to answer customer calls with the aim of increasing automation, efficiency and the amount of borrower information available to call-centre staff. Unfortunately, the project had the opposite results, with loan officers losing business when customers went to rivals, rising customer complaints and 99 per cent of callers zeroing out to a customer-service operator.[101]

One temptation for digitally savvy leaders is to adopt the latest technologies as soon as solutions come onto the market. If they don't, they worry they will fall behind competitors or lose the opportunities the new technology provides. Unfortunately, this approach results in organisations incorrectly focusing on changing their internal processes and systems to fit the technology rather than finding technology to fit the process. This disrupts existing processes, frustrates team members and the organisation's buyers, and can result in poor management behaviours.

This is one of the reasons why the GMACCP CRM implementation failed: the project team didn't define the needs of the end users of the new phone system (their loan customers). This meant customers were getting a voice recording when they needed to speak to a human, and the vast majority circumvented the new system to speak to a human anyway. As Stefan Thomke, Professor of Business Administration at Harvard Business School, writes:

> *Tools—no matter how advanced—do not automatically confer benefits on organisations. They must be integrated into systems and routines that are already in place. Tools are embedded*

within the organisations that deploy them as well as the people that use them. When integrated incorrectly, *they can actually inhibit performance.*[102]

Wasted opportunities

The next reason digital transformations don't achieve the expected results is because organisations often see new technology as a substitute for existing tools or ways of working. In sales, examples might include replacing a sales call or presentation with a recorded, on-demand webinar. This approach can lead to cost savings, but it fails to leverage the bigger opportunities these tools can provide, which include how a buyer's total experience can be reimagined with new technologies.

This point might sound contradictory to the previous one, but they are two different ways of thinking. The previous approach started with technology and looked at how processes and systems could be retrofitted to suit the technology, which didn't take the needs of those engaging with the technology (your team and your buyers) into consideration. This approach starts with the wants and needs of your buyers, looks at how those can be addressed with technology, and *then* looks at opportunities beyond just switching out one tool for another.

Consider the example of your morning commute, and then imagine switching out your current car for a Bugatti Chiron, one of the world's fastest cars at the time of writing.[103] Your commute won't magically become faster because you are in a faster car. Instead, you would need to look at other factors that would take advantage of the car's speed, like a different route, or moving the time of your commute to a window with less traffic.

Organisational tensions

Even in cases where technologies are implemented for the right reasons or in the right way, many organisations are not aware of the organisational tension knots that arise from these transformations. These tensions are instances where there are both positive and negative consequences from a change, and they can be experienced differently at different levels of the organisation.

These tensions include:[104]

- *autonomy tensions:* technology use can lead to higher autonomy but can also have the negative consequence of increased availability. Just consider how digital technologies give individuals the opportunity to choose when, where and how to work, leading to more flexibility and improved work-life balance. At the same time, this technology has resulted in 'always on' work cultures where employees and managers often need to increase their availability during and outside working hours, which can lead to more stress, higher workloads and negative impacts on work-life balance
- *innovation tensions:* these arise when changing from existing to new ways of doing things. In these cases, people can resist the adoption of technologies either because it is too difficult to change, or the value of the technology is not apparent. Lack of adoption becomes frustrating for senior leaders, who want to see a return on their investments, and for middle managers, who struggle with the challenges of persuading their teams to adopt new technologies
- *information tensions:* these relate to situations where technology increases the amount of information available but reduces information quality and security. For example, thanks to digital technologies such as CRM and sales analytics systems, vendor organisations have better access to sales and buyer information and a better understanding of revenue sources, buyer motivation and sales conversion rates. These have positive effects on decision making and enable better access to and dissemination of knowledge. However, with larger quantities of data, it is harder to control quality

- *interaction tensions:* these occur when technology changes the way individuals and teams interact within an organisation and externally. For instance, thanks to multiple communication platforms, salespeople can personalise their communication to suit each buyer's needs, which improves buyer relationships. However, new communication channels can result in concerns for salespeople about their job security because buyers can avoid salespeople and communicate directly with other actors in the vendor organisation
- *resource tensions:* these relate to situations where technology reduces costs or makes better use of human resources but can also result in negative consequences such as increased costs of implementation and management
- *control tensions:* these are the tensions between improved transparency and increased surveillance. Consider situations where technology allows sales managers and sales directors to monitor and control the salesforce. While this is positive for leaders, that increased transparency often increases the pursuit of activity (e.g. more sales calls), which, in turn, increases workload and stress and could divert focus from more effective selling tasks.

If we return to the example of implementing a CRM, most organisations underestimate the amount of change required to adopt a CRM, leading to innovation tensions, or resistance to change. Most organisations underestimate the ongoing cost and resources required to modify and administer CRM systems, leading to resource tensions. Most organisations *over*estimate the value of CRM information to salespeople, leading to information tensions.

And most organisations underestimate the amount of time and effort salespeople need to divert to CRMs, leading to autonomy, resource and innovation tensions (and ultimately reducing the time each salesperson can commit to selling, increasing selling costs and reducing sales efficiency).

As you can see, technology implementation doesn't happen in isolation. Even organisations with the best intentions when introducing new tools to their teams can encounter these tensions if they don't thoroughly consider what the change might mean across the organisation.

The race to adapt

From the birth of the modern sales force to the present day, there have been many changes to vendor organisations' sales approaches. James H Patterson documented the first formalised sales process in the 1880s, which was followed by the rise of countless selling methodologies from the 1930s to the 2000s.

Interestingly, many of these process changes were surface-level — the role of the salesperson remained unchanged, with salespeople acting as consultants and advisers to solve business problems.

Today is different. The past 20 years in particular have seen an explosion of technology, connectivity and accessibility, all of which has led to a landscape of more informed buyers, and vendor organisations that are struggling to adapt to the new landscape. Digital technologies have replaced humans for many common buying and selling tasks and, with the latest boom in generative AI, the pace of change is only accelerating.

The adoption of these technologies has also accelerated the transformation of buying and selling approaches. Buying approaches are now more collaborative, prioritising risk reduction and value enhancement, while selling approaches are more focused on developing relationships to create strategic value for buyers.

Ultimately, buyer and seller adaptation is only becoming more important, with vendor organisations being forced to adapt to the requirements of and the approaches used on the buying side of the equation in order to remain relevant.

CHAPTER 2
RISE OF THE ROBOTS

The past few years have seen an unprecedented explosion of interest in generative AI. Just two months after launching in November 2022, ChatGPT had reached 100 million active monthly users, which climbed to 100 million active weekly users within a year.[105,106]

In the business world, CB Insights' 2023 State of AI report found that AI startups raised USD42.5 billion, with generative AI attracting 48 per cent of all AI funding. This was up significantly from 2022, the growth driven by large language model developers like OpenAI, Anthropic and Inflection. The average AI deal size climbed by 21 per cent to USD23.4 million, while mergers and acquisitions reached a record high of 317 for the year.[107]

Unsurprisingly, 70 per cent of organisations are now in exploration mode with generative AI, with 40 per cent of companies saying they were increasing their investments in AI due to recent advancements.[108,109] OpenAI also revealed that teams in more than 80 per cent of Fortune 500 companies had adopted the technology in 2023.[110]

But does the growth of generative AI really matter for the sales and buying journey?

The short answer is, yes. There is so much potential to easily integrate generative AI into selling and buying practices, as this technology provides the means to effectively cut human involvement in these tasks. In fact, chatbots powered by generative AI are already being deployed by sales organisations as autonomous agents for online enquiries, and as the technology evolves it will be able to take on more complex tasks.

When it comes to the existing use of AI in vendor businesses, 68 per cent of business leaders say AI and automation tools are important to their overall business strategy, with 71 per cent reporting increases in employee productivity and 72 per cent saying their investment in AI and automation tools has returned a positive return.[111] In 2018, 21 per cent of sales leaders said their organisations were already using AI, which we can expect to have grown due to the functionality made possible by large language models.[112]

Ultimately, 82 per cent of large companies believe AI has the potential to make human work in sales and marketing more meaningful and valuable.[113]

So what is AI?

For all the media, business and academic discussion on AI, many struggle to define what this technology is. This is particularly true when there are examples of tools that achieve similar things, but which might be powered by different technology.

Consider chatbots as an example. Since the launch of ChatGPT, many people assume that chatbots are all powered by large language models, using existing content to generate new content. However, many of today's chatbots are based on decision trees that follow pre-defined rules. These rules drive interactions with an if/then framework: if the visitor does A, the chatbot will respond with B. If the visitor does C, the chatbot will respond with D. As far as the end user is concerned, it is a similar experience (they enter a prompt, and get an answer), but the underlying technology is different.

So, what is AI, then?

At its simplest, AI is the process whereby machines learn how to learn.[114]

Outside the world of science fiction (which featured intelligent robots long before the concept was pursued by academics), Alan Turing made one of the first mentions of intelligent machinery in 1947. In 1950, he posed the question 'can machines think?', proposing the idea of the Turing Test.[115]

The term 'machine learning' was introduced in 1969, when Arthur Samuel developed the first self-learning program to play checkers.[116] However, it wasn't until the 1990s and 2000s that machine learning, neural networks and Deep learning started to become more accessible due to the growth in computer processing capacity, rise of the internet, and the explosion in data collection and processing.

While the last generation of AI focused on automating simple and repetitive tasks, the current generation focuses on technologies that use generative models to generate new content based on training data.

The most well-known models used today are Large Language Models (LLMs), which are used in technologies such as ChatGPT, Microsoft Copilot and Google Gemini to generate text in response to prompts. Generative AI tools built on LLMs are capable of performing more complex tasks than the past generation of technologies—apparent reasoning, text production, understanding different viewpoints and more—and were brought to the mainstream with the launch of ChatGPT.

While what these tools can achieve is impressive, do we need to be worried about AI taking over the world in the near future?

This is not a concern at this point in time. *AI—the new intelligence in sales* defines three different types of AI:[117]

- *Artificial narrow intelligence:* programs that are able to perform individual tasks well
- *Artificial super intelligence:* artificial intelligence that is superior to humans
- *Artificial general intelligence:* programs that are able to do anything humans can do.

In books and films that depict robot uprisings, these are examples of artificial general intelligence or artificial super intelligence: it is only because the program is able to perform at the same or higher breadth and depth as humans that it is able to take over.

When many people started engaging with ChatGPT and similar tools, they worried it was an example of AI having reached the level of artificial general intelligence, because ChatGPT's ability to engage using natural language and to respond to prompts made it seem almost human. (Humans also tend to anthropomorphise non-human entities, which means it is natural for us to layer human experience, intelligence and emotion onto text on a screen.[118] This is exacerbated by the fact that many Millennials and Gen Zs have built social and parasocial relationships with people through screens.)

In reality, tools such as ChatGPT are an example of artificial narrow intelligence: they perform a very narrow task and perform it well. Just imagine if you had to engage with ChatGPT using numbers or code, and if the responses it gave you were delivered in numbers or code. It would be achieving the same thing it does now (generating content based on training data) but communicating in a different language that would prevent users from layering human elements on a sophisticated algorithm.

Even though today's AI technologies are still at the level of artificial narrow intelligence, this doesn't mean they can't deliver benefits. Just some of the tasks generative AI can assist with include analysing vast amounts of data; identifying trends, patterns and correlations within that data; and drawing insights to assist with decision making.

However, while there is a lot of potential, there are also obstacles to AI's adoption and limitations to its abilities. Common obstacles include poor understanding of the technology, issues around trust, and lack of resources. Blocks to understanding might include not understanding AI's potential added value, writing it off as the latest fad or buzzword and not knowing how to connect the technology to real-world business problems. When it comes to trustworthiness, there are concerns about data security. Consider ChatGPT: do you know what happens to records of your chats? And resource concerns relate to a belief that it will be too expensive, time consuming or complex to implement this technology.[119]

There are also real limitations to consider. While AI built on LLMs might *sound* human, these programs lack emotions, empathy and social intelligence, meaning they currently fall short of human intelligence. While this may be acceptable in low-cost, low-risk sales and buying environments, as the value of exchanges grows and vendor organisations need to take on a deeper, more consultative role, this human intelligence is essential.

What AI will mean for sales

When any new technology has entered the workforce, the assumption has been that the impact will be limited to blue-collar jobs, and those that don't require a high level of education or training. This has been the case since the industrial revolution, when manufacturing jobs were split into individual tasks where each step could be accomplished by a machine, instead of one person crafting each product.

This may have been the case in the past, but the AI era is one where those narrow tasks are now information tasks, not assembly ones, and many can be completed by AI — even narrow artificial intelligence.

According to Sebastian Thrun, an AI professor at Stanford University known for his work on self-driving cars, 'we are just seeing the tip of the iceberg. No office job is safe'. Jerry Kaplan, another Stanford academic and author of *Humans need not apply*, famously stated that 'automation is blind to the colour of your collar'.[120]

Just some of the white-collar jobs vulnerable to automation include pharmacists, lawyers and doctors, each of which are already undergoing automation.[121]

Let's consider pharmacists. While it takes a great deal of training and education to become a pharmacist, the role itself is very routine, making it ideal for automation. In fact, the University of California in San Francisco has already adopted automated dispensing technology and believes the technology helps avoid many of the risks involved when humans perform the work.

In law, a significant part of entry-level and paralegal roles is reviewing documents, something that can be performed algorithmically using AI (without the billable hours).

Even medicine is open to automation, as demonstrated by Watson, IBM's cognitive computing platform. In 2015, Watson was able to diagnose a cancer sufferer with a rare form of leukaemia that trained specialists were unable to diagnose. Even more impressive is the fact that Watson did this in just 10 minutes. Watson was able to make this diagnosis by cross-referencing the patient's genetic data with its own database, then filtering out any data points that were not relevant (or correlated) to reach its conclusion.[122]

So, what about sales?

The role of sales has always been thought to be a people-based role requiring a high degree of knowledge and above-average communication skills to be successful. For this reason, the role of the salesperson was never seen as under threat throughout earlier waves of automation. After all, there's nothing predictable or routine about sales. Right?

Wrong.

According to research by McKinsey, AI automation technologies can be applied to nearly 40 per cent of an organisation's sales processes. With advancements in natural language processing, that could increase to more than 50 per cent.[123]

Why wouldn't vendor organisations want to leverage this? Just consider the following capabilities of AI that are relevant to the sales profession.

First, AI can process, analyse and draw insights from large amounts of data. In sales, this means AI could identify prospects, communicate with them at the right time via the right channel, analyse prospect data, calculate the likelihood of closing a deal and recommend the best next steps in the sales process. AI could help salespeople build a deeper relationship by testing buyer-specific product configurations, selecting complementary products and calculating the best price for the bundle with the most attractive sales terms. And after the sale, AI could monitor the interactions your buyers have with your organisation and make predictions about future behaviour based on these interactions.

Second, AI can free your team from repetitive and administrative tasks such as data entry, data processing, planning, forecasting, analytics and research. The *Harvard Business Review* found that 51 per cent of large companies expect AI to automate these processes, while HubSpot found that the top three AI use cases in business were automating manual tasks, gaining data-driven insights and writing prospect outreach messages and sales content.[124,125]

Third, generative AI can help vendor businesses, sales teams and sales individuals develop a deeper understanding of their buyers and their needs. Eighty-five per cent of large companies expect AI to create better buyer experiences, with more than half of companies planning to use AI to identify early signs of buyer dissatisfaction.[126]

AI could be used to create comprehensive personas of current and potential buyers, to automatically customise the journey for each buyer, to quickly identify changes in buyer behaviour and to address the buyer with personalised content.

When it comes to implications for B2B marketing, the growth of social media and the IoT has led to an explosion of data that AI can process to reveal insights about the needs, preferences and attitudes of different segments. IBM's Watson is an excellent example of this in process, as the system is able to identify sentiment, emotions, values and attitudes expressed in text.[127]

While any new technology can lead to fear and uncertainty, we don't see the rise of generative AI as one that will put salespeople out of a job. AI is an opportunity for salespeople who have a long-term commitment to the profession to get even better at their roles, as this technology can help them build a deeper relationship with their buyers and help those buyers realise more value.

Eighty-two per cent of large companies also believe that this technology has the potential to significantly improve the alignment between sales and marketing teams (which leads to better buyer experiences). Seventy-two per cent of these companies struggle with tracking their buyers' journeys and attributing conversions, and AI can help fill the gaps in the process and determine which activities are the most effective. Additionally, 38 per cent of these companies believe having a holistic view of their buyers (which can be achieved with AI-driven data collection) will empower them to adjust sales and marketing approaches in real time.[128]

When vendor organisations effectively leverage the capabilities of this new technology, they can expect to experience a raft of benefits.

The most obvious one is efficiency. As we will discuss in more depth in chapter 4, the majority of salespeople's time is currently spent on non-selling activities, and many of these tasks can be automated by AI, freeing up time for serving buyers. HubSpot estimates that AI and automation tools save sales teams more than two hours a day, with 79 per cent of sales professionals saying AI allowed them to spend more time selling, while 72 per cent said it helped them build rapport with their buyers faster.[129]

The next area is effectiveness as, through analysing existing and past business relationships, AI can discover new opportunities that would have otherwise remained unexplored. AI can also generate personalised recommendations on how salespeople can work with each buyer, empowering them to engage with buyers in the right way at the right time. Unsurprisingly, 85 per cent of salespeople using AI say it makes their prospecting efforts more effective.[130]

AI can also reduce the risk of knowledge being lost when employees move on by facilitating the effective knowledge transfer between team members. Even if a team member doesn't perform a thorough handover before leaving, AI can track individuals' activities and discover trends that lead to successful outcomes, then use these to develop recommendations for other team members.

Unsurprisingly, McKinsey analysts estimate that AI has the potential to contribute USD1.4 to USD2.6 trillion of value in marketing and sales in the coming years.[131]

What's next for AI?

AI technologies, and their popularity, will continue to grow from here.

According to Gartner Research available at the time of writing, by 2025, AI avatars will support 70 per cent of digital and marketing communications, with 30 per cent of marketing content being created by generative AI and then augmented by humans (this was less than 2 per cent in 2022).[132]

AI infrastructure will continue to grow, with Nvidia's high-end chips consuming 13 797 GWh in 2024 (this is the same amount of energy as a small nation) and 80 per cent of data centre power expected to be consumed by AI over the next 15 years. It is estimated at the time of writing that, by 2026, we will run out of high-quality text data to train LLMs, which could see AI progress slowing, but it also means that vendors with proprietary content will become valuable licensing and acquisition targets.[133]

Corporate investments into generative AI are also expected to climb, with major tech companies buying tens of thousands of graphics processing units. Similarly, millions are already being invested into LLMs, with the starting price for customising GPT-4 for enterprise starting at USD2–3 million, and one Fortune 500 healthcare company already spending USD5 million a year on OpenAI.[134]

Development in the space is also getting easier. Small language models are already 88 times smaller than LLM GPT-3.5, making them faster to train and cheaper to run. These smaller models are expected to take on narrower tasks across finance, healthcare and law.

Open-source LLMs are seeing rising investor interest and, as more of these open-source models become available, a record number of new AI projects is expected to be built.

The use of AI copilots is also growing across industries. In coding, copilots are expected to become standard-issue tools at the enterprise level. In healthcare, copilots are automating tedious tasks such as documentation. In law, copilots can draft contracts, summarise documents and optimise research.

In sales, copilots like Qoos.ai can integrate directly into vendor CRMs to provide real-time guidance, coaching and insights at the point of need. Some examples of this functionality include:

- lead-qualification scores that highlight pipeline risks and provide clear next-best-actions
- stakeholder insights and psychological profiles to navigate complex buying centres with ease
- in-the-flow-of-work learning, so sales teams can get the guidance they need, exactly when they need it.

Unsurprisingly, the increased adoption of these tools is expected to launch the next boom of white-collar productivity growth.

Putting the professional setting aside, though, it's also worth looking at the generational impact of AI. At the time of writing, nearly half of the workforce is comprised of Millennials (38.6 per cent) and Gen Z (6.1 per cent).[135] This ratio will only grow as Baby Boomers retire and younger members of Gen Z reach working age.

These generations are known for being digital natives. Every day, Millennials spend more than two hours on social media, plus almost three hours online via PCs, laptops or tablets and an additional four hours online on their phones.[136]

Meanwhile, Gen Z spends more than six hours a day on their phones. They turn to the internet first for information (including reviews before making a purchase), consume their media online and curate their online selves more carefully than previous generations.[137]

With this in mind, it isn't surprising that these generations are deeply engaged with AI — even on a romantic level. People aged between 18 and 30 are having less sex than ever before, with the annual California Health Interview Survey (CHIS: the largest sexual health survey in the United States) finding that 38 per cent of the cohort reported that they'd had no sex in the past year.[138] While the younger generations have more opportunities to connect than ever before with dozens of dating apps, the apps don't appear to be working. A study of 12 Tinder users' activity showed that of the 286 477 profiles they were served, only 10 829 led to messages.[139]

With the growth in generative AI, it isn't surprising that dating apps like Bumble and MatchGroup are using these algorithms to make dating less awkward. Even more interesting is that AI girlfriend startups are finding a growing male audience.

Beyond dating, however, generative AI is now even playing a role in friendships. In the post-pandemic world, we are spending more hours alone than ever before. Gen Z in particular spends far less time with friends in person than any other generation.[140] AI is now filling the friendship gap, with more than half of the four million users of Character.AI (a generative AI-powered chatbot web app) being under the age of 24.[141]

This might all seem tangential to the discussion on the evolving sales and buying landscape, but just recall that nearly half the workforce (including business buyers and B2B salespeople) are now Millennials and Gen Zs. As sales was traditionally a relationship-based profession, we need to be prepared when working with buyers and sellers who increasingly prefer to develop relationships using AI.

Will the robots take over?

We expect AI to become the most widely used technology in sales: it will complement sales in a valuable way by becoming an additional resource and being strategically integrated into future vendor organisations. Because of this, it should be seen as an opportunity for organisations ready to leverage it. As with other developments in digital technology, those that don't seize the opportunity will be left behind by the vendors that do.

However, technology alone isn't the answer, and implementing new technology without first addressing an organisation's foundations will only accelerate what isn't working. Becoming a Deep-Selling organisation starts with the shift towards buyer centricity, and buyer centricity starts with understanding today's buyers.

CHAPTER 3
WELCOME TO THE AGE OF THE BUYER

When Graham first began selling enterprise software in 1996, the sales and buying landscape was transitioning from the information technology era into the internet era. This was a time of flux: the efficiencies brought on by the information technology era had been cemented, and buyers and sellers were accustomed to building cooperative, strategic relationships.

In time, the internet era would give buyers access to global supply networks and the ability to conduct independent research, and this would see them prioritising vendors who could provide complete solutions.

However, in 1996, enterprise software was the biggest game in town and most software vendors were experiencing extraordinary growth, making massive profits and attracting all of the best sales talent available. Vendor salespeople were afforded almost rock star status.

Not only were these salespeople earning massive commissions due to exploding sales growth, but they were also highly sought after for their bleeding-edge knowledge and access to game-changing R&D. As a software salesperson, Graham was able to pick up the phone and call almost any business — small, medium or large — and be instantly granted an appointment. It was a growth market where buyers would roll out the red carpet to be educated on how technology could help them reduce costs and enable business growth.

This was a time of massive deals — of 'landing whales' — where the buyer would pay millions upfront with no risk to the vendor, and a salesperson could hit their quota for the year in a single deal.

Mark kicked off his career as a sales engineer five years later, in 2001, selling high-value engineering solutions. When he moved into building products in 2005, buyers were not only open to but also actively seeking out new solutions. Like Graham, he could get a meeting with almost anyone in the industry with a single phone call.

Fast-forward 20 years and everything has changed. The IT market is mature, vendor salespeople are no longer rock stars, and the balance of power has now shifted back to the business buyer. There are also so many vendor salespeople in the field that it's hard to stand out from the noise, which means even getting in the door is increasingly difficult. Rather than focusing on the big win, salespeople now have to take a more methodical and incremental approach, prioritising buyer loyalty and long-term sustainability and gradually building revenue streams.

And the landscape is still changing, with 90 per cent of executive leaders surveyed in 2022 believing that buyers had changed in the previous 12 months alone. When asked how buyers had changed, 51 per cent said buyers were conducting more research prior to engaging vendor businesses, 43 per cent said they preferred a digital-first experience, 42 per cent said they were looking to peers for vendor recommendations and 37 per cent said buyers had increased expectations of value-added insights (something that is key to the Deep-Selling approach).

In this chapter, we will discuss how buyers have changed through four broad themes: digitalisation, the shifting power dynamic from vendors to buyers, higher buyer expectations and the crisis of customer confidence.

The impact of digitalisation on the buying process

Every sales professional is familiar with the buyer journey, which comprises the three broad stages of awareness, consideration and purchase.

At the awareness stage, buyers become aware that they have a problem that needs solving. They start researching ways they can address this problem, often taking a top-down approach—starting with more general questions and enquiries before considering specific solutions.

Once they reach the consideration stage, they have narrowed their search to just a few solutions, or vendors, that they believe will be able to address their problem. This stage involves more research, delving deeper into each of the offerings and how they might address the buyer's pain points. By this stage, the buying organisation will have defined internal criteria for the solution and will measure offerings against those criteria.

At the purchase stage, the buyer has decided to move forward with a particular solution. The solution is then refined to meet the buyer's needs, after which testing, implementation and training will ensue.

Figure 3.1 (overleaf) illustrates the three stages of the buyer journey.

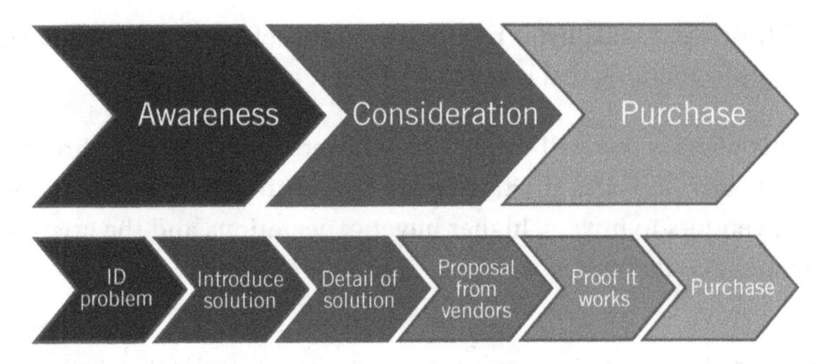

Figure 3.1: the three stages of the buyer journey

The sales cycle has always run in parallel with the buying journey, and switched-on salespeople understand and leverage this connection to ensure success. This relationship is depicted in figure 3.2.

For most of the 140-year history of modern sales, buyers have relied heavily on the specialist knowledge and expertise of vendor salespeople. Historically, the only way buyers could access this knowledge was via their vendors and, as a natural consequence of this knowledge gap, vendors held the power and were often viewed as trusted advisers in almost every buying organisation. Consequently, salespeople were able to work alongside buyers throughout the buying journey to create awareness, discover needs and then sell solutions.

Today, the buyer journey has changed significantly, and digitalisation is one of the major culprits behind this change.

Digitalisation has resulted in more decentralised and multi-channel approaches, with the average B2B buyer using more than nine channels on their buying journey, including older channels like email and phone calls as well as newer ones like mobile apps and web chats.[142] These multi-channel buying approaches have increased both the amount and speed of information that can be accessed for decision making, and mean that many stages of the buying process are completed electronically with less manual effort required.[143,144]

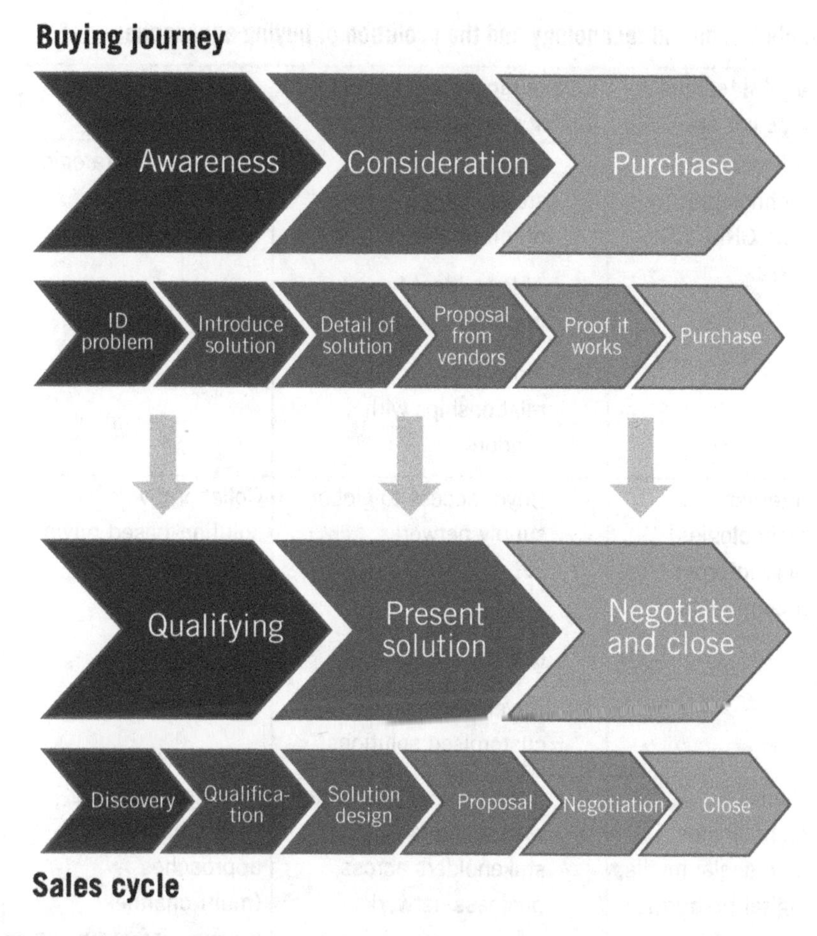

Figure 3.2: the parallel nature of the buying journey and the sales cycle

At an organisational level, complex systems consisting of the IoT, AI and digital platforms have enabled interconnection, information transparency, decentralised decision making and improved decision support, all of which have led to more efficient transactions and better coordination and control of buying tasks (see table 3.1, overleaf).[145]

If we return to the buyer journey, buyers still move through the three stages of awareness, consideration and purchase, but they no longer need the assistance of a vendor to enter the funnel or move through the stages.

Table 3.1: digital technology and the evolution of buying approaches

Digital technology type per era	Role of technology type in buying approaches	Resulting buying approach
Information technologies (e.g. CRM, EDI, ERP)	• Improved collection, storage and processing of information • Able to identify important suppliers • More strategic relationships with vendors	Cooperative/strategic buying (based on vendor relationships)
Internet technologies (e.g. internet, e-commerce)	• Buyer access to global supply networks • IT solutions becoming increasingly commoditised • Buyer need for customised solutions	Collaborative/ solution-based buying (customised over out-of-the-box solutions)
Digital technologies (e.g. social media, digital platforms	• Improved communication with multiple stakeholders across business networks • More effective data analysis • Enabled decentralised decision making	Decentralised and multi-channel approaches (multi-channel buying, rise of buying committees)
AI technologies (e.g. artificial intelligence, ChatGPT)	• Advanced analysis of large datasets • Predictive capabilities • Vast amounts of data searched and interpreted • Personalised information delivered	Digitalised and automated buying (AI reviewing options and recommendation generation)

Instead, today's buyers are highly educated and have access to huge amounts of information. Rather than receiving a visit from a field salesperson or contacting a retailer to learn about their options, buyers can gather all the required information themselves.

First, they might become aware of a product via PR, online advertising, social media or word of mouth. At this stage, social media is playing a larger role than ever before with 82 per cent of B2B buyers saying the winning vendor's social content had a significant impact on their purchase decision.[146]

Next, they will learn more about the product by searching online, with buyers preferring to do pre-sales research online by a factor of three to one. Eighty-one per cent of salespeople say buyers increasingly conduct research before they reach out and 55 per cent of consumers start their online product research with Amazon reviews.[147,148,149] While it's easy for those of us in sales to say that online research can't hold a candle to a one-to-one conversation with a salesperson who has an in-depth understanding of the product and how it might meet the buyer's needs, the truth is that the majority of B2B buyers feel that product recommendations shown on websites are as valuable as recommendations made by sales representatives (50 per cent versus 16 per cent).[150]

At the purchase stage, nearly 75 per cent of today's buyers feel that buying from a website is more convenient than buying from a salesperson.[151] Fifty-nine per cent of buyers prefer not to interact with salespeople, and 93 per cent prefer to buy online when they have decided what to buy.[152] In fact, buyers have become so comfortable with online buying that they are happy to close deals of more than USD500 000 without ever meeting a vendor salesperson in person.[153]

This trend has been accelerated by the rise of generative AI.

Consider using a tool like ChatGPT to make a purchase decision as a consumer. You are in the market for a luxury car, and you want it to be less than two years old. You open a chat and ask for a list of all the luxury cars released in the past two years. Once you have your list, you can ask ChatGPT to recommend the top three of these. If there are certain criteria that are important to you, like budget, fuel consumption or safety features, you could ask ChatGPT to make a new recommendation based on your preferences.

While this is a business-to-consumer (B2C) example, it is a clear illustration of how buying has evolved. Since the beginning of the digital era in 2010, buyers have become increasingly digitally proficient, able to use Google to learn about different solutions and read user reviews. In the AI era, they don't even need to search for the information themselves: all they need is to know their selection criteria, and they can ask a bot to do the work.

Beyond making the work itself easier, these tools have access to information far broader than what any one individual buyer (or even the average buying committee) could access. It is well known that B2B buyers are rational, and that vendor salespeople can't pull emotional levers the same way that B2C salespeople might. However, that rationality is bounded.

What we mean by this is that there is a limit to what a business buyer can know. Consequently, they may have the intention of reducing risk and increasing value when making a purchasing decision, but they will never have full visibility of all the available information. This means they need to make the best decision they can with the information they have available.

Theoretically, AI technologies do not suffer from bounded rationality (at the time of writing, tools like ChatGPT are drawing on finite knowledge libraries, but in the future, these tools could have access to boundless information). This means buyers have access to a tool that is completely rational without those bounds.

So, where a buyer might have made a decision based on likely risk and reward in the past, there would also have been an element of their relationship with the vendor organisation and the individual salesperson they were working with—and the level of trust that had been built between them—that would factor into their decision. That trust would help fill the gap between what the buyer does and doesn't know, and would mean that the buying decision could never be entirely rational.

When it comes to AI, there is no trust gap. It knows everything at once and any relationship between the buyer and seller has no impact (unless the buyer asks it to take this into consideration). This is a complete upheaval of the traditional buyer-seller relationship.

This means the buyer no longer has the same need to engage with salespeople. Only 17 per cent of buying activity time is spent meeting with potential suppliers, with 70.2 per cent of buyers preferring to wait to engage a vendor until after they have a clear understanding of their needs and 20.2 per cent preferring to wait until solutions are evaluated.[154,155] As a result, the average buyer now completes up to 87 per cent of their buying process before even approaching a salesperson.[156] Figure 3.3 illustrates this new trend.

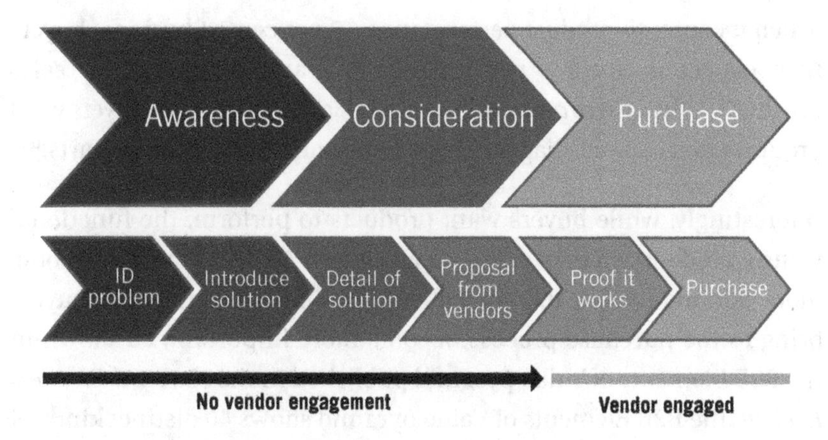

Figure 3.3: vendor engagement in the new buyer journey

Despite the many myth-busting arguments attempting to undermine the assertion that salespeople are arriving late to the buying journey, the facts are clear: buyers are doing huge amounts of research before they engage with vendor salespeople. This pre-engagement knowledge reduces the risk that the vendor might lead them down the wrong path and it obviously puts the buyer on a stronger footing for negotiations.

Consequently, vendor salespeople no longer influence the buying journey as they once did, and anyone who has sold anything knows that being called into a sales opportunity late simply limits your ability to influence the sale.

Buyer expectations are higher than ever before

When a buyer does engage a vendor salesperson, their expectations are higher than ever before. These include their expectations of product performance, their expectations for the buying process, and their expectations for their relationship with vendor organisations.

When it comes to product performance, 78 per cent of business buyers now expect to receive performance guarantees during the sales process.[157] When there *are* performance issues, 73 per cent of buyers want products that can self-diagnose issues and automatically order parts.[158]

Interestingly, while buyers want products to perform, the functional value a product will deliver is seen as a given. As B2B offerings become more commoditised, the subjective, personal concerns that buyers bring to the purchase process become more important, as shown in the B2B Elements of Value pyramid published in the *Harvard Business Review*. The B2B Elements of Value pyramid shows 40 distinct kinds of value B2B offerings provide buyers that go beyond the function of the product itself.[159]

The pyramid is a similar model to Maslow's Hierarchy of Needs. The base layers of physiological needs and safety needs are non-negotiable, but assuming these are met, they are not something that a person would aspire to. Similarly, in the B2B Elements of Value pyramid, the base layers are table stakes (including meeting specifications, price, regulatory compliance and ethical standards) and functional value (including product performance and economic value).

The current buying environment is one of global competition where many markets are hitting maturity and fighting against commoditisation. In this environment, all established vendors would be expected to meet their legal obligations, offer a product that works and deliver economic value to their buyers. These elements are essential, but they are the price of entry.

Buyers' expectations of value have increased. They don't just want a product that works, they want one that will deliver value to their organisation. The most common sources of buyer value are increased productivity and reduced costs, but buyer value can also be delivered through a stronger relationship with their vendors (this might include high stability, internal expertise or responsiveness), as well as the simplicity of accessing the provided solution.

Further up the hierarchy, buyers will also be considering the individual value of choosing different solutions. Which ones will have the biggest impact on their careers, their network, and their growth and development? Closely linked to their ongoing relationship with the vendor, which solution will result in lower anxiety for the buyer — or more fun?

Finally, at the top of the values pyramid are those factors relating to purpose: the buyer's overarching vision, hope and social responsibility.

The takeaway is that business buyers see different types of value when choosing which vendors to work with. Product and business hygiene are only one part of the equation, and savvy vendors who can meet deeper business and individual needs are those who will come out on top.

Closely linked to the B2B Elements of Value are the expectations buyers have for the buying process. Eighty per cent of buyers say that the experience an organisation provides is as important as its products and services, yet 63 per cent say that most buying experiences fall short of what they know is possible.[160]

Again, delivering a product that does what it says it will is barely scratching the surface when it comes to the expectations of the modern buyer.

What do buyers want from the buying experience? Simpler, on-demand, omnichannel engagement that puts their needs first.[161]

Seventy-two per cent of business buyers say they expect real-time/always-on customer service.[162] Keep in mind that this doesn't mean you need a customer support team that is available around the clock. Self-service is the norm, with many Millennials and Gen Zs saying that a phone call *isn't* the best way to solve their problems. Instead, they expect chatbots, virtual assistants and voice-enabled technologies.

Modern buyers also expect an omnichannel experience. Fifty-six per cent of all buyer interactions take place across multiple channels, with 71 per cent of buyers preferring different channels depending on context.[163,164] While 72 per cent of business buyers want the ability to purchase from any channel, 72 per cent also highlighted the importance of having a consistent experience across all channels.[165]

When it comes to which channels buyers prefer, the preference was overwhelmingly for digital channels, with more than three-quarters of B2B decision makers preferring remote and digital sales methods.[166] Buyers also get frustrated when being forced to engage in a channel that isn't their preferred one, with 74 per cent of buyers expecting to be able to do anything online that they can do in person or over the phone.[167]

Vendor organisations that successfully deliver an omnichannel experience reap the benefits, retaining an average of 89 per cent of their buyers, compared to just 33 per cent for organisations with weak omnichannel strategies.[168]

If buyers do not feel their needs have been met during the buyer journey, or if they have a poor experience, 70 per cent of them say they will happily consider other vendors.[169] And, as we shared earlier, the ideal buying experience is one where buyers do not have to engage a vendor salesperson, with 75 per cent of buyers saying they would prefer a seller-free experience.[170]

The final area where buyers have high expectations relates to the ongoing relationship they have with their vendors (or, before making a purchase decision, the relationship they believe they will have with the vendor organisation). Eighty-seven per cent of business buyers expect sales reps to act as trusted advisers.[171] Seventy-eight per cent of business buyers expect companies to adapt to their changing needs and preferences, with 73 per cent wanting them to anticipate their needs and make relevant suggestions even before making contact.[172] Buyers are also making purchase decisions based on higher standards of ethical corporate behaviour, illustrating, once again, that a product that does its job is no longer enough to close the deal.[173]

Unfortunately, most vendor organisations are failing to meet these expectations. According to Bain and Company, while 80 per cent of vendors believe they deliver superior customer service, only 8 per cent of buyers believe they experience superior customer service.[174] Similarly, Forrester found that 80 per cent of sales engagements fail to meet buyer expectations.[175]

The changing balance of power

The combination of information parity and higher buyer expectations has led to a shift in power from the vendor to the buyer.

In the early years of our careers, buyers actively sought guidance from vendors and would rapidly embrace solutions that could give them a competitive advantage, regardless of the complexity involved. These buyers would cobble together solutions across disparate platforms, crafting a veritable patchwork quilt of semi-temporary IT platforms and applications, all connected via bespoke systems and networks.

Buyers took pride in dealing with dozens, if not hundreds, of specialist vendors over multi-product generalists, believing that this was the way to achieve the best outcome, and CIOs of the time would wear their complicated tech stacks as a badge of honour.

With hindsight, it is easy to see how this ad-hoc approach to custom-built environments would result in long-term disadvantages for businesses needing to respond to increasing levels of change. Consequently, complexity is the sworn enemy of today's CIOs, who prefer custom-built, all-encompassing solutions and have been consolidating vendor contracts for more than a decade in order to achieve this.[176]

Rationalising software vendors comes with a range of benefits for modern buyers. It is easier to manage fewer relationships, while efficiencies can be gained through a multi-product vendor's ability to streamline internal processes and delivery. Working with fewer vendors also creates opportunities for cost savings via volume pricing discounts.

Additionally, doing more business with fewer vendors addresses concerns about risk. Chosen vendors tend to be those who have already proven themselves in one or more areas, meaning buyers are more likely to trust them to deliver in other areas as well. (Meanwhile, if something *does* go wrong, there are fewer vendors to chase: 'one throat to choke', as they say.)

This process of vendor rationalisation begins with buying organisations ranking their suppliers in terms of strategic importance or level of priority. This vendor stack encompasses a small number of 'prime' — or Tier 1 — vendors, who usually receive the bulk of the organisation's spend. Tier 2 features a larger number of vendors, who are deemed to be a lower priority and who receive a smaller portion of the organisation's spend, while Tier 3 contains the remaining vendors.

The problem with simply reorganising existing vendors into tiers is that this arrangement often creates a high level of friction without a corresponding increase in value.

Consider National Australia Bank (NAB), which had five Tier 1 vendors, 31 Tier 2 vendors and 1100 Tier 3 vendors in 2013 (see table 3.2). Imagine having to engage with 1100 individual vendor salespeople (and account teams), each of whom is being driven to sell NAB more and more each month, quarter or year!

Table 3.2: NAB vendor stack, December 2013

Vendor tier	Number of vendors
Tier 1	5
Tier 2	31
Tier 3	1100

This creates confusion and complexity. In many cases, it would slow down the acquisition of new products and services; the cost is likely higher as NAB won't have enough volume with any of those suppliers to benefit from volume discounts; and it increases the risk that something will go awry.

It's hardly surprising that NAB, like many buyers who are looking for more efficient and cost-effective processes, was aiming to reduce the quantity of its Tier 3 vendors by 50 per cent.

Similarly, Qantas also broadly categorised its vendors into three tiers, and aimed to cut its Tier 3 vendors from 363 down to 100 (see table 3.3). Even more interesting, however, is the split of IT spend among the different tiers: the nine vendors in Tier 1 received 86 per cent of Qantas' entire annual spend, averaging almost 10 per cent each. By contrast, the 13 Tier 2 vendors received 7 per cent of Qantas' IT spend, or about 0.5 per cent each, while the 363 Tier 3 vendors also received 7 per cent, or less than 0.02 per cent each.

Table 3.3: Qantas vendor stack, August 2013

Vendor tier	Number of vendors	% total annual IT spend
Tier 1	9	86
Tier 2	13	7
Tier 3	363	7

Why wouldn't Qantas see if their nine Tier 1 vendors could cater to all their IT needs? Most of their budget was already going to these vendors, and nine vendors would be far easier to manage than 385.

What does this mean for vendor organisations?

Thanks to the increase in digital technologies, buyers have access to more information than ever before and are able to complete most of their buying journey independently. Because of this increased access to information, they are able to compare more solutions and more vendors than at any other time in history and can use tools such as ChatGPT to analyse different offerings. The wider range of options means their expectations have also increased: a product performing to expectations is the bare minimum, and they are instead looking for vendors who can meet needs that go beyond product performance and business hygiene.

With hundreds, if not thousands, of potential vendors at their fingertips, if one can't meet their expectations in terms of process, quality, relationship or price, they can easily find another that will. And when they do, they are more likely to return to that vendor for their future needs than to try someone new.

Ultimately, the power is in your buyers' hands.

The crisis of customer confidence

While the new sales and buying landscape appears to be overwhelmingly in the business buyer's favour, increased power and higher expectations on the buyer side have resulted in higher levels of buyer indecision than ever before.

According to Gartner, 77 per cent of B2B buyers state that their latest purchase was very complex or difficult.[177] And while there is a mistaken, yet long-held, belief among salespeople that their greatest challenge is overcoming their buyers' status quo, only 44 per cent of deals that are lost to inaction are due to the buyer's preference for the status quo. In 56 per cent of deals, buyers want to move away from the status quo, but they are unable or unwilling to commit to a new approach.[178]

This is why more than 94 per cent of buyers have taken part in a buying process that ended in no decision, and when a decision *is* made, it takes twice as long as expected.[179,180]

Why is this happening in an environment where buyers seem to hold all the cards?

First, there is the buyer struggle with information overload. Gartner found that 89 per cent of buyers said they received high-quality information from vendors during the purchase process, yet it was a challenge to make sense of it all, and 95 per cent of buying groups reported having to revisit decisions at least once after getting new information.[181,182] Buyers having additional information leads to higher uncertainty, not higher clarity. And the more information buyers have, the longer the decision cycle becomes because of the time it takes to digest the information required to make the best decision. All in all, more information means buyers are more likely to end the buying journey with no decision, or to settle for a decision that is less disruptive than what they had originally sought.

Even though more information can be a hindrance to buyers, there is a mistaken belief among many sellers that more information is better. A *Harvard Business Review* piece reported that 86 per cent of salespeople agreed that 'helping the customer consider all possible options and alternatives [was] important', while 68 per cent agreed that 'more information generally helped customers make better decisions'.[183] In reality, the article shared that less was often more when it came to successful sales, with a prescriptive approach increasing purchase ease by 86 per cent, and buyers perceiving prescriptive salespeople 'as being one step ahead, anticipating and eliminating obstacles'.[184]

The second reason why deals are ending in 'no decision' outcomes is due to decreased risk tolerance in buying organisations. Salesforce's *State of the Connected Customer* shared that 78 per cent of buyers said their organisations were more careful about spending money than in the past, while Forrester Research reported that 43 per cent of business buyers made defensive buying decisions more than 70 per cent of the time.[185,186] Fourteen per cent of buyers had a higher number of C-level decision makers to answer to than in the past, and 43 per cent said they needed more information than before to justify any new purchase (which presents an interesting dichotomy to the problem of information overload).[187]

Business buyers are also prioritising solutions they have used before (which leads us back to the discussion on vendor rationalisation), with 51 per cent of buyers referring to their previous experience to inform purchase decisions, and that experience being one of the top three factors guiding their business purchases.[188]

We are now in an environment where most B2B buyers are so terrified of making the wrong decision that they will stick with the status quo rather than make a potentially career-ending decision. As one article aptly put it, 'executives in large corporations are reluctant to propose and advocate for risky projects. They quash new ideas in favour of marginal improvements, cost-cutting and "safe" investments'.[189]

And it won't matter how amazing your ROI looks or how brilliantly you have presented your business case in the context of competing priorities and risk aversion.

The third factor contributing to this confidence crisis among your buyers is the rise in consensus buying. One of the most effective sales strategies throughout history has been to build a relationship with the company decision maker — an executive who can single-handedly approve any purchase — and sell directly to them.

The issue today is that a single decision maker rarely exists. Forrester reported that 94 per cent of B2B vendors sell to groups of three or more individuals, with 38 per cent selling to groups of more than 10 buyers.[190] Gartner found that buying groups were even larger, with six to 10 decision makers in B2B deals, which rose to between 14 and 23 decision makers in the average tech purchase.[191,192]

Any modern purchasing decision likely rests with a group of individuals — many of whom are cross-functional and from different regions, all with their own agenda — each of whom has the power to veto any decision.

The combination of information overload, lower risk tolerance and the ever-growing buying committee means that the buying journey itself is more complex than ever before. Remember the three stages of the buyer journey we shared in figure 3.1 — awareness, consideration and purchase? The modern B2B buying journey no longer takes place in these three linear steps (see figure 3.4, overleaf). Instead, it is a tangled mess: a 'buyer spaghetti bowl', to use a term coined by sales and marketing adviser, Brent Adamson.

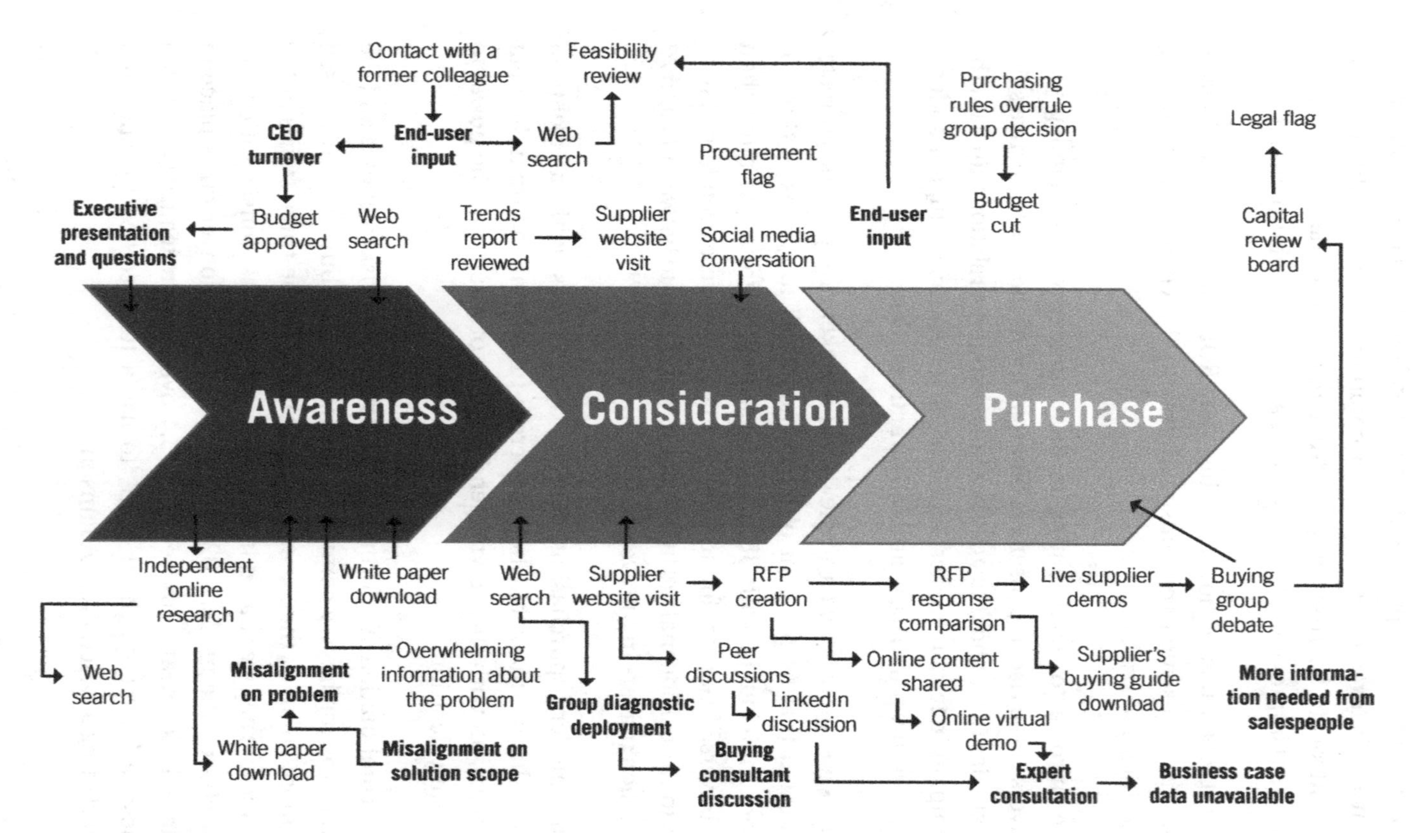

Figure 3.4: the modern B2B buyer journey[193]

Unsurprisingly, this adds significant hurdles to the decision-making process, resulting in longer sales cycles, with 58 per cent of buyers saying sales cycles are longer than they used to be.[194] And this is if a decision is made at all. As we've discussed, 'no decision' outcomes are becoming ever more common, especially when there are multiple decision makers: 81 per cent of purchases are made when there is a single decision maker, which plummets to between 50 and 60 per cent when there are two-to-four decision makers and falls again to 31 per cent when there are six decision makers.[195]

One of the benefits of building a relationship with a buyer is the ability to personalise your pitch and your solution to meet their needs. The issue with having multiple decision makers involved is that personalising your pitch to each of them can highlight conflicting goals and priorities in the group, hindering a consensus. It can also highlight that you, as a salesperson, are trying to influence them down a particular path for your own vested interests.

Add to this the fact that people are changing jobs more frequently, and it becomes more difficult than ever to build and maintain a personal relationship with the necessary people. We have lost count of the number of times we have worked on a large enterprise deal, developing close relationships with people across the buying organisation, only to find that a key stakeholder has just moved on, and we've had to start afresh with strangers who couldn't care less about our solution and who have previous experience with a competitor who they then invite to the bidding war.

Frustrating, yes, but this happens all the time.

The final factor brings us back to risk tolerance, but this is on the individual level rather than the organisational level. This is FOMU: the fear of messing up.

FOMU relates to the psychological concepts of commission bias and omission bias. Omission bias is the phenomenon where people prefer inaction (omission) over action (commission), and this phenomenon is why people tend to feel more regret when there are negative consequences due to their actions, than when consequences arise due to not taking action.[196] This is especially true in business buying, where buyers worry about choosing the wrong option, worry that they haven't done enough homework to make a good decision, and worry they won't get the value that they have paid for. In a business environment, the consequences of this might include being passed over for a promotion, or even losing a job.

This means there's much more incentive for buyers to make the 'safe' choice. CEO and founder of Membrain, George Brontén, has shared an excellent discussion on LinkedIn about this phenomenon in the world of CRM implementation, where he writes that no-one ever gets fired for buying Salesforce.[197] No-one gets fired for going with the market leader or the tried and tested option, so if your business buyers are afraid of messing up, why would they try someone new?

(As a side note, the same is true within vendor organisations. No-one gets fired for doing things the way they have always been done, which is why so many sales organisations are persisting with outdated, ineffective, push-selling approaches instead of moving forward with what really works: a buyer-centric, Deep-Selling approach.)

In short, buyers have more information and responsibility than ever before. At the same time, they don't trust salespeople to guide them, meaning the weight of making the correct investment is entirely on buyers' shoulders, as is the fear of messing up.

Walking the buyer tightrope

Buyers overwhelmingly prefer to perform research, find solutions and complete transactions online, which means vendor organisations that follow traditional sales approaches can actually inhibit buyers from having their preferred experience.

At the same time, buyers are experiencing a crisis in confidence, where the purchase experience is more complex than ever before and the growing size of buying committees, and the growing fear of messing up, is resulting in an increasing number of deals ending in no decision.

This leaves vendor organisations in a challenging situation. On the one hand, buyers increasingly prefer self-serve, seller-free experiences and no longer value the traditional salesperson's role as a trusted adviser. On the other, buyers with complex needs and/or complex buying environments have a greater need for salespeople to fill that role than ever before. Nowhere is this dichotomy clearer than in recent research, with Gartner finding that 75 per cent of B2B buyers prefer a seller-free experience and Salesforce finding that 84 per cent of business buyers expect sales reps to act as trusted advisers.[198,199]

This is one of the major reasons why an increasing number of salespeople are struggling to perform. Vendor organisations that are unable to find the balance required for their buyers will find that their sales performance and business outcomes will continue to decline as a result.

CHAPTER 4
THE FALLING EFFECTIVENESS OF SALES TEAMS

Sales teams are facing the most challenging sales and buying landscape in history. The modern, buyer-led era is one where vendor organisations and sales teams can seemingly do everything 'right', yet still not get the results they want.

For instance, in 2018, CSO Insights released a white paper titled *The growing buyer-seller gap*, which introduced the concept of the apathy loop vendor that salespeople find themselves in.

Interestingly, the paper revealed that even though buyers are generally satisfied with vendor salespeople—61.8 per cent of buyers felt that salespeople *were* meeting expectations, almost one-third believed that salespeople exceeded expectations and 65.2 per cent of buyers found value in discussing solutions with salespeople—less than one-quarter chose vendor salespeople as a top-three resource for solving business problems. Vendor salespeople ranked ninth on a list of 10 potential resources, including colleagues and third-party experts, but also sources made possible due to the past few decades of digitalisation: websites, web searches, social media and online forums.[200]

Consequently, business buyers are engaging vendor salespeople later in their buying journey than ever before. As we discussed in the previous chapter, 70.2 per cent of buyers said they preferred to wait until after they had a clear understanding of their needs before engaging a vendor, with 20.2 per cent saying they preferred to wait until solutions were evaluated and they were ready to negotiate terms.[201]

As sales professionals, we know that getting involved this late in the process severely limits a salesperson's ability to provide value and act as a trusted adviser, which means it isn't surprising that more than half of buyers saw little difference between vendors, and 10.4 per cent saw no difference between them at all.[202]

This brings us to the sales apathy loop. According to a CSO Insights report from 2018[203], vendor salespeople regularly meet, but don't exceed, expectations. This means that many buyers see salespeople as product representatives rather than advisers who can help solve business problems. Buyers, therefore, wait until they have already found a solution before engaging a vendor and see little difference between vendors due to them being engaged so late in the journey. The chosen vendor then meets the buyer's expectations by delivering the chosen solution, but this fails to build a Deep relationship or any long-term loyalty. If vendor salespeople are not careful, they can get caught in this apathy loop where they continue to the be treated as a commodity, and never realise the opportunity to add real value to their buyers.

Is it any wonder, then, that many buyers are cutting salespeople out of their buying process entirely? Vendor rationalisation means it's more difficult for smaller vendors to get any direct face time with buyers, resulting in them often having to sell through larger vendors. And the crisis in customer confidence means that even when salespeople *can* get in front of a buying committee, the sales process is taking longer than ever before, and 40 to 60 per cent of the time the process will end with no decision.[204]

With all of this in mind, it's not surprising that many salespeople feel sales is harder than it used to be. Eighty-two per cent of sales professionals say they've had to adapt quickly to new ways of selling, with 69 per cent believing that their job is harder now.[205] Salespeople have also reported a 40 per cent drop in prospecting efficiency as the budget for new vendors has dried up.[206] Meanwhile, 83 per cent of CSOs and senior sales leaders report that their sellers struggle to adapt to new buyer needs and expectations.[207]

The result? Seventy-eight per cent of salespeople are underperforming.[208]

The real question, though, is why is this happening? We have already discussed digitalisation and trends influencing the buyer side of the equation, but what is happening within vendor organisations and sales teams?

As technology and buyers evolve, so do sellers, with the sales role and vendor business models both having changed significantly when compared to just a few decades ago.

How the sales role has evolved

The sales role is not what it used to be. Since Dale Carnegie released *How to win friends and influence people* in 1936, personal relationships have been seen as the foundation on which the sales process is built.

Like most sales professionals, we have spent most of our careers with personal relationships at the centre of our daily activities. We have honed our relationship-building skills and our ability to build trust and value throughout the sales process, believing that this is the key to closing deals.

However, the world has changed over the past 30 years, and we now find ourselves in a new dynamic: one where buyers don't need a personal relationship with us at all. In fact, today's buyers are actively looking for ways to *avoid* having any kind of personal relationship with salespeople. As we shared in chapter 3, nearly 75 per cent of B2B buyers think buying from a website is more convenient than buying from a salesperson, while 93 per cent prefer to buy online once they have made a decision and just need to make a purchase.[209]

Personal relationships in business are never as strong as we like to think they are. They are often built on very thin foundations that are misleading to salespeople, because it's in the buyer's best interest to coerce naïve salespeople into thinking that your relationship is important. As long as the buyer keeps receiving high value for a declining cost, the relationship continues. As soon as prices go up or value goes down, the relationship is over.

If you don't believe us, try telling your most important buyers that you've just raised your prices by 10 per cent and see what happens. Let's see how strong your 'critical' buyer relationship is when your buyer is forced to go to their management and argue for more budget due to your price increase. Let's see how strong the relationship is when a new, low-cost substitute comes along offering 20 per cent savings for a similar output.

A modern buyer is not going to stay with a vendor just because they like them. Your relationship will never be justification enough for the buyer to pay 'overs' for any product or service when there are cheaper alternatives.

The truth is that the days of having a relationship that's strong enough to influence buyer decision making are gone. Buyers simply don't value personal relationships with their vendors anymore, and sales teams need to be able to adapt to that change.

If personal relationships are no longer the crux of the sales role, then what is?

The answer might surprise you. Where a traditional field salesperson's role used to revolve around prospecting, building relationships with buyers in their territory and closing deals, today's salespeople are expected to do far more than close sales.

While salespeople often work longer than the typical 40-hour week, a study conducted by Pace Productivity Inc. found that only 22 per cent of that typical working week is spent selling. The rest of their time is spent on activities that don't directly result in sales, such as administration, order processing, planning, travel, service and other duties.[210]

Similarly, academics Moncrief and Marshall reviewed selling activities in 1986, and again in 2005, and discovered 49 new selling activities required of modern salespeople that hadn't been present two decades earlier.[211,212]

Most of us will have some familiarity with the dangers of multi-tasking and the importance of making time for focused work. With this in mind, the logical assumption would be that salespeople should reduce the breadth of their activities to focus on selling. However, there is disagreement on this point. On the one hand, new digital technologies can enable systematisation and automation, allowing sales professionals to focus on the 'important' things.[213,214] On the other, higher service expectations from buyers are forcing vendor organisations to make buyer-specific investments, including allocating dedicated resources and co-creating value with these buyers, adding yet another aspect to the salesperson's role.[215]

This also means there is an increasing demand for new skills among sales professionals, with 80 per cent of sales leaders ranking analytical and quantitative skills among the top capabilities for individual team members, and 85 per cent agreeing about the importance of solution selling as a core sales capability, requiring strong product knowledge and solution design as well as account-planning skills.[216]

This leaves sales teams with a growing list of responsibilities beyond selling and a lack of clear direction on where they should focus their energy: on leveraging new technologies and systems, or on customised solutions where they co-create value for strategic buyers?

Business model evolution

Just as the sales role has evolved, so too has the business model of many vendor organisations.

The traditional sales model focused primarily on the 'close'. Particularly in high-tech industries, vendor salespeople would sell highly customised software or services contracts with multi-year terms and then receive the bulk of the revenue upfront. See figure 4.1.

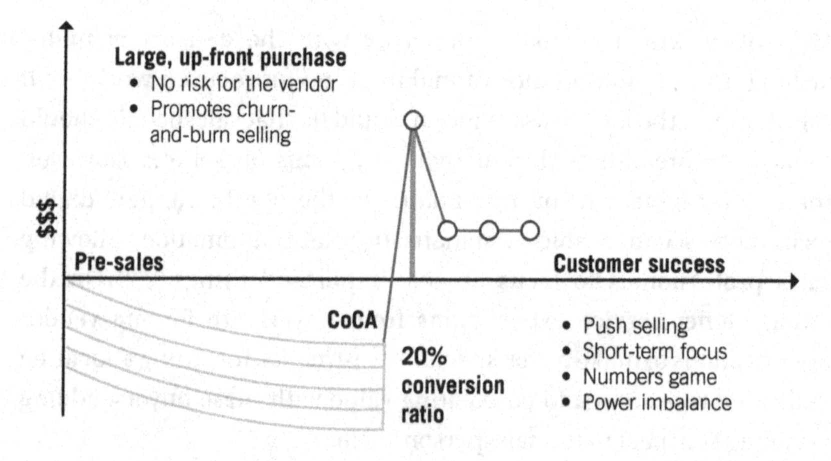

Figure 4.1: the old, up-front revenue model

From here, the salesperson would celebrate their win, take home the commission and move on to the next opportunity. While not every sale would close, and the acquisition costs of each opportunity were significant whether or not the buyer went ahead, the deals that went through were often so large that they made up for the costs of those that didn't close.

There are several issues with this approach. The first is that it is focused on a short-term vendor outcome rather than the lifetime buyer value, and this has exacerbated the distrust between vendors and buyers. Vendors often overpromised and then underdelivered, leaving a sour taste in the mouths of their buyers.

The second issue is that this old model encourages salespeople to push hard to close any lead, regardless of fit. Because there's a big upfront purchase, there's no risk to the vendor if the buyer is unhappy with the product or service. If the buyer chooses to move on, the vendor has already been paid in full.

The third issue is that this model allows sales teams to get away with underperformance. This old-world, push-selling model bred the mindset of many current C-suite members with a background in traditional sales. It is all a numbers game: just put as much in the top of the funnel as you can and push it all down until something falls out the bottom.

Unfortunately, the numbers often don't hold up under closer examination. Acquisition costs in this model are high and conversion rates are low, yet these inefficiencies get swept under the rug as soon as there is a large sale. This model allows continued underperformance, because no-one sees a need to improve pipeline efficiency as long as those 'whales' keep coming in.

With changing buyer expectations and new technology, those large upfront purchases rarely happen. Buyers no longer choose to transform their technology infrastructure by replacing all their legacy technology. Instead, an increasing number of buyers invest in consumption-based models where they purchase a monthly subscription to a servitised version of what would have formerly been sold as a one-off product purchase (see figure 4.2).

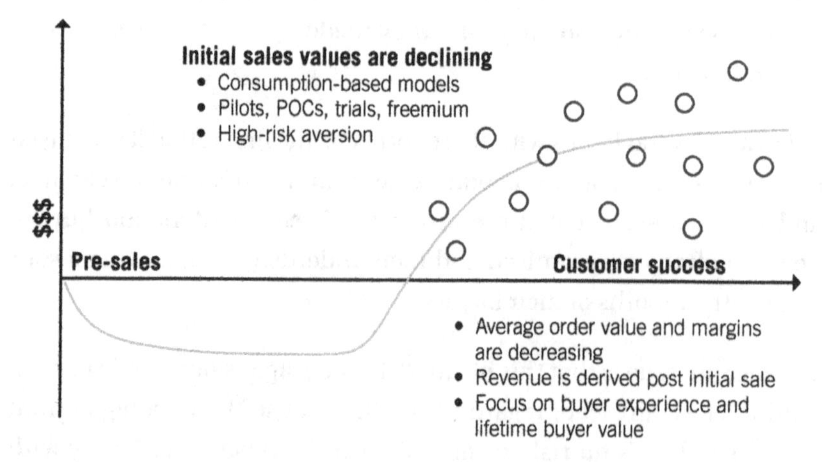

Figure 4.2: the new, ongoing revenue model

In this model, acquisition costs and conversion rates need to be closely monitored, as there is no big win that will level the balance sheet. Instead, acquisition costs need to be recuperated via a steady string of small purchases over time, with 70 to 80 per cent of total buyer revenue taking place after the initial sale.[217]

Consequently, vendor organisations must have a vested interest in the ongoing success of their buyers.

This is why many successful companies are removing the word 'sales' from their organisations, instead designing roles focused on customer experience, customer success and relationship management.

The challenge goes beyond the transition from big wins to micro-transactions, however. There have also been changes to how long it takes to reach that point in the buyer journey. As we discussed in chapter 3, the rise of consensus buying and fear of messing up mean that the typical solutions purchase takes twice as long as buyers think it will, and this is if they reach a purchase decision at all![218]

The impact of long acquisition times and ongoing revenue models means that it is very easy for acquisition costs to blow out, especially when considering the high cost of traditional field sales forces.

According to Payscale.com, the average salary (including commissions, bonuses and shares) for an outside sales representative ranges from USD60000 to almost USD150000.[219] Table 4.1 compares US salaries with the UK, Australia and Canada.

Table 4.1: average outside salesperson salary

	United States (USD)	UK (GBP)	Australia (AUD)	Canada (CAD)
Salary	55356	25789	62714	53564
Bonus	30000	36000	17000	23000
Profit sharing	15000	4000	4000	15000
Commission	49000	4000	14000	31000
Total	149356	69789	97714	122564
Total (USD)[220]	149356	87275	63797	105876

Keep in mind that these numbers are just averages—when filtered to certain cities or industries, they climb exponentially. In the high-tech space in Melbourne and Sydney, Australia, the average outside sales representative has a base salary of AUD150000, and if they hit their numbers, they can often earn another AUD150000 in bonuses and commissions.

At a total package of AUD300000, plus expenses like travel and entertaining clients, it's easy to see how people become the largest cost of a sale. Additionally, Forrester Research's 2009 report *Uncovering the hidden cost of sales support* found that technology vendors are spending, on average, 19 per cent of their selling, general and administrative costs — or USD135 262 per quota-carrying salesperson — on support-related activities.[221]

So, what's the problem? Haven't salespeople always received good salaries?

While this is true, we have entered a time when the relative cost of salespeople is higher than ever before.

First, the time required to bring a new hire to full productivity is longer than ever, with 65.2 per cent of businesses saying it takes at least seven months to bring new hires up to speed, and 28.8 per cent of businesses saying it takes at least one year.[222]

Meanwhile, average tenure has dropped to 1.4 years (or 16.8 months).[223] If we combine this with the previous statistic, this means most salespeople only have four to seven months of full productivity in any position!

Add this to the growing length of sales cycles, ranging from six to twelve months in B2B technology sectors, and the fully trained salesperson only has time for a single sales cycle before they are off to their next job.

Once upon a time, B2B salespeople accepted that it would take them around 12 to 18 months to build relationships in a given territory or set of accounts, and that the subsequent two to three years would be where they would see the fruits of that early labour. Today, fewer than 5 per cent of salespeople stay on board for more than three years.[224]

And when it's time for businesses to find a new salesperson, the expenses come to an average of USD114 957, including separation costs, replacement costs, training costs and acquisition costs.[225]

In the past, this was swallowed as a cost of doing business. Products needed to be taken to market, after all, and there were no other options.

Today, things are different.

Vendor organisations have reached a crisis point where traditional sales is both more expensive and less effective than ever before. At the same time, there are more alternatives to the traditional outside sales force and—with natural market forces driving businesses to become more cost effective without sacrificing revenue or market-share growth—business leaders are looking to move away from the rigid resource models of the past and become more flexible and effective.

The impact on sales teams

If we move from changes to vendor organisations and sales roles to sales individuals, the impact shouldn't come as a surprise. The changing environment leaves salespeople putting in more work for worse results, which then has a detrimental impact on team morale, engagement and retention.

Only 19 per cent of sales professionals consider themselves to be actively engaged in their work, with 30 per cent being actively disengaged.[226] Forty-three per cent feel like their work environment is toxic, and 67 per cent of salespeople feel close to burnout.[227]

This has a significant cost for sales leaders and vendor organisations when you consider that highly engaged salespeople achieve up to a 19 per cent increase in sales, with 18 per cent higher productivity.[228,229]

A salesperson's mood directly impacts the experience a buyer has with them, and 80 per cent of buyers say the experience a vendor organisation provides is as important as its products and services.[230] Sixty-one per cent of buyers say they have a positive sales experience when a salesperson isn't pushy or aggressive, and 88 per cent agree that the salespeople they ultimately buy from are those they see as trusted advisers.[231,232]

When sales team engagement and morale falls, though, this affects the attitude and enthusiasm they bring to buyer interactions. This influences the buyer's perspective, making them less likely to move forward with a deal, which then has a negative impact on sales results. This further lowers morale, creating a vicious cycle.

And nowhere is this cycle more evident than in the number of salespeople who are missing quota. A Bravado report that surveyed 300 000 salespeople across 75 000 US organisations found that only 22 per cent of salespeople hit their quota in the fourth quarter of 2022, compared to 53 per cent just one year earlier.

What's even more concerning is that these results were after many of the surveyed companies had *lowered* their targets: 30 per cent of companies lowered their targets for 2022, and nearly 100 per cent lowered their targets for 2023.[233]

In other words, if the quotas being measured were the same as those from 2021, an even higher number of salespeople would have missed them.

Unsurprisingly, this environment has led to increasing turnover among salespeople.

More than 57 million people in the United States quit their jobs from 2021 through to early 2022, with the median annual turnover among sales professionals hitting 50 per cent.[234,235]

When it comes to future plans, in September 2022, the Salesforce *State of sales* report shared that 27 per cent of sales leaders were either currently looking for a new role or planning to start looking within 12 months, with a further 21 per cent considering leaving their current role within 12 months. That's nearly half—48 per cent—of sales leaders who are either looking for a new role or considering leaving their current one (the numbers for sales reps and sales operators were 45 and 39 per cent respectively).[236]

Why do sales professionals want to leave? Table 4.2 offers some reasons.

Table 4.2: reasons for turnover among sales professionals[237]

Sales leaders	Sales reps	Sales operations
1. Lack of advancement opportunities 2. Too much admin work 3. Unrealistic sales targets 4. Uncompetitive pay/benefits 5. Not enough flexibility/autonomy	1. Unrealistic sales targets 2. Uncompetitive pay/benefits 3. Want to leave sales entirely 4. Uncompetitive product 5. Bad company culture	1. Lack of advancement opportunities 2. Inadequate technology/tools 3. Unrealistic sales targets 4. Uncompetitive product 5. Uncompetitive pay/benefits

While the reasons varied depending on role, there were common elements. Across the board, sales professionals all cited unrealistic sales targets and uncompetitive pay and benefits in their top five reasons for leaving. Meanwhile, both sales leaders and sales operations staff mentioned a lack of advancement opportunities as a reason for leaving, while both sales reps and sales operations mentioned uncompetitive products.

What is clear is that an increasing number of sales professionals across all levels are dissatisfied with their careers, which is leading to higher attrition and falling performance across the board.

The new reality for salespeople

Sadly, so much of the modern sales role runs in a fog of automatic and habitual behaviour due to outdated leadership that has failed to recognise the new, buyer-led era.

Under the old regime, salespeople were forced (in many cases) to use crude tactics to control, persuade and manipulate buyers into purchasing before they were ready, and those old tactics created a dynamic where the buyer and seller were pitted against each other as adversaries. In this dynamic, salespeople were taught how to conquer the buyer, rather than how to help them solve their problems.

In such a dynamic, real trust can never exist. Can you imagine any other scenario where someone would treat an important stakeholder with such contempt?

The pendulum has now swung and buyers have the power and access to information required to solve their own problems.

The challenge for sales teams and vendor organisations is how to adapt to this new dynamic.

Today's buyers will only engage with credible sales professionals who possess specialist insights and who understand that buyers want to be taken on a long-term journey. The successful sales teams of the future will be digitally driven, socially connected, subject-matter experts with deep domain knowledge that can offer their buyers unique perspectives and commercial insights.

These sales teams must learn how to attract (not chase) their buyers by creating value before trying to extract value. This will affect the vendor organisation's sales structure, models, daily activities and compensation, all of which must change to drive the right behaviour and culture.

Simply, sales teams and vendor organisations need to make the shift to Deep Selling to survive.

CHAPTER 5
THE AGE OF DEEP SELLING

Deep Selling is foremost about buyer centricity, buyer success and buyer experience. And while buyers have always been the lifeblood of any vendor organisation, they are now more at the forefront of business consciousness than at any previous point in history.

In October 2022, 178 000 LinkedIn users held the position of 'customer success manager' — up from just 3900 in 2015.[238] The Customer Success Association was established in 2012 and, at the time of writing, had over 65 000 members worldwide.[239] Dozens of in-person and virtual customer success conferences were launched, with several 'best conferences' lists available online.[240]

And Google trends results for 'customer success' show that the term is at its highest level of interest in 20 years at the time of writing.

With this in mind, it is unsurprising that 63 per cent of executives are increasing their spend on customer loyalty.[241]

What has led to this boom?

As we discussed in the previous chapters, buyers are not only more discerning than ever before, but they are more demanding. It is, therefore, getting harder for vendor salespeople to engage with them. Online shopping and e-commerce platforms enable buyers to search for, identify and acquire products and services on a global scale, often without the need for any human interaction. Buyers can now diagnose their own problems and prescribe an online purchase to solve those problems, meaning they no longer need salespeople the way that they once did.

Meanwhile, competition has intensified across almost every industry, segment and category globally, with lower barriers to entry than ever before. As a result, buyers have more options and more information than they used to, resulting in the increased commoditisation of most products and services.

Additionally, time-poor buyers are looking to simplify their solutions wherever possible, so they are striving to do more business with a smaller number of vendors, which drastically reduces the opportunities available to most vendors across the market.

Simply, the needs and wants of the modern buyer have changed. And, where once a vendor held the power in a sales conversation due to being the holder of proprietary information and knowledge, today buyers have the power, with easy access to information, the ability to self-serve, increasing commoditisation and the imperative to rationalise the number of vendors that they deal with.

This leaves vendor organisations needing to fight commoditisation, declining prices and margins. To achieve this, 65 per cent of the world's manufacturing capacity has switched from production to services as the main revenue source as vendors attempt to shift from being product centric to buyer centric, offering buyers solutions instead of simply manufacturing products.[242]

One well-known example of a traditional product vendor that has successfully made this shift is Hilti. Hilti is a tool manufacturer that, in the early 2000s, received a request from a buyer for a holistic tool management solution. Hilti realised that when its buyers purchased a tool, they were also taking on the responsibility of tracking usage, maintaining the tools, repairing them and upgrading them, all of which required significant overhead. By contrast, by leasing the tools, the buyers could still experience the productivity gains that a wide range of tools enabled, while Hilti could take care of maintenance and upgrades, ensuring its buyers would always have access to reliable tools. Hilti received guaranteed monthly income, experienced less buyer churn and discovered that its buyers were willing to lease more tools than they had ever purchased.[243]

In other words, Hilti recognised that its buyers weren't purchasing tools, but were instead purchasing the value those tools enabled them to create. In this partnership, Hilti is rewarded for making tools available that enable its buyers to be more efficient and effective, and the buyer is rewarded with lower costs as well as an ongoing relationship with and the advice of Hilti's reps, which can help them optimise their own processes.

As more vendor organisations shift from large, one-off sales to providing ongoing solutions, the financial burden of the purchasing relationship has shifted from the buyer to the seller. However, buyers take on far less risk than they used to in this model, which means they are more likely to churn before the vendor breaks even on the cost of the sale. This requires a new approach to relationship management. Hence the rise of buyer centricity.

The road from buyer centricity to Deep Selling

Deep Selling is a new sales approach where vendor organisations leverage data-driven insights to sell more value to their buyers. Deep Selling involves the strategic use of technology to uncover data and derive actionable insights about your buyers, which can be used to drive buyer-centric sales behaviours and success measures.

In other words, Deep Selling is not just another sales methodology, but a holistic approach to how the vendor organisation of the future needs to work in order to keep pace with the ever-evolving needs of buyers, and the volatility, uncertainty, complexity and ambiguity of the modern sales and buying environment.

This approach empowers Deep-Selling organisations to sell in a way that modern B2B buyers are more receptive to.

Research tells us that only 3 per cent of buyers are in a buying window at any point in time.[244] Any approaches to buyers outside of this window can be detrimental to the vendor's brand and lower its chances of establishing a valuable relationship with that buyer. Yet, Shallow sales approaches encourage vendor salespeople to approach these buyers anyway, leading to activities and actions that can upset and annoy even the most patient of buyers.

By contrast, Deep-Selling approaches encourage salespeople to spend more time understanding the buyer before engaging with them. They guide vendors to make use of technology and data to identify when a buyer is nearing the buying window—for example, by analysing their interaction with websites, company profiles and online content—and then approach the buyer with valuable information and insights that match the buyer's intent.

Deep-Selling experts waste less effort on buyers who don't want to purchase, and more time developing deep and mutually beneficial relationships with buyers who need their solutions. Therefore, Deep Selling is more valuable to both buying and sales organisations and makes better use of one of a business's most costly resources: its salesforce.

The simplest way to contextualise Deep Selling is by contrasting it with the old-world, product-centric approach.

Product-centric organisations are focused on capturing value from their buyers and measure success based on internal outcomes such as growth in new products, profitability per product and market share. These organisations are transaction oriented: instead of focusing on an ideal buyer persona, they sell to whoever will buy their products. Their positioning highlights their product's features, and the organisation is structured around those products with product managers, product sales teams and product profit centres.

Deep-Selling organisations prioritise buyer value creation and improving buyer success. These organisations are relationship oriented, centring on serving their buyers over the long term. With this focus, their product positioning highlights the benefits their product offers in terms of meeting the needs of their buyers. The organisational structure also supports these buyers, with roles like customer relationship managers and customer success managers, and teams organised with the objective of delivering a delightful buyer experience. Deep-Selling organisations measure success using the key metric of buyer health, which includes elements such as buyer relationship quality, product usage and buyer value realisation (see table 5.1, overleaf).

When we look at sales specifically, this approach has a significant impact on sales culture, as depicted in figure 5.1 (overleaf).

Table 5.1: comparing product-centric and Deep-Selling approaches[245]

	Product-centric approach	Deep-Selling approach
Philosophy	Sell products; sell to whoever will buy	Serve buyers; all decisions start with the buyer and opportunities for advantage
Business orientation	Transaction oriented	Relationship oriented
Product positioning	Highlight product features and advantages	Highlight product's benefits in relation to meeting individual buyer needs
Organisational structure	Product profit centre, product managers, product sales teams	Buyer segment centres, customer relationship managers, customer success managers, buyer-segment sales teams
Organisational focus	Internally focused, new product development, new account development, market share growth	Externally focused, buyer relationship development, profitability through buyer loyalty, employees are buyer advocates
Performance metrics	Number of new products, profitability per product, market share by product	Share of wallet of buyers, buyer satisfaction, lifetime buyer value, buyer equity
Management criteria	Portfolio of products	Portfolio of buyers
Selling approach	How many buyers can we sell this product to?	How many products will deliver value to this buyer?
Buyer knowledge	Buyer data are a control mechanism	Buyer knowledge is a valuable asset

Why it's time to go Deeper

No longer a mile wide and an inch deep, Deep-Selling organisations focus on *developing quality relationships* with their buyers over *the quantity* of buyers. This is how vendor salespeople build trust, which leads to co-creating real business value with their buyers and long-term success for both the vendor and buying organisations.

Figure 5.1: different types of sales cultures

This is why, in this buyer-led era, it is every sales leader's imperative to push their organisation to achieve Deep-Selling excellence.

Going Deep means being genuinely buyer centric, and there is a raft of benefits to putting your buyers at the centre of your organisation's strategy. Buyer-centric organisations are 25 per cent more profitable than their product-centric counterparts, with 5.1 times higher revenue growth.[246] Buyers are also willing to pay 4.5 times more for the excellent experience that these organisations deliver.[247]

Additionally, when buyers perceive that an organisation is putting their needs at the centre of everything it does, this perception has a positive impact on both sales revenue and buyer loyalty, as well as moderating a buyer's impression of price (to the extent that if an organisation charges high prices, the perception of buyer centricity has a positive, significant impact on sales revenue, yet there is no significant impact on organisations that charge low prices).[248]

This is why Deep-Selling organisations benefit from 25 per cent higher retention than product-centric organisations.[249] In the traditional, acquisition-focused sales model, every single buyer is hard earned. In the B2B sales environment, this process often takes months, with sales and marketing introducing the new buyer to their brand, engaging them, qualifying them and converting them through sales conversations. Once the sale is closed, the process starts again.

This is why Deep Selling promotes an organisational philosophy of doing more with existing or past buyers: these buyers already know you and your offer. Focusing on your existing and past buyers leads to a plethora of business benefits:

- The top 1 per cent of buyers is *18 times* more valuable than the remaining 99 per cent.[250]
- Once a buyer has been doing business with an organisation for more than 30 months, they spend 67 per cent more than in their first six months.[251]
- Fifteen per cent of an organisation's most loyal buyers account for anywhere between 55 per cent and 70 per cent of the organisation's total revenue.[252]
- Repeat buyers have a conversion rate of between 60 and 70 per cent, compared to between 1 and 3 per cent in the general market.[253]
- Adobe found that repeat buyers (who have already purchased at least two times) are nine times more likely to convert than new buyers.[254]

With all this in mind, it's not surprising that if an organisation increases its buyer retention rate by just 5 per cent, this can increase profits by 25 to 95 per cent. When you also consider that acquiring a new buyer can be anywhere between five and 25 times more expensive than closing an existing one, it's imperative for vendor organisations to shift their focus from closing sales to long-term buyer success.[255]

Putting aside the obvious financial benefits of having happy and loyal buyers, vendors that shift from the old, sales-driven culture to a buyer-obsessed one find that their employees consider their work more meaningful and are more likely to stay for the long term.

SurveyMonkey found that 76 per cent of employees whose work had a direct impact on buyers (like salespeople) found their work meaningful, compared with just 49 per cent whose work had little impact on the organisation's buyers. Seventy-three per cent of employees at organisations that had buyer satisfaction as a key priority found their work meaningful, compared with just 55 per cent at organisations that didn't have this priority. And *83 per cent* of employees who worked at organisations that prioritised buyer satisfaction were at least pretty sure that they would still be at the organisation in two years. This is essential considering current levels of attrition in sales.[256]

The four elements of Deep-Selling excellence

Even though the benefits of becoming a Deep-Selling organisation are clear, and the concept of buyer centricity has become more mainstream over the past two decades, many organisations fail to successfully make the transition.

Fewer than 9 per cent of organisations are buyer centric. And while 56 per cent of organisations with more than 2500 employees have adopted a 'customer journey strategy', just 29 per cent would rate these strategies as effective.[257] When it comes to buyer perceptions, even though 75 per cent of organisations believe themselves to be buyer centric, only 30 per cent of buyers agree.[258]

Why is there such a disconnect between organisations' intentions and their results? Because achieving Deep-Selling excellence requires an organisation-wide commitment to delivering buyer-based outcomes through the mastery of four key elements.

The first is *people*, spanning an organisation's team, structure and culture. Organisational cultures are notoriously resistant to change. However, in order to become a Deep-Selling organisation, a vendor's culture must be held together by the central value that every decision begins and ends with your buyer. This is supported by integrating and aligning all functional activities to deliver superior value to your buyers. The result is a deeply aligned workforce that understands and has been trained to support buyer success and value creation with the organisation's resources.[259]

The second element is *technology*. We have discussed the pitfalls of poor digital transformation attempts in depth; however, Deep-Selling organisations don't ignore the opportunities that new technologies provide in order to avoid these challenges. Successful Deep-Selling organisations have a deeply developed and integrated tech stack. The key is that this tech stack supports your people in delivering your buyer-centric strategy, thereby enabling buyer success and value creation.

The third element is your organisation's *success metrics*. The right metrics drive the right behaviours, as reconfiguring the organisation's definition of success means the team is rewarded for truly buyer-centric behaviours. This demonstrates a deep commitment to buyer success and value creation and is reflected in the organisation's approach to compensation and incentives.

The final element is *strategy*. Deep-selling organisations require deeply developed sales processes, measures and methodologies that support buyer success and value creation. The right strategy and processes are the difference between executing transactions with your buyers and building and sustaining ongoing relationships with them instead.

Note that while we've listed these four elements in a linear order, it is important to take a holistic view when it comes to implementing changes in any one area. Each element will influence the others: your strategy will impact the metrics you prioritise when defining success. These metrics will, in turn, dictate how your people are rewarded and will drive their behaviour and how they work with your buyers to co-create value. Your technology will be required to support all three areas, and your tech stack could then reveal areas for further growth in each.

Consequently, all four elements should be kept in mind as you work your way through the Deep-Selling roadmap, which is also an ongoing, evolving process that you will continue to revisit as your organisation increases its level of Deep-Selling maturity. Figure 5.2 serves as a handy reminder of the four elements that combine to achieve Deep-Selling excellence.

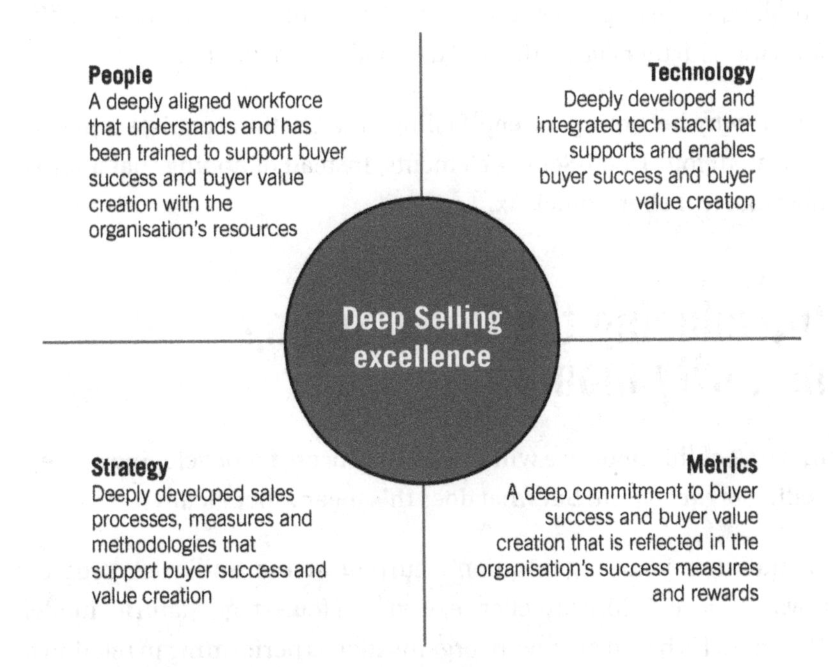

Figure 5.2: the four elements of Deep Selling

After reviewing the elements of Deep Selling, you're probably starting to gauge the scope of becoming a Deep-Selling organisation. These elements are not restricted to the sales team, but require changes to an organisation as a whole. And this is one of the reasons why the majority of vendor organisations never truly become buyer centric: because the journey is typically longer and more complex than expected.[260]

New digital technologies add further complications to the process: while 91 per cent of organisations claim to have adopted a digital-first strategy, the average use of these technologies is far from optimal, with nearly two-thirds of enterprise subscription applications not being used to their full potential. [261,262]

This is then compounded by the number of technology implementations in vendor organisations that are treated as a band-aid solution to problems of falling performance, profit and revenue without addressing the underlying issue: relying on old-world, Shallow sales tactics that are not effective or relevant for modern buyers. Instead of solving the problem, these implementations accelerate the organisation's existing activities, further cementing unsustainable behaviours.

This is why becoming a Deep-Selling organisation requires a holistic look at all four Deep-Selling elements, instead of hoping that another new tool will offer a quick fix.

Introducing the Deep-Selling maturity model

In part 2 of this book, we will share our process for developing a Deep-Selling organisation. But what does this mean, specifically?

To measure your organisation's current status and your progress towards Deep-Selling excellence, we use a four-stage maturity model. This model is based on how an organisation is performing in relation to each of the Deep-Selling elements summarised in figure 5.2.

Organisations in stage 1 of the maturity model are what we would consider to be Shallow organisations. These organisations have a product-centric culture and no defined buyer success strategy. Their processes and workforce are digitally immature and they have low technology use across the organisation. If technology is used, it enables or accelerates product-centric behaviours.

At stage 2, organisations are Emerging. Emerging organisations have developed a vision for a buyer-centric culture, have audited their processes and supporting technologies, and have developed a roadmap for change. They have also identified the processes and resources that need to change in order to facilitate that roadmap.

Stage 3 organisations are Exploring the world of Deep Selling. At this stage, a Deep sales strategy has been developed, approved and is supported by the organisation, from frontline employees to senior leadership. The transformation is underway: processes, training and technologies are beginning to change, and resources have been diverted to support the project. In Exploring organisations, energy is high and positive effects are being observed.

The final stage of the maturity model is when organisations become Deep-Selling organisations. In stage 4, organisations have a strong, buyer-centric culture, strategy and process. They are digitally mature, with an evolved tech stack that enables the buyer-centric strategy and processes. They also have a well-trained and engaged workforce, committed to the long-term success of their buyers.

Figure 5.3 (overleaf) illustrates the four-stage Deep-Selling maturity model.

In part 2, we share the roadmap that will empower your organisation to move from Shallow to Deep, which consists of three phases.

In the first phase, you will assess your current state to commence the move from Shallow to Emerging. This will include auditing your organisation's current state and analysing the gaps between your ideal and current state.

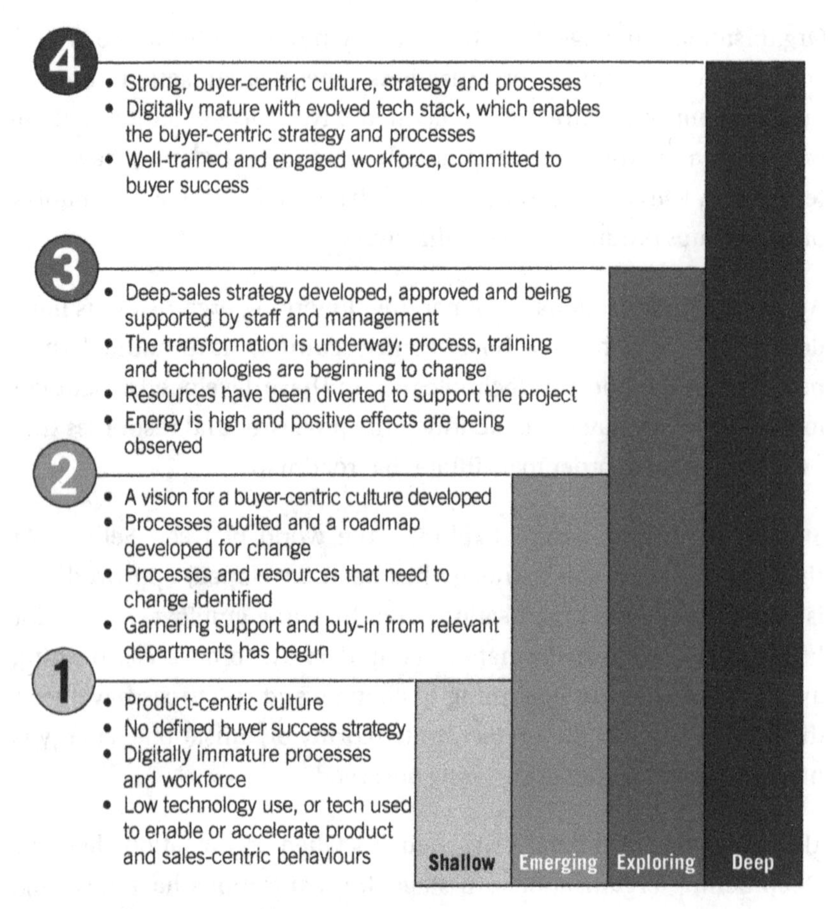

4
• Strong, buyer-centric culture, strategy and processes
• Digitally mature with evolved tech stack, which enables the buyer-centric strategy and processes
• Well-trained and engaged workforce, committed to buyer success
3
• Deep-sales strategy developed, approved and being supported by staff and management
• The transformation is underway: process, training and technologies are beginning to change
• Resources have been diverted to support the project
• Energy is high and positive effects are being observed
2
• A vision for a buyer-centric culture developed
• Processes audited and a roadmap developed for change
• Processes and resources that need to change identified
• Garnering support and buy-in from relevant departments has begun
1
• Product-centric culture
• No defined buyer success strategy
• Digitally immature processes and workforce
• Low technology use, or tech used to enable or accelerate product and sales-centric behaviours
Shallow
Emerging
Exploring
Deep

Figure 5.3: the Deep-Selling maturity model[263]

In phase 2, you will develop the roadmap for change, moving from Emerging to Exploring. This will include developing a Deep understanding of your buyers and evolving your sales execution model.

In the final phase, you will implement, embed and routinise the changes to move from Exploring to Deep (see figure 5.4). In this phase, you will create a buyer-oriented, high-performance culture and stay the course with the Deep-Selling balanced scorecard.

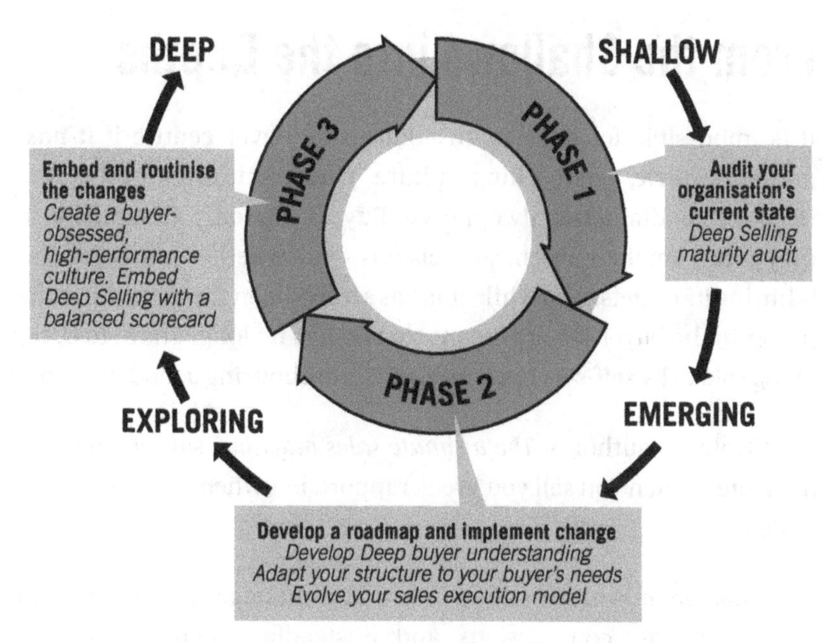

Figure 5.4: moving from Shallow to Deep Selling

Like the four Deep-Selling excellence elements, this roadmap should be seen as a loop rather than a series of linear steps.

Having worked with hundreds of vendor businesses, including those at the enterprise level, we recognise the complexity of making widescale changes and know that many organisations will need to take an incremental approach. Additionally, the buying and sales landscape will continue to evolve in parallel with technological developments, meaning successful Deep-Selling organisations will need to continue to evolve to succeed.

This is why we treat this roadmap as one to be implemented and built upon on an ongoing basis. Once you have embedded an initial round of measures, you can re-audit your organisation, determine your new position on the Deep-Selling maturity model, and look at adopting new measures to move up the maturity ladder.

From the Shallows into the Depths

It is impossible for any organisation to be buyer centric if it has a product-centric, push-selling culture. Quota smashing and buyers' interests are diametrically opposed. Buyers care only about the value they gain from their purchase decisions — not whether your sales team is hitting its targets. And while this has always been the case, the shift of power in the buyer-led era means that buyers no longer have to accept being sold to by self-serving opportunists harbouring a hidden agenda.

Chet Holmes, author of *The ultimate sales machine*, said it best when he wrote, 'When you sell you break rapport, but when you educate you build it'.[264]

If vendor organisations still measure and manage their salespeople around quotas, commissions and a steadfast focus on top-line revenue attainment, they will be surpassed by the savvy vendors who have already woken up to the new reality. The game has changed and it's time for vendors to drop the relentless focus on revenue and profit maximisation.

Those vendors that commit to becoming Deep-Selling organisations — those that shift their culture to one with their buyers' interests at the forefront — see top-line revenue, profit margins and sustainability increase as a natural by-product. Delivering a stellar buyer experience is the key to loyalty, repeat business, buyer advocacy and financial success for your organisation.

PART II

THE ROADMAP TO DEEP-SELLING EXCELLENCE

PHASE 1
SHALLOW TO EMERGING

Welcome to the journey to becoming a Deep-Selling organisation. In the first phase of this roadmap, here is what you should expect to start seeing in each of the Deep-Selling elements described in chapter 5:

- *People:* You understand your people's current commitment to buyer centricity, including the level of commitment to buyer relationship quality, the available skills to deliver value to buyers and a structure that supports this commitment.
- *Technology:*
  - You understand your organisation's level of digital maturity and readiness to change.
  - You have assessed your current tech stack in relation to Deep-Selling maturity levels and understand typical functions available at each level of maturity.
  - There is a defined scope for technology change based on current-state audits and levels of readiness.
- *Metrics:*
  - Current sales performance and levels of buyer success have been audited.
  - You understand existing internal and external metrics in the context of buyer centricity.

- *Strategy:* Key processes and sales measures have been audited to foster a deep understanding of the organisation's current state.

You will achieve this by performing an audit of your organisation's level of buyer centricity, digital readiness and current tech stack.

Let's dive in!

CHAPTER 6
AUDIT YOUR CURRENT STATE

Anyone working in sales knows that the landscape has changed. Buyers have higher expectations than ever before yet are simultaneously less likely to move forward with new solutions. For many products and services, buyers prefer to use self-service options that circumvent working with a vendor salesperson altogether. And both vendor organisations and the sales profession as a whole are struggling as a result.

To start building your organisation's Deep-Selling strategy, the first step is to take stock of where you are now. This doesn't just mean having awareness of industry-wide changes, but also the challenges confronting your organisation, your position as a sales leader and the performance of your sales team.

Unfortunately, even in the face of lower order sizes, falling buyer tenure, salespeople failing to hit quota and more, many vendor organisations refuse to admit they have a problem. Or, if they *do* admit that something is wrong, that 'something' is external to the organisation: difficult buyers, stiff competition, the economy and more.

Consider BlackBerry. The first BlackBerry device was released in 1999 as a two-way pager in Germany.[265] Focusing on email functionality—with its unique QWERTY keyboard and using internet data instead of charging per text message like other service providers at the time—BlackBerry quickly grew in popularity.[266] In 2008, the company had a market value of nearly USD80 billion and in 2009, the company held 56 per cent of the American smartphone market and 20 per cent of the global smartphone market.[267,268,269]

Then Apple launched the iPhone in 2007, which was followed by Android devices in 2008, and we all know how the market developed from there. BlackBerry quickly fell behind as new devices offered more sought-after features, including bigger screens, better multimedia players, a better browser experience and touchscreens.[270]

Confronted by falling sales, market share and share prices, BlackBerry entered an era of strategic confusion. At the time, Apple had an exclusivity contract with mobile network AT&T, which left other networks looking for a way to compete. Verizon Wireless approached BlackBerry to develop an 'iPhone killer', but BlackBerry's failed attempt led Verizon to turn to Motorola and Google instead. In the same period, former co-CEO and board member Jim Balsillie attempted to shift the company's focus to instant-messaging software, only to cut all ties to the company when the plan was opposed by founder Mike Lazaridis. And, in 2012, then-CEO Thorsten Heins proposed the launch of a new, slim device with a glass touchscreen (the BlackBerry Z10) that would compete with iPhones and Android devices. This was also opposed by Lazaridis, who argued that BlackBerry should stick with keyboard devices. When the Z10 eventually launched (six years after the first iPhone release), its marketing campaign didn't have a clear value proposition. iPhone and Android users preferred their existing devices (which already offered the benefits of the Z10), while BlackBerry's raving fans found the new system to be too different from the classic experience.[271]

The Globe and Mail described BlackBerry's demise as 'Once a fast-moving innovator that kept two steps ahead of the competition, [BlackBerry] grew into a stumbling corporation, blinded by its own success and unable to replicate it.'[272]

Ultimately, BlackBerry wasn't listening to its buyers. The leadership team wasn't listening to the wider market and addressing what consumers wanted in a smartphone, nor were they listening to what their existing users valued in the original devices.

Within four years, BlackBerry's global market share had collapsed to less than 3 per cent, and its value dropped from a peak of almost USD80 billion in 2009, to just USD6 billion in 2016.[273] In the first quarter of 2024, the company's global market share was just 0.11 per cent.[274,275]

Houston, we have a problem

The first step to moving forward is admitting your organisation has a problem. Understanding your current state, particularly what is not working (or what isn't working as well as it could be) puts you in a powerful position to make the case to senior management and the wider organisation about why change is necessary.

By the end of this chapter, you will understand the scope of the change required in order to achieve Deep-Selling excellence. This empowers you to set expectations with leadership regarding the investment required for the change; it sets accurate expectations among both leadership and sales teams for how quickly the change will progress and when they can expect to see results; and this then means the organisation is more likely to give the change the time it needs to become embedded and fully pay-off, rather than cutting resources partway through the process.

If you don't take this step, your organisation might not understand the urgency for change, because they don't see a problem with the way things are done now—something that can be an issue both in leadership and within sales teams. Or the change might be endorsed initially, but if the understanding of your current state is incomplete, the change might then be deprioritised or resources might be pulled because the project is taking longer or is more complex than expected.

But where do you start?

We will determine where your organisation sits on the Deep-Selling maturity model by assessing your current level of buyer centricity, your digital readiness and your tech stack.

Articulate and quantify the problem

In part 1 of this book, we have explained why vendor organisations need to become more buyer centric, why they need to leverage technology and data more effectively, and why modern buyers want to deal with Deep-Selling organisations. And while Deep Selling is an aspiration for modern vendor organisations, sales leaders might not fully recognise the problems their Shallow sales tactics create.

When we talk about 'problems', these sit on a range. At one end of the spectrum, there are minor issues such as leaking sales, poor pipeline efficiency and long sales cycle times, a high portion of sales ending in 'no decision' outcomes, and an inability to forecast accurately due to the number of deals that are getting stuck in the middle of the funnel. This could then result in the wrong deals being made—for example, buyers getting shoehorned into a proposal because sales teams need to hit their internal targets instead of deals being made because they are the best fit for the buyer.

After a deal goes through, poor buyer alignment may lead to those buyers not experiencing the full potential of your products, with low feature usage and penetration rates across the buying organisation. In fact, this can even happen in cases where there is excellent buyer alignment if the internal customer success function isn't effectively supporting those buyers in realising value.

At this end of the spectrum, the organisation is still getting deals and delivering results. It is still functioning, but not at an optimal level, with wasted time and resources, and subpar results.

If these patterns continue, the issues become more significant. Increasing sales cycle times and stuck deals lead to a higher cost of acquisition. Poor feature usage and low user numbers increase the risk of churn among your buyers. These then impact profit margins and revenue levels and, over time, will result in falling market share and investor returns. The longer these issues persist, the greater the impact on the organisation's bottom line and the more urgency there is to address them.

Eventually, organisations lose buyers and market share to competitors. Revenue and profit decline further, resulting in the need to cut costs, potentially leading to layoffs and reduced research and development. This prompts a vicious cycle, where fewer resources lessen an organisation's ability to innovate and remain relevant to its buyers.

Ultimately, these issues are all symptoms of having a Shallow sales organisation. The good news is that they can be addressed, and the earlier you catch these problems, the quicker and easier it is to get back on the right track.

How do you determine where your organisation sits on the spectrum?

These issues might be occurring in your buyer relationships, within the sales team or they might be organisation wide. Consider the examples in table 6.1 (overleaf) as a starting point.

Table 6.1: common vendor organisation issues

Buyer relationship issues	Sales performance issues	Wider organisational issues
• Falling average order value and lifetime buyer value • Increasing sales cycle times • Low buyer satisfaction • Poor buyer relationships • Short buyer tenure • Inconsistent buyer experience	• Low team morale • High attrition/low tenure • Increasing number of team members not meeting sales quotas • Mismatch between sales approach and buyer preferences • Mismatch between sales approach and product requirements	• Poor integration between different buyer-facing teams (e.g. marketing, sales and support) • Mismatch between organisational objectives and team KPIs • Product development not reflecting buyer preferences and usage

Consider the issue of poor morale in your sales team as an example. Poor morale leads to lower productivity, which means salespeople are meeting with fewer prospects. When they do meet with these prospects, the salesperson's lack of engagement means they are less likely to go above and beyond, meaning they are more likely to do the bare minimum (following a script about product features and benefits instead of actively looking at how they can co-create value with the prospect).

This then means the prospect is less likely to buy and, if they do, they are less likely to adopt the full range of products or services required for them to experience maximum value. Because they aren't getting the value they'd hoped for, they are less likely to become repeat buyers or to refer other buyers to your organisation. This has a long-term impact on costs and revenue, as your organisation loses the revenue of repeat business and referred business and, with the cost of acquiring a new buyer ranging from five to 25 times more than retaining an existing buyer, the opportunity cost is significant.[276]

Your organisation likely already has ways of tracking and measuring its performance across buyer relationships, sales and the wider organisation.

For buyer-related issues, this can include the following metrics:

- Buyer trust
- Buyer satisfaction
- Net promoter score (NPS)
- Number and percentage of repeat buyers
- Number of referrals from existing buyers to new prospects
- Average order value
- Average buyer tenure
- Lifetime buyer value
- New product activations
- Product use (including ongoing use, number of users within a buying organisation, changes in frequency or depth, breadth of feature activation)
- Value received from product use (increased buyer productivity, reduced costs, achievement of other goals).

Issues relating to your sales team, might be the result of a mix of the following metrics:

- Conversion rates (lead to marketing-qualified lead; marketing-qualified lead to sales-qualified lead)
- Average sales cycle time

- Sales team quota, and how this has changed over time
- Percentage of team hitting quota
- Performance range (what is the mean performance, and how far are the outliers from the stated quota?)
- Average tenure on your sales team (both how this has changed over time, as well as how this compares to other teams)
- Percentage of team members who consider themselves to be engaged
- Team attrition rates
- Qualitative data from employee engagement surveys.

Finally, the wider organisation is likely to consider the following metrics:

- Revenue
- Gross margin
- Market share
- Share price trends
- Cost of sales team
- Revenue per sales rep.

While most organisations track many of these metrics, they might not be clearly visible to the sales team, or there might be a higher emphasis placed on some metrics over others. For example, we commonly see organisations prioritise revenue, volume and gross margin over buyer relationships metrics. While this is understandable, considering an organisation's focus on creating shareholder value, there are significant benefits for organisations that prioritise buyer-focused metrics. In phase 3, we will introduce you to the Deep-Selling balanced scorecard, which helps vendor organisations strike the balance between internally-focused sales metrics and metrics that drive the organisation's buyer relationships and Deep-Selling competencies.

For now, concentrate on getting a picture of your organisation's current state, remembering to focus on the trend over individual numbers. Trends tell you how your buyers, your team and your organisation are evolving—ideally, the positive metrics will be going up over time and the negative ones will be going down. You have a problem when metrics are moving in the wrong direction, or when they aren't improving quickly enough (for instance, if average order value and repeat buyers are not increasing quickly enough to offset higher costs, which is having a negative impact on revenue over time).

Deep-Selling maturity assessment

The goal of the three-phase roadmap is for your organisation to develop Deep-Selling excellence, or to move your organisation from being a Shallow sales organisation to a Deep-Selling organisation, using the Deep-Selling maturity model as a guide.

Where your organisation sits on the model will tell you what you should expect to see in the four elements of Deep Selling: people, technology, metrics and strategy.

After reading the previous chapters, you might already have a sense of where your organisation sits in the model. We will confirm that (or provide further insight, if you are unsure) with three exercises:

1. The buyer-centricity audit
2. The digital-readiness audit
3. The tech-stack audit.

After completing each audit, you will have a numerical score for each of the elements of Deep Selling, which you can then use to plot your position in the Deep-Selling maturity model. As you implement the next phases in the roadmap, you can revisit these audits over time to chart how your organisation is progressing through the stages.

Buyer-centricity audit

Throughout this book you'll notice that we emphasise buyer centricity as the cornerstone of being a Deep-Selling organisation. And, in the modern, tech-driven buying and sales landscape, this focus is more important than ever.

As we shared in part I, one of the dark sides of digitalisation is the temptation for organisations to adopt the newest tools—without fundamentally transforming their organisation's culture, structure, processes and success measures—to take a buyer-first perspective.

This can lead to wasted resources (time, financial and human) as teams adopt new tools, but those tools don't lead to a buyer-centric approach. Consequently, they don't improve sales results. In fact, this is one of the reasons why many organisations are wary of digital change programs: they have undergone transformations like this in the past and have not seen the expected benefits.

A separate challenge is dealing with resistance around the accusation that a team or organisation is not buyer centric. Many organisations believe they are buyer centric because they have values or missions that talk about putting the buyer at the centre of everything they do. However, truly buyer-centric organisations aren't those that simply talk about being buyer centric. They are ones where the organisation is structured around the buyer, processes are built around the buyer, success is measured based on buyer outcomes and team members are rewarded for putting the buyer first. (We will dive deeper into each of these areas in the coming chapters.)

In other words, buyer-centric organisations have buyer-centric cultures, people, strategies and metrics.

To contrast this with product-centric organisations, in product-centric organisations the culture focuses on selling products, and highlighting product features and advantages with the goal of processing transactions. In a Deep-Selling organisation, the culture focuses on serving buyers, with product benefits being highlighted in relation to buyer needs and the goal being to build long-term relationships. In a product-centric organisation, business strategy focuses on product growth, profitability and sales. Deep-Selling organisations have both a business strategy and a buyer strategy, with processes that create dual value, facilitate an omnichannel buyer experience, and effectively collect and analyse buyer data. In a product-centric organisation, metrics focus on the number of new products, profitability per product and market share by product. In Deep-Selling organisations, the leading metric is long-term buyer health.[277]

To assess your organisation's level of buyer centricity, you will perform a qualitative assessment on your organisation's people, strategy and metrics. Note that this assessment is based on your organisation's *current* state and scores should be based on where your organisation is now, regardless of any improvement plans that might already be in motion.

Rate your organisation's level of performance based on each of the areas listed in tables 6.2, 6.3 (overleaf) and 6.4 (see page 106), where 5 is the highest level of commitment and performance you could imagine (there isn't anything else the organisation could do to be more buyer centric), and 1 is where your organisation is entirely product focused.

For each of these areas (people, strategy and metrics) you will have a score ranging from 5 to 25. Remember these scores for later, as you will input them directly into the overarching Deep-Selling maturity model.

Table 6.2: people audit

Topic	Description	Rating				
		1	2	3	4	5
People						
Vision	To what extent does the organisation have a defined buyer vision, with everyone in sync and working towards its achievement?					
Culture	To what extent does the organisation enthusiastically pursue superior quality buyer relationships and emphasise buyer and market issues?					
Structure	To what extent does the organisation's structure enable it to focus on and commit resources to prioritising buyer outcomes?					
Skills	To what extent does the organisation have the required level of skills, experience and willingness of employees to create superior buyer value?					
Leadership	What is the extent of leadership commitment to buyer value creation and buyer success?					
People score		/25				

To understand your organisation's level of buyer centricity independently of the wider maturity model, combine the ratings for the three areas to get a total score ranging from 15 to 75. Your rating will determine your position on the buyer-centricity dial, which will tell you how far your organisation needs to go to become fully buyer centric (which is essential to achieve Deep-Selling excellence):

- level 1 (<20) = fully product centric
- level 2 (21–35) = mostly product centric
- level 3 (36–50) = balanced product/buyer centric
- level 4 (51–65) = mostly buyer centric
- level 5 (>65) = fully buyer centric.

Table 6.3: strategy audit

Topic	Description	Rating				
		1	2	3	4	5
Strategy						
Processes	To what extent do business processes support and adapt to provide quality and efficient buyer interactions?					
Governance	To what extent does the organisation adopt clear standards and regulations regarding everyone's role and responsibilities for supporting buyer success?					
Innovation	To what extent does the organisation have defined innovation processes, use agile innovation methods and have a willingness to change?					
Products and services	To what extent does the organisation develop and deploy smart, connected or digitalised product and service offerings?					
Business model	To what extent has the business model been digitalised, and what is the level of its use of digital technologies to create or capture value?					
Strategy score		/25				

At level 1, your organisation is only focused on sales metrics, including revenue, margin, profit and volume. These organisations have a pushy sales and sales management culture, and no-one truly cares about the buyer. There is no specific guidance to how salespeople should interact with buyers and no focus on buyer outcomes or buyer sentiment. The goal is to win the sale at all costs. The buyer perception of these organisations is, 'they're only in it for themselves'.

At level 2, organisations are still mostly focused on sales metrics and on each salesperson's volume of activity, rather than the quality of their buyer interactions. There are no specific measures of buyer happiness or success. Buyer outcomes are usually superseded by lagging financial performance metrics. There is no specific guidance on which types of buyers to target. The focus is on persuading the buyer that you have the best solution. The buyer perception of these organisations is, 'they're not here to help me'.

Table 6.4: metrics audit

Topic	Description	Rating				
		1	2	3	4	5
Metrics						
Buyer-focus of metrics	To what extent does the vendor organisation focus on and reward its salesforce for external buyer outcomes (rather than sales or internal financial outcomes)?					
Buyer prioritisation	To what extent are buyer outcomes prioritised over sales or internal financial outcomes?					
Visibility of metrics	To what extent are buyer outcomes represented on a performance scorecard visible to the entire organisation?					
Transparency of metrics	To what extent would the organisation be comfortable discussing or showing its metrics to its buyers?					
Buyer insight	To what extent does the firm engage its buyers in developing and contributing to its metrics?					
Metrics score		/25				

Level 3 organisations have a mix of leading and lagging performance metrics. For example, some of a salesperson's bonus might be linked to financial performance but is also linked in some way to buyer interaction or success targets. These organisations are focused on helping solve buyer problems and they have a team selling structure with a relationship selling culture to facilitate this (so no lone wolves). There is some guidance provided to salespeople to help them identify ideal potential buyers, to guide how to engage with those buyers, and to identify and resolve their problems. Salespeople identify the buyer's problem and solve it with the organisation's products or service. The buyer perception of these organisations is, 'they're here to help me solve my problem'.

Organisations at level 4 make heavy use of lead measures over lag measures, but metrics are still internally focused (for instance, salesperson activity volumes or NPS). The focus is on how the organisation can deliver value to its buyers through its products, services and solutions, but organisational alignment to buyer value creation is sporadic. The salesforce focuses on understanding buyer needs and working collaboratively to achieve them, but the wider organisation lacks the systems and processes to consistently deliver on these buyer solutions. Buyer relationships are valued as a source of the organisation's success. The buyer perception of these organisations is, 'they're here to help me perform better'.

Finally, at level 5 organisations are heavily focused on lead measures that result in improved buyer outcomes such as performance improvement, better product utilisation or buyer satisfaction. The focus is on buyer success and mutual value creation. Salespeople are encouraged to challenge their buyer's perspective and to bring valuable insights to buyer interactions, and there are specific processes and systems designed to help salespeople to work with buyers to co-create value. There is organisational alignment with other departments that share the same vision, and these departments are resourced effectively to assist. These organisations strive to make their buyers successful. The buyer perception of these organisations is, 'they are fully aligned with my business and capable of making a big contribution to my success'.

Deep-Selling organisations typically sit at level 5 on the buyer-centricity dial. However, there is some nuance here. In the previous descriptions, there is an emphasis on working with buyers to co-create value, and the implication that the vendor organisation is building custom solutions to help its buyers meet their goals. While this is an important element to keep in mind for the time being, note that vendor organisations selling simpler products and packaged solutions can still achieve Deep-Selling success: the key is offering an experience and solution that meets your buyer's needs.

We will discuss this in more detail in chapter 9.

Digital readiness and maturity audit

While buyer centricity is essential for Deep-Selling success, in this data-driven, technology-led era, simply being buyer centric isn't enough. Going Deep requires the use of technology and data to deliver the best possible buyer experience. This is required for vendor organisations and sales individuals to position themselves as trusted advisers; to meet buyer expectations of a personalised, omnichannel buyer journey; to co-create value with their buyers; and to accurately measure the value their buyers are receiving as a result of their relationship.

Before implementing new technologies to facilitate this, however, it is important to understand your organisation's readiness to implement said technologies. At an individual level, salespeople and managers will have varying skills and experience with digital technology, and this will impact their ability to learn, adapt and create value from these technologies. And at the organisational level, differences in factors such as systems, processes and culture will dictate an organisation's ability to derive value from digital technology use.

Different organisations have different levels of digital readiness stemming from their current levels of digital maturity. Understanding your level of digital readiness will help you make recommendations based on what is possible for your organisation, as well as increasing the likelihood of the success of any digital transformation.

By contrast, not having an understanding of your organisation's digital readiness can lead to wasted resources as you try to implement changes that are inappropriate for the organisational environment.

Like the buyer-centricity audit, the digital-readiness audit is a qualitative survey where you will rate your organisation's performance based on each of the areas listed in table 6.5, where 5 is the highest level of commitment and performance you could imagine, and 1 is where these attributes are non-existent.

Table 6.5: digital-readiness audit

Topic	Description	Rating				
		1	2	3	4	5
Digital readiness/maturity						
Digital strategy	Does the organisation have a digital roadmap linked to the achievement of long-term business objectives?					
Digital culture	To what extent do behaviours and attributes support and enhance digitalisation efforts (e.g. risk-taking, no-blame culture)?					
Technology (tools)	To what extent does the organisation have available and effective digital tools and support for the sales team?					
Operations and processes	To what extent are the organisation's processes supported by technology?					
Digital ecosystem	To what extent are the digital systems and processes integrated (vertically and horizontally), enabling everyone to work within the same digital ecosystem?					
Digital readiness/maturity score		/25				

Your rating out of 25 points will determine your level of digital readiness and maturity:

- level 1 (<7) = digitally immature
- level 2 (8–12) = early stages of digitalisation
- level 3 (13–17) = maturing

- level 4 (18–22) = strong digital maturity
- level 5 (>22) = digital excellence.

Organisations at level 1 have few processes and systems for digitalisation. The organisations use few digital tools and/or those tools are not well integrated. In these organisations, the digital vision and/or leadership is weak or not visible.

At level 2, organisations are in the early stages of digitalisation. Leadership might be committed to digitalisation, but digital capabilities are low, tools are evolving, employees are learning new systems and processes, and technologies are not well integrated or aligned with buyer expectations.

At level 3, organisations are digitally maturing. Leadership and employee capabilities are improving and there is integrated use of digital tools across the organisation. The focus in these organisations is on using digitalisation for the benefit of their buyers, and there is strong governance and a focus on digital innovation.

At level 4, organisations are digitally proficient. At this level, they have a digital vision and roadmap that aligns with their long-term objectives. Leadership is committed to digital innovation, employees are digitally capable and digital tools add value to their buyers. Some digitalisation of products and services is underway at this level.

Organisations at level 5 have developed a fully integrated digital ecosystem that is connected to buyers and drives business operations and growth. These organisations have servitised their products, and these services have been integrated with smart/connected solutions. The organisation's business model has been heavily digitalised.

An interesting note to keep in mind about this assessment is the relationship between digital readiness and digital maturity, as these don't always go hand in hand. It is possible to have an organisation with low digital maturity but a high level of digital readiness — that is, there is leadership buy-in for digitalisation, the team is proficient in the latest tools and technologies and there is a roadmap to digitalise. This is a powerful position to be in. Although you might have a lower score, you have all the foundations required for successful change.

The opposite scenario is a more challenging one: an organisation with what seems to be a high level of digital maturity, but low readiness when it comes to digital evolution. These tend to be large enterprises with custom software and systems that were implemented years ago. At the time of implementation, they may have achieved a good score in this assessment, but as technology continues to evolve they struggle to keep up due to the complexity of making technology changes in such a large organisation.

Simply, the organisation may have been digitally mature in the past, with integrated ecosystems and an innovation roadmap, but they have become stagnant. In these cases, it's possible for an organisation that was at level 5 in the past to drop to level 4 or level 3 as the wider landscape outpaces it.

If you are in an organisation like this, it is important to keep this in mind when performing this assessment. Don't consider only the level of technology that has been implemented, but also the appropriateness of that technology in the current sales and buying landscape, and your organisation's ability to evolve as the market and your buyers do.

Tech-stack audit

Where digital readiness and maturity look at *how* technology is implemented across your organisation, including your organisation's ability to continue to evolve, the tech-stack audit looks at *what* technology is implemented across your organisation—that is, the specific tools you are using, what they can achieve, and how effectively they are being used.

Unfortunately, many vendor businesses are barely scratching the surface of what is possible with today's digital technologies. Many have a CRM and some marketing automation, but that's it.

The result is that they find themselves reacting to changes in the market and their buyers' behaviour, rather than proactively using new methods to connect with their target market. They have no insights about what their target market wants and how they want to interact, which means their sales and marketing teams are constantly working on assumptions and hoping for the best.

They have no structured way to manage their intellectual property—that is, nothing is properly stored, managed or documented. In some cases, the vendor's IP isn't even understood, as it only exists in the heads of their key staff members. When they move on, that knowledge is then lost.

There is also a lot of duplication of effort, with ad hoc processes and a lack of visibility, not to mention the poor management of resources.

From the perspective of the salesperson, productivity is lower, and the internal burden of administration bottlenecks gradually kills job satisfaction. They find themselves managing everything offline and struggling to keep track of the paper trail. They also find themselves having to do everything—spending 23 per cent of their time on admin, 12 per cent on order processing and 10 per cent on service requirements—because there is a lack of resources and tools to allow them to focus on connecting with buyers.[278]

This is compounded by a lack of clear key performance indicators (KPIs), and sales leaders are unable to gauge what is going on in their team. Rather than being able to accurately monitor progress and performance, they need to rely on informal conversations and sales individuals holding themselves accountable.

This is underpinned by a backdrop of continued underperformance. As we discussed in part 1, an increasing number of salespeople are struggling to meet their quota and effectively engage with buyers, which leads to retention and acquisition rates falling.

Not only is the lack of supporting and enabling technology preventing salespeople from doing their jobs effectively, but it's also leading to higher sales staff turnover. An increasing proportion of the workplace consists of Millennials and Gen Z, who expect to be able to join a vendor organisation and have the tools and technology they need to succeed. When vendor organisations don't have those resources set up, that talent will look elsewhere.

The right technology stack is critical in helping vendors meet modern buyer expectations. With the right combination of tools and platforms, salespeople will have accurate buyer insights and can make more educated decisions about how to engage with buyers. IP is recorded and organised in a way that allows the entire team to leverage the knowledge the vendor business has built over the years and achieve the best results. And buyers are delighted that their needs are seen to quickly and easily, and actively look for further ways to work with the same vendor.

Digital tools are the key to sales productivity, funnel efficiency, effective market research and targeting, lead nurturing, and sales conversions. It's only by implementing an efficient sales technology stack that vendor organisations will be able to keep up with changing buyer demands, continue expanding their market reach and hit their target sales output.

To help you assess your organisation's current tech stack, in table 6.6 (overleaf) we have mapped out the typical technologies that can assist with each of the following stages:

- buyer understanding
- awareness
- consideration
- purchase
- buyer success
- sales enablement.

These stages align with the buyer journey, with sales enablement acting as a supporting layer that runs across the entire journey.

Table 6.6: tech-stack maturity levels

	Shallow	Emerging	Exploring	Deep
Buyer understanding	• Internet search • Lead clipping • Lead list building • Web visitor tracking	• Call-back lead capture • Email autoreply mining • Match prospects to IBP/MBP	• Buyer intent data • Account targeting • Predictive lead scoring • Data cleanse/append • Recommend prospects based on IBP/MBP • Refine IBP/MBP with market trends	• LinkedIn integration with CRM technologies • AI-based market intelligence & social listening • Data-dictated direction
Awareness	• Static web content • Inactive professional social presence • Low share of voice	• Automated media monitoring • Automated social listening • Automated content calendar • 100% complete LinkedIn profiles • Regular content publication • Actively growing network • Automated social listening • Automated content calendar	• Engagement analytics content recommendations • Audience outreach based on existing buyer demographics and behaviour • Content creation and distribution tools • Content amplification (paid and unpaid) • Auto profile visit • Auto follow	• Automated content creation and targeting • Predictive outreach • Automated email messaging • Lead scoring • Predictive analytics • White space identification

Consideration	• Phone & email • Online meeting • Meeting schedulers • PowerPoint	• Sales prospecting & engagement • Presentation builders • A/B content testing • Gated content & automated nurture sequences	• Video selling • Personalisation/social • AI email outreach • Buyer portals • AI meeting note taking • Reference management • Channel management	• AI-driven value mediation • Sentiment analysis • Conversational analytics • Automated proposal generators • Automated simulators and calculators • Dynamic pricing
Purchase	• Website • PowerPoint • Spreadsheets • Documents • Email	• ROI calculators • Buyer consensus • Value selling • eSignatures • Proposal creation • CPQ (configure, price, quote) software • e-commerce store • Marketing/sales integration, digital/mobile commerce	• Account & opportunity management • Sales process & action management • Contract life-cycle management • Digital marketplace (joined) • Omnichannel buyer life-cycle management • Guided web search capabilities • Chatbots	• AI-driven sales processing • Automated scanning of legal documents • Digital marketplace (owned/orchestrated) • AI-driven sales orchestration • AI-assisted web search capabilities • AI-enabled chatbots

(continued)

Table 6.6: tech-stack maturity levels (*cont'd*)

	Shallow	Emerging	Exploring	Deep
Buyer success	• Spreadsheets	• CRM • Buyer experience & success • Onboarding process	• Buyer engagement • Revenue management • Renewal management • Referral management	• Data-driven buyer success management • Automated buyer onboarding
Sales enablement	• Spreadsheets • Face-to-face training • Human-led coaching • Manual sales reporting	• CRM • Sales compensation planning & admin sales portal • Some gamification • Skills development & reinforcement • Digital-supported coaching • Basic CRM with pipeline management • Sales analytics	• Forecast analysis & machine learning • Sales performance management • Territory management • Video practice & role play • Sales call recording & coaching • Data-led coaching • CRM with sales operations/ marketing integration • Sales analytics with self-service capabilities	• AI-assisted/AI-driven training • AI-enabled coaching systems • AI-driven predictive CRM • Predictive sales analytics

As you review table 6.6, make note of the technology you currently have supporting each step of the journey. For each step, does your organisation predominantly sit at the Shallow, Emerging, Exploring or Deep maturity level?

Note that it is common for organisations to sit across multiple maturity levels (for instance, you might find you have some Emerging buyer understanding tools and some evolving buyer understanding tools). In this case, simply mark your organisation based on which level has the highest number of tools (so an organisation with three tools in the Emerging level and two in the Exploring level would be marked as Emerging).

Using table 6.7, rate your organisation for each level. Shallow will give you a rating of 1, Emerging will give you a rating of 2, Exploring will give you a rating of 3 and Deep will give you a rating of 4.

Table 6.7: tech-stack maturity audit

	Rating			
Topic	**Shallow: 1**	**Emerging: 2**	**Exploring: 3**	**Deep: 4**
Tech stack				
Buyer understanding				
Awareness				
Consideration				
Purchase				
Buyer success				
Sales enablement				
			Tech stack score	/24

As in the previous exercises, your total score will define your overall level in the tech stack audit:

- level 1 (<6) = Shallow
- level 2 (7–12) = Emerging

- level 3 (13–18) = Exploring
- level 4 (>18) = Deep.

Level 1, or Shallow, organisations are using the most basic of the current available tools to support the buying journey and to enable their sales force. Their buyer understanding relies on internet searches and basic website tracking, while their ability to reach buyers through the awareness step relies on a static website and inconsistent social media content. The consideration and purchase steps are managed by phone, email and online meetings, with basic Microsoft Office or Google Drive tools to share information, and post-purchase usage is tracked with spreadsheets.

Emerging organisations build on their previous tech stack. At level 2, their ability to understand their buyers is more advanced, with call-back lead capture, email auto-reply mining and the ability to match prospects to their ideal and minimum buyer personas. They have more automation in the awareness step, including automated media monitoring, social listening and content calendars. When communicating with buyers, they have more sophisticated tools at their disposal, such as presentation builders, automated nurture sequences, ROI calculators and the ability to process purchases online. Post-sale, they can track usage with a CRM and have tools to support a customer success function.

Exploring organisations continue to build on these tools, with buyer intent data, predictive lead scoring, regular data cleansing and the ability to recommend and target ideal prospects. Level 3 organisations have more targeted campaigns with engagement analytics able to recommend ideal content for prospects, and outreach based on existing buyer demographics. Buyer communication includes video selling, personalised recommendations, AI email outreach and advanced reference and channel management tools, and there are automated account and opportunity management and sales process management tools in place. Post-sale usage data includes buyer engagement, revenue management and referral management information.

At level 4, organisations have achieved a Deep tech stack. Their understanding of their buyers is deeper than ever before, with LinkedIn and social integration with their in-house CRM, which facilitates automated buyer signal recognition. These organisations exploit AI-based market intelligence and social listening, and data dictates the direction they pursue. The awareness step of the buyer journey is largely computerised, with automated content creation, email messaging and targeting facilitated by predictive outreach and analytics. During the consideration step, these organisations are more informed than ever, with sentiment analysis and conversational analytics at their fingertips. These data empower Deep organisations to further streamline and personalise the process with AI-driven value mediation, dynamic pricing and automated proposals, simulators and calculators.

At purchase, Deep organisations leverage AI to drive sales orchestration and processing with chatbots to answer buyer questions. The scanning and processing of legal documents is automated, and post-purchase customer success management is data driven with automated onboarding and usage reports to drive further success.

Importantly, it is possible for organisations to have a deeper tech stack at one step of the buyer journey than another. For instance, an organisation might be in the Exploring category for buyer understanding, but in the Shallow category for buyer success. Rating each area separately and determining your overall score will give you a bird's-eye view of where your organisation sits and valuable insight into the areas where there is the most opportunity for improvement.

Bringing it all together

To determine your level on the Deep-Selling maturity model, you will combine your ratings for each of the four elements of Deep-Selling excellence: people, strategy, metrics and technology (see figure 6.1, overleaf).

Simply combine your scores from the previous three exercises to get your total score:

- *people:* score of 5–25 from the buyer-centricity audit
- *strategy:* score of 5–25 from the buyer-centricity audit
- *metrics:* score of 5–25 from the buyer-centricity audit
- *technology:* this combines your digital readiness score of 5–25, and your tech stack score from 6–24.

Customer-centricity			Technology			
Strategy	People	Metrics	Digital readiness	Tech stack	Total	
-/25	-/25	-/25	-/25	-/24	≤30	1 Shallow
-/25	-/25	-/25	-/25	-/24	31–65	2 Emerging
-/25	-/25	-/25	-/25	-/24	66–95	3 Exploring
-/25	-/25	-/25	-/25	-/24	≥96	4 Deep

Figure 6.1: Deep-Selling maturity scores[279]

If your total score across all the assessments is below 30, you are in a Shallow sales organisation. As discussed in chapter 5, these organisations have a product-centric culture with no defined buyer success strategy. Their processes and workforce are usually digitally immature, and they have low levels of technology use across the organisation.

If your score is between 31 and 65, your organisation is Emerging. At this stage you have likely developed a vision for a buyer-centric culture along with having audited your processes and developed a roadmap for change. The organisation has also begun garnering support for becoming more buyer centric and data driven.

Organisations scoring between 66 and 95 are Exploring organisations. At this maturity level, a Deep sales strategy has been developed, approved and is being supported by staff and management. The transformation is underway, with processes, training and technologies beginning to change, and resources have been diverted to support the project. In these organisations, energy is high and positive effects are being observed.

Finally, organisations with scores over 96 are Deep-Selling organisations. These organisations have a strong, buyer-centric culture, strategy and processes. They are digitally mature with an evolved tech stack that enables the strategy and processes, and they have a well-trained and engaged workforce, committed to their buyers' success.

Regardless of where your organisation currently sits on the maturity model, the roadmap in this book is designed to increase your Deep-Selling maturity, as vendor organisations (along with the sales and buying landscape) are constantly evolving. We see the process as cyclical. You should periodically return to this phase and perform a new audit to determine where your organisation now sits on the maturity model and to understand the next actions that will help you go deeper.

Looking to the future

Now you have an understanding of your organisation's level of Deep-Selling maturity, including your current sales performance, where the organisation sits on the buyer-centricity scale, your level of digital readiness and the sophistication of your current tech stack.

In phase 2, you will start to increase your Deep-Selling maturity by developing a deep understanding of your buyers, rethinking the structure of your buyer-facing teams, and choosing the best sales execution model for your organisation and your buyers.

PHASE 2

EMERGING TO EXPLORING

Now that you have laid the foundations for your Deep-Selling journey, phase 2 will build the roadmap to move your organisation from Emerging to Exploring on the maturity model.

As your organisation moves from Emerging to Exploring, you should expect to see the following:

- *People:*
  - There is high motivation and positive energy being diverted to executing a Deep-Selling strategy.
  - The key buyer-facing teams are being reorganised to achieve your organisation's buyer-centric strategy, resulting in higher inter-team communication and a better total buyer experience.
- *Metrics:*
  - You have developed a deeper, data-driven profile of your buyers, which gives your organisation a better understanding of what your buyers want, when they want it and how your organisation is delivering to those expectations.
  - As teams are restructured, managers will start looking at new ways to measure success in this cross-functional structure, rather than in siloed buckets.

- *Technology:*
  - New technologies are implemented to support the collection and analysis of data, which can drive buyer-led and aligned sales actions.
  - Similarly, the implementation of new sales models and structures develops requirements for the required technology to support and optimise the change.
- *Strategy:*
  - Your organisation has a deeper understanding of your buyers than ever before, including your ideal and minimum buyer personas.
  - The ideal buyer experience dictates your organisation's sales strategy, execution models and roadmap for change.
  - Sales execution models and organisational structure are refined to align to the ideal buyer experience.

This phase in the journey consists of three chapters:

1 *Develop a deep understanding of your buyers.* Chapter 7 takes a holistic look at your buyers. You will be introduced to technologies that can help you acquire data that can be used to understand your buyers at a deeper level. You will develop deeper insights into your buyers' motives, actions and expectations. And you can use these insights to develop deeper and more meaningful buyer personas and experience maps, which will facilitate more meaningful and valuable interactions.

2 *Restructure the team to align with the buyer journey.* Buyer-centric organisations have structures that reflect their buyer's needs. In chapter 8, you will align your resources to the buyer journey.

3. *Evolve your sales execution model using Deep-Selling tactics.* With Deep buyer understanding and an aligned team structure forming a solid foundation, in chapter 9 you will begin to execute a Deep-Selling sales model for your buyers and your products and capture this in a one-page sales playbook.

It's time to move your organisation out of the Shallows.

CHAPTER 7
DEVELOP DEEP BUYER UNDERSTANDING

So many vendor organisations proclaim they are buyer centric, or even buyer *obsessed,* but in most cases, those are mere words on a website or sales brochure. Most vendor organisations are anything but buyer obsessed, with the majority still chasing, interrupting, pushing, pitching and verbally vomiting on the most important stakeholder in their business.

Buyer obsession is the key to Deep Selling: placing your buyer at the core of your business strategy, including aligning your organisational structure, execution models, culture and metrics to the goal of delivering value to your buyers, and leveraging technology to optimise the experience.

In chapter 6, you laid the groundwork for becoming a Deep-Selling organisation by understanding your current state. In this chapter, we put the rubber to the road by developing Deep buyer understanding and re-orienting your organisation to become truly buyer obsessed.

We know you've done this before. You've done the surveys and the interviews, the post-support call ratings and the NPS feedback. You already know your buyers.

We acknowledge that you've done the work. And we recognise that objections might crop up because of this, especially if you're in an organisation that is more excited about leveraging new technologies than focusing on buyer centricity.

However, we strongly advise you to take this step. As we discussed in part I, focusing on digitalisation without looking at the foundations underpinning your organisation means you run the risk of implementing new tech that accelerates bad habits, rather than paving the way for change.

In the best-case scenario, taking this step will mean you have a deeper understanding of your buyers than ever before, which you can use to design an ideal buyer experience. Any subsequent technology implementations or organisational changes will help drive that experience, leading to a more successful sales team, higher business revenue and happier buyers. In the worst-case scenario, you'll realise that you already have a clear understanding of your buyers, and that is still a worthwhile outcome as far as we're concerned.

How do buyers see you as a vendor?

Let's first look at how our buyers perceive us as vendors. While many vendor organisations strive to become valued business partners of their buyers, in reality, most buyers will categorise vendors based on the strategic importance of our solutions to their businesses.

For example, an organisation that sells stationery to a multinational manufacturing company might never be as important as a vendor that sells rare manufacturing additives, or one that manages the maintenance for the machines that keep that company producing. Simply, the importance of each vendor is dictated by how strategic the vendor is to the operation of the buying organisation, and how easy it is to acquire the vendor's solutions from other suppliers.

Vendors with solutions of the highest strategic importance are categorised as Tier 1 vendors, as per the vendor rationalisation approach we discussed in chapter 3. Those vendors are not easily replaceable.

Strategically important vendors supply items that are critical to the operation of the buying organisation. Vendors with low strategic importance are those that supply items that are not crucial to the core operation of a buying firm. A strategically important vendor to a computer hardware producer would be the vendor that supplies its microchips. One with low strategic importance would be the vendor that supplies coffee for the staff kitchen: while the team might not be happy to run on less caffeine, coffee is not critical to the organisation producing its product.

Rare or strategically risky items are those that are not readily available or are offered by a limited number of vendors. By contrast, items that are readily available and offered by many vendor organisations present very little supply risk to a buying organisation.

The vendor positioning matrix shown in figure 7.1 (overleaf) illustrates how buyers categorise and analyse the strategic importance of different types of vendors based on the overall importance of their products or solutions to the buying organisation. The matrix categorises items into four groups—strategic, leverage, bottleneck and non-critical items—and provides strategic advice for how the buyer should interact with vendors in each category.

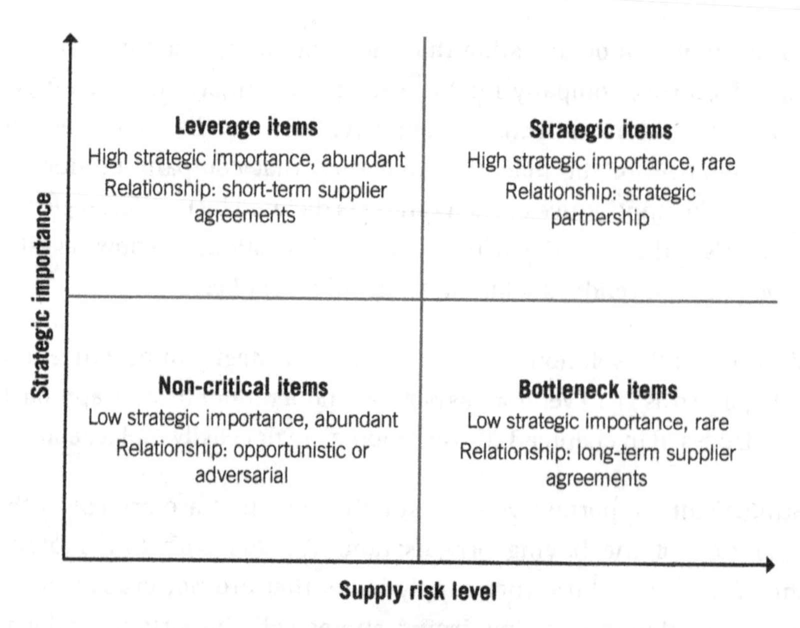

Figure 7.1: vendor positioning matrix (adapted from the Kraljic matrix)
Source: Adapted from the Kraljic matrix.

For example, buying organisations will generally look to form strategic long-term partnerships with vendors that provide solutions that are strategically important and rare. Alternatively, they will tend to take an opportunistic or adversarial approach to vendors that offer abundant and less critical items. For items in the other two quadrants, supplier-based agreements — where vendors agree to medium-term, fixed price supply contracts — are common, as these reduce the risk for buying organisations and provide certainty of supply to vendor organisations.

As a vendor, you can objectively analyse your organisation's position within the matrix by surveying or interviewing your buyers, or by analysing your interactions with them. You will need to consider the following:

- *How strategically important are you to your buyers' operations?* While it is common for vendors to believe that their solutions are critical, the reality is that some items are more critical than others. Consider what would happen if your buyer was unable to buy your solution at all. Would their operation shut down? Or could they easily find a substitute or alternative?

- *How rare is the solution you provide?* It is also common for vendors to consider themselves to be the best and, in some cases, the only supplier who can service their buyers' needs. Ask yourself, how true is this really? If you were to go out of business tomorrow, who else would be able to offer your solution? Would your buyers find it difficult to replace you?
- *What type of approach do your buyers take when interacting with you?* While vendors like to be in control of interactions with suppliers, it is common for buyers to approach vendors differently based on their strategic importance. Do buyers invite your firm to provide input into critical decisions, or do they keep you at arm's length? Do you have trouble finding time to see key stakeholders, or are you constantly consulted throughout the buying process?
- *What stage of the process are you invited into?* Modern B2B buyers typically complete 87 per cent of the buying process before even consulting a vendor.[280] This is especially true if you are a non-strategic vendor. So, are you often involved in competitive tenders before a buyer has decided what they need to buy? Or do you usually get invited to the table only after the buyer has decided what they need?

The answers to these questions will help you analyse your position in the eyes of your buyers, and these insights will provide you with an indication of where you sit on the scale of strategic importance. This will provide you with a starting point for analysing your ideal sales model, which we will discuss in detail in chapter 9.

Understanding your buyers

Now that you have a better understanding of how your buyer classifies you as a vendor, you can start to uncover insights that can be used to clearly define, segment and prioritise your buyers.

Proper segmentation and prioritisation of buyers is an important determinant of a vendor organisation's success. However, many B2B vendors struggle to understand their buyers effectively, leading to confusion and misunderstanding regarding who their most important buyers are. There are several reasons for this:[281]

- *The rationality of B2B buyers.* Unlike B2C buyers, who primarily make purchasing decisions based on emotions, B2B buyers need to be able to demonstrate the return of any investment. This makes it more challenging for vendors to identify buyer needs, as there are fewer behavioural and needs-based segments, and this often results in segmentation based on superficial factors such as business size and turnover. (Note that these are still important to consider, but they shouldn't be the be-all and end-all of segmentation.)
- *The complexity of B2B products.* B2B products, particularly in the high-tech space, are highly complex and tailored to buyer requirements. This raises the question of whether segmentation is even possible in some markets: if each buyer's needs are unique, how does a vendor group them in meaningful ways?
- *The size of B2B markets.* B2B markets are often small, with each niche dominated by a handful of large buyers, resulting in fewer possible segments existing in the first place. It is also challenging to gather data on those segments.
- *B2B customers are long-term buyers.* Because many business purchases are made via long-term, rolling contracts, vendors often see less of a need to define and target segments. A long-term buying environment means the buyers in that

environment are less likely to churn. The risk is that vendors can then become complacent in their segmenting and targeting efforts.

- *The increasing number of decision makers in any B2B sale.* As we have discussed, the average tech purchase involves between 14 and 23 people.[282] This not only makes it more difficult to target decision makers, but results in longer sales cycles and a higher likelihood of a 'no decision' outcome.

Because of these challenges, vendor organisations have typically left segmentation to chance or made use of only the most basic tools available to them—for example, keeping buyer information in poorly configured and static CRM systems, simple databases or Excel spreadsheets.

Deep-Selling organisations leverage technologies such as social media, dynamic CRM systems and AI to identify, categorise and monitor their buyers in real time. This enables them to gain a deeper understanding of their buyers and helps them develop meaningful and actionable buyer segments.

Use technology to gain deeper buyer insights

As described above, vendor organisations now have access to advanced technologies that are capable of finding, storing and disseminating data far more effectively than ever before. Organisations that can embrace this technology as part of their buyer-centric strategies will be at a significant advantage to those that can't.

Just some of the capabilities now available to Deep-Selling organisations are:

- *monitoring and analysing lead actions:* most modern CRM platforms are now equipped with data mining capabilities. Organisations can use these capabilities to monitor their buyers' actions — for example, their interactions with your social media content, contact with customer service representatives or website visits. These 'lead actions' can help you to uncover valuable insights about their needs, their past engagements with your organisation and past associations with other successful accounts, and can be used to guide when and how to engage with them in the future

- *buyer intent data:* this functionality is also available in many CRM platforms with built-in analytics features and AI tools that can alert you to when a buyer demonstrates suitable intent. By monitoring profile information, support calls and chats, purchase history, social media sentiment and website behaviour, alongside market research, AI can identify trends in the data to reveal common pain points, preferences and buying triggers, and alert the salesperson when the buyer has shown sufficient intent to warrant an approach. Many CRM platforms also have advanced relationship mapping features that allow vendors to understand how actors across their network are connected, thereby empowering salespeople to leverage existing relationships to find more buyers from within that network
- *digital footprint:* to build deeper relationships between sales individuals and buyers, it is important to develop an effective digital footprint. Having a coordinated digital footprint across an organisation creates a consistent experience for buyers who perform independent research online before contacting a vendor. As many buyers will only approach vendors who can help them to achieve their goals, a vendor's digital footprint should include information about their capabilities, qualifications and prior successes with important clients. This helps to establish trust and instil confidence before the buyer has interacted directly with your salesforce.

See figure 7.2 for a visual representation of sources of buyer data for data-led selling.

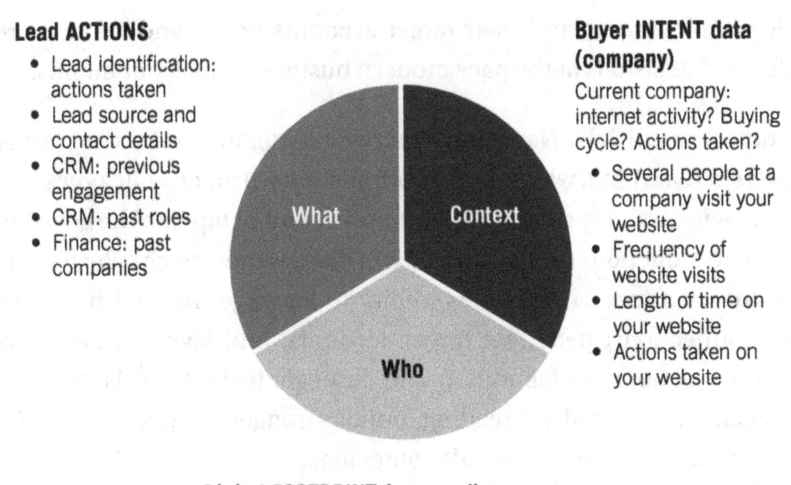

Figure 7.2: sources of buyer data for data-led selling

LinkedIn is taking the lead when it comes to leveraging technology for data and Deep buyer insights, having recently launched the world's first Deep sales platform: LinkedIn Sales Navigator.[283] This platform is designed to give sellers the unparalleled ability to find and connect with the right prospects, build and nurture relationships, and stay informed about important changes and trends among their target buyers.

This data can then be used to prompt sales actions. For example, if a key stakeholder changes jobs, the vendor can be prompted to reach out to other contacts at that business. Likewise, if a 'friendly' stakeholder starts a new job at another firm, sellers are prompted to reach out to understand if they require any assistance in their new position.

AI is significantly enhancing the capabilities of LinkedIn Sales Navigator, with features such as AI Account IQ, which provides deep insights and analytics about key accounts. This feature helps salespeople understand their target accounts better and make more informed decisions at the pace modern business velocity demands.

Another critical Sales Navigator feature for better understanding target buyers is TeamLink, which reveals connections through colleagues and team members, empowering sales professionals to tap into the power of warm introductions (something we will discuss more in chapter 9). This feature enhances salespeople's ability to leverage internal networks and connections; penetrate target accounts; and leverage networks for introductions, collaboration and strategic insights. This deepens engagement and multi-threading, builds stronger relationship equity and ultimately drives better sales outcomes.

Importantly, LinkedIn's platform can now be bi-directionally integrated with leading CRM systems such as HubSpot and Salesforce. This integration means that contact and company information can be updated in real time by the contacts themselves. In effect, this creates a self-populating and self-healing CRM that works for salespeople, rather than the other way around.

One of the key problems with current CRMs is that the information contained within them is often input by salespeople themselves. This means they are notoriously inaccurate and time consuming to maintain. As a result, salespeople avoid updating their CRM unless pushed by their managers, and sales managers often don't trust the information in the system anyway.

Self-fulfilling CRM systems like those powered by LinkedIn's data, avoid these problems by facilitating a direct transfer of the buyer's own information into the vendor's CRM. The vendor is then free to configure its CRM and associated sales enablement systems to leverage insights provided by this data and to drive sales actions that lead to better results. No more delays, no more inaccuracy, no more double handling or duplication. The data that a contact wants you to see is readily available and accessible inside your own system in real time.

LinkedIn's platform is just one example of a technology that enables better information and data synergy between firms, but there are many other technologies that enable vendors to monitor their prospects and identify the best time to approach them.

For example, leading software website *G2.com* lists 262 social listening platforms that are available to sales organisations to help them listen to market trends, identify buzz words, find and monitor potential buyers and more. *Captiv8*, *Scout* and *Konnect Insights* are just a few of the social listening tools available to modern sales and marketing teams that can help organisations to better understand their buyers.

Vendors can use AI-enhanced social listening platforms to analyse social media data and online conversations to identify trending topics, influencers and pain points among those that fit your target market. Similarly, integrating website analytics platforms with AI can give you deeper insights about prospects before they convert by identifying patterns in most visited pages, most downloaded content, interaction with website chatbots and more.

There is also a growing number of AI-based sales intelligence tools that organisations can use for everything from analysing their own buyers and their previous interactions with them to prospecting for new leads and opportunities using deep insights about their previous and ideal buyer profiles. *Apollo.ai* and *Zoominfo* are just two of the dozens of platforms that have these advanced functions.

AI can be used to analyse activity among your existing buyers as well as in the wider market, both of which can be helpful for developing buyer understanding.

Ultimately, these technologies provide sales teams with better information, which can be used to develop a much deeper understanding of your buyers. This information can be used for better segmenting and targeting, and to create more accurate and useful buyer personas. This leads to increased efficiency, as your organisation is free to engage with those buyers in a more meaningful way and to deliver value from the very first interaction.

Note that while we have identified a range of tools that are available to help vendor organisations identify and target potential buyers and to improve their buyer understanding, we don't recommend haphazardly implementing these solutions. Instead, we believe it is important to understand which tools are available and to integrate these tools intelligently into your sales process when needed.

Next, we will learn how to develop a picture of your ideal and minimum buyer persona.

Buyer segmentation and targeting

Buyer segmentation relates to the process of aggregating buyers into groups based on common needs, or how buyers respond to your organisation's products or solutions. Segmentation is important for focusing a salesforce on its most important customers, and this reduces wasted resources and effort chasing customers who are not likely to buy or are not strategically important to your business.

Most vendors base their segmentation process on macro-level criteria such as business size or location. For example:

- *Size:*
  - micro (1–4 employees, turnover <$2 million)
  - small (5–19 employees, turnover $1 million–$3 million)
  - medium (20–199 employees, turnover $3 million–$10 million)
  - large (200+ employees, turnover $10 million+)[284]
- *Geography:* the regions and areas in which your buyers reside, their location's population density and geographic differences that impact demand for your solutions (metro versus rural, hot versus cold climates, etc.).

However, by gaining a deeper understanding of your buyers using the technologies and techniques described, we can now consider more relevant and informative micro-level characteristics such as:

- *purchasing behaviour:* purchase history, brand loyalty, usage level, benefits sought, distribution channels used, reaction to past sales and marketing activity
- *benefits sought:* What benefits does each segment seek from your product or service? Consider:
  - *current problems/pain points:* What are they currently struggling with? Which problems would they pay to solve?
  - *potential risks:* What risks might they face now or in the near future? Would they place value on mitigating these?
  - *potential opportunities:* What opportunities might the organisation be able to leverage, now and in the near future?
  - *existing plans for growth/development:* What are their existing growth and development plans?
- *buyer interaction preferences:* how buyers prefer to interact with vendors, including:
  - *preferred mode of interaction:* social media, email, phone, in-person, self-service, other digital channels
  - *buyer needs:* Does the buyer need help, or do they know what they want and just want to purchase?
- *similarity to previous successful buyers:* What factors are common to previous win/loss buyers? What factors were critical to previous wins and losses?

The factors that will be relevant for defining market segments vary from vendor to vendor, so choose those that are most relevant to your organisation and complete a table like table 7.1 (overleaf) with the characteristics relevant to each of your audience segments.

Table 7.1: segmentation characteristics chart

	Macro-segment 1 criteria: ________	Macro-segment 2 criteria: ________	Macro-segment 3 criteria: ________	Macro-segment 4 criteria: ________
Micro-segment 1 characteristics				
Micro-segment 2 characteristics				
Micro-segment 3 characteristics				
Micro-segment 4 characteristics				

You should consider macro-level criteria for segmentation on the top of table 7.1. This includes considerations such as the buying organisation's size, geographic location, the nature of its product application or its buying situation.

Below each macro segment, you should consider micro- or buyer-level characteristics such as its buying behaviours, the personal characteristics of the buyer, the buyer's preferred interaction method or the benefits they seek.

By combining these macro-level criteria with micro-level characteristics, you will build powerful target segments, which will guide your team's sales activities.

Defining your ideal and minimum buyer persona

Technology and data can provide you with a more granular and dynamic understanding of the buyers your organisation and sales team intend to reach. And a good way to solidify that understanding is to define your ideal buyer persona.

Just some of the benefits of developing buyer personas include:

- These personas become clear target profiles for salespeople to pursue and gives them a simple way to qualify opportunities.
- Buyer personas determine which content sales and marketing need to develop to connect with their target market.
- Personas set the tone, style and delivery strategies for content and the sales approach.
- Accurate buyer personas tell vendor businesses where to find their buyers: which platforms they use online, which events they attend offline, which associations and communities they

are members of and so on. This helps sales and marketing teams create a range of networking strategies for connecting with that market.

When creating your buyer personas, you want to create two versions for each of your target buyers.

The first version is your *ideal* buyer—someone who not only meets all of your organisation's requirements but exceeds them. These requirements will vary from organisation to organisation, and even product to product, but some factors to consider include:

- *the solution required.* What is the premium solution you offer?
- *their budget.* How much of a budget do they need to purchase your premium offering?
- *their time frame.* How quickly do you want the buyer to move? How much time do you need to deliver a top-quality solution without stress or cutting corners, and how quickly does the buyer need to move to ensure you aren't wasting time?
- *their priorities.* Do you want them to be focused on getting the job done quickly, or getting the job done well? Should they need to choose? Are there other priorities that matter to you?
- *potential upside.* What are the ideal benefits a buyer can experience from your solution? What value would the ideal solution provide for the ideal buyer? How much revenue, how much new business, and what level of efficiency and savings?
- *lifetime buyer value.* Do you want them to become a lifetime buyer? What is the potential value of the buyer if they do? Do you have offerings to achieve this?
- *their attitudes/behaviour.* How should they work with you? This might include communication styles, payment policies, ability to stay within scope (or allow extra time/budget for scope creep) and so on.

- *your current capabilities*. What is your organisation able to deliver?
- any other criteria important to your team and organisation.

Again, what is required in an ideal buyer will vary from organisation to organisation, and even from product to product. However, in every organisation, and for every product, the definition of an ideal buyer should rest at the intersection of your organisation's goals, the buyer's requirements and goals, and the buyer's ways of working, as illustrated in figure 7.3.

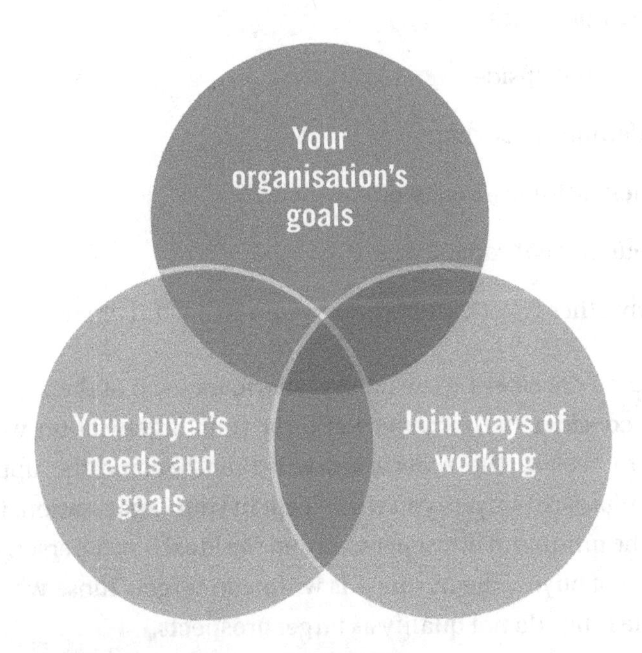

Figure 7.3: the ideal buyer persona intersection

Once you have defined what is an ideal buyer for your organisation, the second persona to consider is your *minimum* buyer. This is a buyer that meets the base criteria for your products or services, but they fall short of the ideal.

This might be a business that wants a basic solution rather than the premium one, that doesn't have the required budget; that has a lower potential upside or lifetime value; or that potentially meets all of your timing, budget and product requirements on paper but has ways of working that aren't a good match for your organisation.

Again, consider the following criteria:

- The solution required
- Their budget
- Their time frame
- Their priorities
- Potential upside
- Lifetime buyer value
- Their attitudes/behaviour
- Your current capabilities
- Any other criteria important to your team and organisation.

Rather than considering the ideal scenario for each of these elements, instead consider the *minimum* criteria your organisation would be willing to accept. These personas will then become the upper and lower limits of the buyers you will accept in your organisation. In other words, the minimum buyer persona and the ideal buyer persona define the range of buyers the business is willing to target. Those who do not fall in the range do not qualify as target prospects.

What you end up with is a range between ideal and minimum, and these are the prospects that you *will* engage. This will also give you a clear picture of what the less-than-ideal persona looks like, which can be equally important in guiding salespeople around carefully qualifying where, and with whom, they spend their time.

Create the personas

To create the personas, take all the information you've gathered and create profiles for individual businesses (even individual stakeholders/decision makers) that meet your ideal and minimum requirements.

When building your personas, consider these questions:

- *Background/story.* Where have they come from? What is their experience to date? Which industries/businesses do they belong to? How many years have they been in this field? What is their level of seniority? What is the decision-making structure like?
- *Goals.* What are the goals for the business and the individual stakeholders/decision makers? For individuals, they may include personal career goals as well as those for the wider team and organisation.
- *Needs.* What are their challenges and requirements?
- *Pains.* What are they currently struggling with? What problems would they pay to solve?
- *Interests.* What are their professional interests? What topics do they Google, read about and research?
- *Sources of information.* Where do they find this information? What formats do they prefer: print or online; articles, videos or podcasts; books or audiobooks (and so on)?

You will need to create two personas for each of your target segments: the ideal buyer persona and the minimum buyer persona.

AI-driven personas

While identifying your ideal and minimum buyer personas has value, the exercise itself comes with limitations. Sales and marketing managers use their own judgement to predict how each persona will react at various points in a buyer journey, meaning the outcomes of these predictions are racked with bias. For example, an airline operator might map the buyer journey as a series of steps, including booking a ticket online, checking in, dropping off baggage, boarding the flight, experiencing the in-flight service, disembarking the airline and then collecting their luggage at the end of the flight.

As the airline team considers how different personas experience each stage of the process, they make assumptions about how each persona will react to various situations. A difficult persona will get annoyed with long wait times for check-in or boarding, whereas a friendly persona might have no problems with the same wait times or processes.

In reality, though, this is all guesswork until a real buyer embarks on that journey. To continue the airline example, a passenger might commence the journey in a good mood, but after several poorly experienced touch points — long wait times, lost baggage, poor inflight service — they might become upset or irritable.

This brings us to a second limitation of static personas: they don't allow for nuances and changes in human behaviour.

The problem is, we have never been able to interact with our personas. Until now.

Using generative AI, sales teams can now generate authentic buyer personas and interact with them as though they are real people. This provides more authentic and dynamic predictions of a persona's pain points across the buyer journey, and enables the organisation to derive more interesting and holistic insights into how a buyer will react in different situations. This also gives vendors the opportunity to refine their offerings and test their sales models in an artificial environment before executing their strategies in the real world.

For instance, do you want to know how a prospect will react to a direct and unsolicited approach from a salesperson in your firm? With AI, you can now ask your persona directly.

The same goes for determining the best sales model or communication methods: simply ask your persona.

While these interactions are artificial, and AI-personas are not expected to exactly match your real buyer's actions and reactions, they can be an excellent starting point for testing strategies and tactics—certainly far better than the old and static personas we had to work with previously.

Plus, with picture-generating software engines such as Adobe Firefly or DALL-E, you can further bring your persona to life by giving it a real face, name and identity. While this might be unsettling to some, it is the next best thing to interacting with a real buyer, not to mention being far simpler, faster and more cost-effective.

Let's illustrate this with an example using ChatGPT.

> ***Scenario:*** *Your organisation is launching a new line of eco-friendly household products, including reusable water bottles, bamboo utensils and organic cleaning supplies.*
>
> ***Persona attributes:*** *Environmentally conscious individuals aged between 25 and 40 who are interested in sustainable living and reducing plastic waste*
>
> ***Generate personas:*** *Enter your list of attributes into ChatGPT and ask it to generate the required number of personas based on those attributes. Note that the more comprehensive the prompt, the more detailed your persona will be.*

After submitting this information, ChatGPT will create personas based on the specified parameters. Its profiles are generally quite detailed, including demographic information, interests, lifestyle habits and pain points.

The following persona was generated by ChatGPT based on the information above.

> ***Persona 1: Eco-warrior Emily:*** *Demographics: Female, 30 years old*
>
> ***Interests:*** *Sustainable living, outdoor activities, healthy cooking*

Behaviours: *Regularly shops at eco-friendly stores, follows environmental influencers on social media, participates in beach clean-up events*

Pain points: *Frustrated by single-use plastic waste, seeks convenient and affordable eco-friendly alternatives.*

After generating your personas, you should review them and make any refinements needed. You can provide feedback to ChatGPT to tweak the personas according to their specific needs. For instance, you might want to adjust the personas to include more information about their preferred communication channels or purchasing behaviours.

Once the personas are finalised, you can interact with them by asking questions in ChatGPT. For instance, you might ask, 'What keeps Eco-warrior Emily up at night?' ChatGPT will then generate an answer from the viewpoint of the persona. Ultimately, the persona will act as though it is a real person.

Use these personas to tailor messaging, content and advertising campaigns to resonate with your target audience effectively. For example, you might create social media content featuring Emily and highlighting how the eco-friendly products align with her values and lifestyle.

Remember that developing personas is not a one-time task; it's an iterative process. The sales and marketing teams can continually refine and update the personas as they gather more data and insights from their campaigns and interactions with buyers. ChatGPT can assist in this process by generating new personas or updating existing ones based on evolving criteria.

To create great AI-based personas in ChatGPT, keep the following tips in mind:

- Explain the situation in detail.
- Provide comprehensive information about the persona: background, goals, needs, interests, pain points and sources of information.

- Explain your product, company and solution in detail.
- Provide any context or issues that might impact your persona.
- Be objective. Don't infuse your persona with bias.

Once you have created your personas, ask ChatGPT to provide you with a detailed prompt or code that can be input into a picture generator such as DALL-E or Adobe Firefly. By generating a picture of each persona, you can bring it to life, and it will feel more authentic when you interact together.

While this process might seem strange, it is the future. Embrace the technology to understand your buyers at a deeper level than ever before.

Mapping the buyer journey

We've already discussed the three broad stages of the buyer journey: awareness, consideration and purchase. These are the three stages most sales teams, and most vendors, consider when establishing their sales processes and go-to-market strategy.

However, the truth is that the buyer journey has evolved to be much longer than before. The stages of the new buyer journey are:

- *status quo and the window of discontent.* The first stage — the status quo — is the buyer before they have recognised a need or a problem that needs to be solved. The window of discontent is after they have recognised a need. This may have been triggered by a bad experience with an existing supplier, changes or transitions within the buyer business, or changes to awareness of an existing risk or problem.
- *awareness.* As in the old buyer journey, at this stage buyers are becoming aware that they have a need and may be questioning whether there is a solution for them. They are likely researching the problem itself. First, they are researching the problem in

relation to their business through surveys and interviews with staff, suppliers and their own buyers. Second, they are performing more general research through Google searches, reading whitepapers, looking at articles on LinkedIn, and so on, to learn about market trends and how other businesses have solved the same problem or addressed the same needs.

- *consideration*. At this stage, buyers are aware they need a solution and are investigating the different options in the market. They might be researching different vendors, including reviewing their websites, their social media profiles and the content the vendors are producing (such as whitepapers, podcasts and articles). They may also be looking into specific products, including reviews, case studies, comparisons and tutorials. Some buyers may contact vendors at this stage with questions and requests for more information.
- *purchase*. If they haven't already, this is when buyers connect with vendors for proposals. In many cases, they have already chosen their desired product and simply need to make the transaction, and some might be reaching out to additional vendors beyond their chosen one to meet due diligence requirements. For a vendor, the challenge at this stage isn't simply closing the deal — it's identifying the real buyers and those who are just filling out their options.
- *success and loyalty*. Most sales teams consider the purchase to be the end of the buyer journey. However, in today's sales and buying landscape, it is just the beginning. It's after the sale that vendors create long-term, trusting relationships with their buyers. At this stage, buyers want to know how they can get the most value out of their products, as well as how they can get even better results, whether that is with further education, upgrading or taking up additional products.

If the buyer has an outstanding experience with a vendor, and that experience becomes the norm as the vendor continues to deliver insights and further value, this generates loyalty and additional revenue for the vendor with repeat buyers spending 67 per cent more than new ones.[285]

- *advocacy*. Finally, those loyal buyers become advocates, referring similar buyers to the vendor. Continuing to engage with buyers after the sale is predominantly about ensuring they get the highest possible value from their relationship with you. When looking at traditional financial metrics, not only does this increase the revenue they bring to the organisation, but it also opens up the potential value of their networks.

At this stage, buyers start sharing vendors with those networks, both online via social media and through in-person networking events, conferences and informal chats.

Most vendor organisations track buyer progress through their sales and marketing funnel, often with clearly mapped out top of funnel, middle of funnel and bottom of funnel activities.

Unfortunately, the majority of these organisations have detached the internal sales process from the buyer journey. This means the buyer journey is left to chance, as you need to wait for the buyer to discover information when (or if) it becomes relevant for them, and then wait for a call. It also isn't an ideal experience, as not only are buyers not getting the right information at the right time, but the sales process is focused on hitting internal targets and not meeting buyer needs.

In the modern, buyer-led era, the focus of vendor organisations can no longer be on these internal processes—it needs to be buyer facing. Sales resources, processes and technology all need to be structured around the buyer journey and how buyers want to buy, rather than trying to retrofit the buyer's preferences into existing sales processes.

By designing an ideal buyer journey, you can encourage buyers to find the right information and resources at the right time, empowering them to experience even more value when they engage with your organisation. Your marketing, sales and customer-success teams will have a better understanding of what your buyers are experiencing at each stage of the process, empowering them to provide more value. This includes:

- understanding of the buyer business model during the status quo and window of discontent — that is, moving beyond the buyers' articulated needs and identifying key value drivers
- identifying value propositions that are relevant to those drivers
- clearly communicating their ability to deliver the promised value
- monitoring, verifying and documenting that the estimated and promised value has been realised in the buyer success stage.

Consequently, this new buyer journey is the foundation upon which vendors can build a truly buyer-aligned sales process.

Buyer question mapping

The first step towards creating a buyer-aligned sales process is determining the key questions, concerns and goals that your ideal buyers have at each stage of the journey, as well as the sources they use to find more information. This process is depicted in figure 7.4.

Based on the information gathered so far, work with the marketing, sales, customer success and customer support teams to answer the questions presented in table 7.2 (overleaf) for each stage of the journey.

Note that while your sales, marketing and support teams can brainstorm the answers to these questions, the best source of information is still your buyers. With this in mind, if you haven't already, we strongly recommend organising interviews with the buyers who match your ideal buyer persona, as well as sending out a broader survey to your buyers in general.

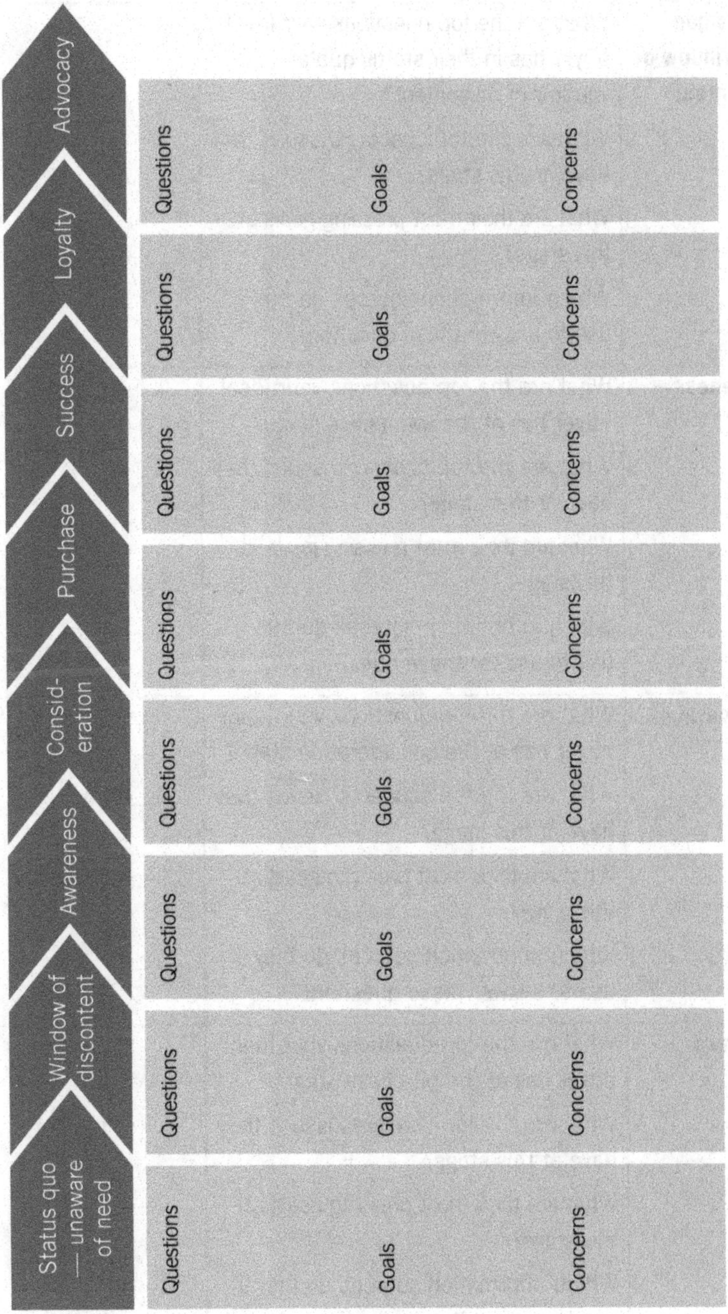

Status quo — unaware of need	Window of discontent	Awareness	Consid-eration	Purchase	Success	Loyalty	Advocacy
Questions	Questions	Questions	Questions	Questions	Questions	Questions	Questions
Goals	Goals	Goals	Goals	Goals	Goals	Goals	Goals
Concerns	Concerns	Concerns	Concerns	Concerns	Concerns	Concerns	Concerns

Figure 7.4: buyer question, goal and concern mapping

Table 7.2: a buyer question template for buyer journey mapping

Status quo and window of discontent	What are the top questions your ideal buyer has in their status quo and window of discontent? What are the top concerns/issues they have at this stage? What are their most pressing goals at this stage? Which information sources do they use to answer these questions?	
Awareness	What are the top questions your ideal buyer has at the awareness stage? What are the top concerns/issues they have at this stage? What are their most pressing goals at this stage? Which information sources do they use to answer these questions?	
Consideration	What are the top questions your ideal buyer has at the consideration stage? What are the top concerns/issues they have at this stage? What are their most pressing goals at this stage? Which information sources do they use to answer these questions?	
Purchase	What are the top questions your ideal buyer has at the purchase stage? What are the top concerns/issues they have at this stage? What are their most pressing goals at this stage? Which information sources do they use to answer these questions?	

Success	What are the top questions your ideal buyer has at the success stage? What are the top concerns/issues they have at this stage? What are their most pressing goals at this stage? Which information sources do they use to answer these questions?	
Loyalty	What are the top questions your ideal buyer has at the loyalty stage? What are the top concerns/issues they have at this stage? What are their most pressing goals at this stage? Which information sources do they use to answer these questions?	
Advocacy	What are the top questions your ideal buyer has at the advocacy stage? What are the top concerns/issues they have at this stage? What are their most pressing goals at this stage? Which information sources do they use to answer these questions?	

Improve internal processes

Before you can map out the ideal buyer journey, it's important to understand the *current* experience your buyers have with your organisation. To map out your current internal processes, we recommend setting up a series of workshops with the teams involved at each stage of the journey:

- *Before the sale (status quo, window of discontent, awareness):* marketing, marketing analytics

- *During the sales process (consideration, purchase):* inside sales, core sales
- *After the sale (success, advocacy):* customer success, customer support.

In the 'Before the sale' workshop, ask the following questions:

- How do prospects first hear about your organisation/solutions?
- What are the most common Google searches relating to your brand name and product names? Which unbranded search terms also lead prospects to discover your organisation/solutions?
- What content do prospects engage with before connecting with the sales team?
- Which pieces of the content generate the most interest (measured in traffic, open rates, downloads and subscriptions)?
- Which channels do prospects use to learn more about your organisation and solutions (e.g. social media, newsletter, blogs, media coverage, review sites, free trials)?
- How long do prospects spend engaging with marketing content before converting or contacting your sales team (measured based on time of signing up for a free trial/download/email campaign and conversion to paid subscription/making a deposit/sales enquiry)?
- Who owns the different stages of the process?
- Who owns the different platforms and channels?

Most of the information at this stage in the journey will come from built-in analytics available for the various channels your marketing team is using. However, some do rely on feedback from prospects and buyers, which is why it is always valuable for sales and customer success staff to ask where prospects and buyers first heard about your organisation and solutions.

In the next stage of the journey, the buyer is considering your offering, and may have converted to a free trial, or will have reached out to speak to your team about their needs. In the 'During the sale' workshop, consider the following questions:

- What is the average and typical sales cycle time, from enquiry to purchase?
- How many people are typically involved in this decision (on the buyer's side), and what are their roles?
- If there is a final decision maker, who is that person and what role do they hold?
- What are the typical questions/concerns that arise during sales conversations?
- Which factors stop prospects from converting?
- Which factors convince prospects to move forward?
- Is there any missing information that would help prospects make an informed decision?
- Are there any critical needs that your organisation's offerings are currently failing to meet?
- Who owns the different activities or stages of the process?

Finally, in the 'After the sale' workshop, work with your customer success and support teams to ascertain the following:

- What happens once a salesperson makes a sale?
- How does the salesperson hand the buyer over to the customer success team?
- What is the onboarding process? When is a buyer considered to be 'onboarded'?
- What happens after the onboarding process?
- Are there any ongoing processes and touchpoints once a buyer is onboard?

- What happens if a buyer complains?
- What are the typical events that happen and/or communications that go out *before* a buyer complains?
- How is the billing process handled?
- What communications does the customer receive throughout this process?
- Which channels do customers use to interact with us throughout this process (e.g. phone, web, online chat, in-person meetings, social media, online portal)?
- Who owns the different stages of the process?
- How do we report on buyer experience, for individual customers and at scale?

You have now mapped out the journey requirements from the buyer perspective, as well as the current process from an internal perspective. The next step is to look at what needs to change in order to meet your buyers' requirements.

Consider the following questions:

- Where are there disconnects between the buyer's questions/desires and the current sales and marketing process?
- Where are there clear gaps in the process?
- Which areas don't work well/are clunky/don't run as smoothly as they could—from both an internal and a buyer perspective?
- At which stages does the buyer get handed between teams? What problems typically arise during handover?
- At which stages do the most issues/complaints arise?

When considering each of the issues or complaints that have been identified, ask whether it is a buyer-facing problem or a problem with internal processes.

Buyer-facing problems should be addressed by incorporating the top buyer questions, concerns and goals into communications buyers receive at each part of the journey. This might include:

- marketing content they consume in the status quo, window of discontent and awareness stages
- resources shared by inside sales and core sales during the consideration and purchase stages (some resources might include PDFs, webinars, videos or training for free trials)
- information shared when presentations are made to buyers during the consideration and purchase stages
- training and resources provided by customer success and customer support teams after purchase.

Problems with internal processes are usually related to information lost during handover. This information can range from records of discussions with a buyer to date—which can result in downstream teams sharing content the buyer is already familiar with (or skipping over information they need to know)—all the way to information about the buyer's product requirements or subscription level, which could lead to the buyer being incorrectly charged or the customer success team taking them through the wrong onboarding process. These are all detrimental to the buyer's experience, though the impact can vary significantly.

To address internal process issues, it is important to involve representatives of the team that is responsible for the activities before the issue occurs (meaning, before handover) and the one experiencing the issue (after handover). Work with them to define the following:

- What is going wrong in the current process?
- For the team doing the handover, what would the ideal scenario look like?

- For the team receiving the buyer after handover, what would the ideal scenario look like?
- What is preventing the ideal scenario from happening (e.g. lack of resources, inadequate technology, underperforming team members, lack of understanding of what is required)?
- What is the minimum viable approach to addressing this issue?

The final question is key. There are cases where poor handover is a result of inadequate training, or team members who are not performing well in their roles. However, these issues can also occur in the most high-performing teams. In this case, they are often a result of being under-resourced, whether that resourcing means a lack of manpower to perform the work required, a lack of tools to support the work, or tools that make the work more complex than it needs to be.

In these scenarios, it's important to understand the minimum viable approach to prevent issues that will negatively impact the buyer experience, with the understanding that more can be done as more resources become available.

Map out the ideal state

The final step is mapping out the ideal buyer experience you would like to create. To achieve Deep-Selling excellence, your entire organisation needs to take a systematic approach to improving the buyer experience and helping your buyers get the best value from your products and services.

It isn't enough to task customer success managers with creating a better experience and then leaving them to their own devices. What one person considers to be a good experience can vary wildly from another's expectations, paving the way for inconsistency and unhappy buyers. By mapping out the ideal buyer experience, everybody (not just the sales team) across the vendor organisation will know what is expected at each stage and your buyers will have a better experience overall.

This map should include all process stages, steps and possible communication channels that buyers can use across their buying journey. It's also important to consider potential complaints at each stage, as figuring out ways to address them in advance will help ensure that those complaints either don't arise at all or are managed effectively and that buyers remain happy throughout the journey.

Figure 7.5 (overleaf) provides an illustrative example of a completed buyer experience map. It describes the user actions, touchpoints and intent processes of a typical buyer across the six stages of the buying journey once the buyer is actively looking for a solution and will vary from buyer to buyer.

Note that the example in figure 7.5 shows the buyer's actions and touchpoints at each stage of the journey (user actions and touchpoints), and the vendor organisation's processes for managing the buyer experience at each stage (intent processes).

When building and managing a buyer experience map, it is important that all user actions and touchpoints are identified, and that intent processes are put in place to manage the buyer at each stage and across all channels and touchpoints.

While it might not be possible to achieve this experience immediately, understanding the ultimate end state will inform investment decisions regarding technology and people, as well as where work should be prioritised.

The end result will be clear, consistent processes that result in buyers who aren't only satisfied, but who also become raving fans.

	Awareness	Consideration	Purchase	Success	Loyalty	Advocacy
User action	Talks to co-workers Google search	Visits vendor websites Reads reviews	Selects product Checks out	Reads training materials Starts using products	Sees business results from product Onboards other team members	Recommends product to colleagues Rates on review websites Interacts with vendor social media
Touchpoints	Banner ads Social media posts	Landing page Webinar Free trial	Phone/Zoom call e-commerce platform	Onboarding call Training sessions	Results reports Support calls for other business needs	NPS surveys Feedback requests Case study preparation
Internal processes	Content creation Advertising Marketing analytics	Webinar hosting/recording Free trial support and follow-up	Sales script/proof points Demo account Contracts	Training materials Onboarding schedule and process	Process for assessing other business needs based on similar buyers	Process for recording positive feedback Process for addressing negative feedback

Figure 7.5: a completed buyer experience map

Buyers as the foundation of Deep-Selling success

Understanding your buyers is the cornerstone of making the shift to becoming a Deep-Selling organisation.

Even though you are likely to have done some of these exercises before, we strongly recommend revisiting them here. Buyer understanding and the new buyer journey form an essential foundation for the next steps in this method, as this will inform how you develop buyer-centric teams and which sales execution models are the most effective in the new, buyer-led era.

Taking the time now to ensure your organisation's buyer understanding is up to date will ensure you take the most relevant approach with the following steps in this methodology, and you avoid the risk of changing your sales structure and models only to later realise they are based on an out-dated understanding of your buyers.

CHAPTER 8
ADAPT YOUR STRUCTURE TO YOUR BUYERS' NEEDS

For more than 140 years, sales teams have been made up of autonomous agents who effectively own and operate an entire territory or set of accounts, regardless of their skill set, knowledge or experience.[286]

As more vendors are starting to realise, this model no longer works in the buyer-led era.

First, field salespeople are expected to perform each and every role required to close a deal—prospecting, opportunity identification, solution design, pitching, proposals, nurturing, even customer support—with no regard for where their specific skills are. Why do sales leaders expect this of their reps when they could easily leverage other team members for improved execution? Where is the logic in allowing your worst presenter to deliver a critical presentation to an important client simply because the client is in their territory?

Traditional, autonomous lone wolves cannot be expected to perform every task optimally.

Second, individual salespeople have limited capacity to manage concurrent opportunities. Consider the current sales capacity at your organisation, which you can calculate by multiplying the total possible sales cycles per year by the maximum number of deals your average salesperson can work on at any one time, multiplied by your total number of reps.

Total sales capacity = total possible sales cycles × max. concurrent opportunities × number of sales resources

For example, if you have a team of eight sales reps, each rep can manage three opportunities at a time and the average sales cycle is four months, this would look as follows:

12 months ÷ 4-month average sales cycle = 3 sales cycles a year

3 sales cycles a year × 3 concurrent opportunities × 8 reps = 72 sales a year

Then, consider the size of your pipeline. In most organisations, there is a massive opportunity cost simply due to sales capacity constraints.

Third, running a traditional field sales force is one of the most expensive fixed (and variable) costs on every vendor's balance sheet. As we shared in part 1, the average salary for a field salesperson ranges from USD60 000 to almost USD150 000, depending on location and exchange rates.[287] In our experience in the high-tech space in Melbourne and Sydney, though, we've found the total package for a field can be closer to AUD300 000.

Ultimately, against the backdrop of shortening product lifecycles and increasing business velocity, the traditional methods of structuring a sales force are no longer effective, which limits a vendor's potential revenue and adds significantly to the bottom line.

From a buyer perspective, we know that most buyers no longer want to engage with traditional sales reps. However, even in cases where they do, the current structure is still unsustainable!

Because buyers are used to dealing with a single salesperson, if that person moves on or even goes on a holiday, they will potentially be working with a new member of the team who lacks the context for the buyer business and working relationship, leading to a poor buyer experience.

Additionally, because individual salespeople can't be experts at every task required for the end-to-end process, buyers are invariably left with a subpar experience because they are not receiving the best service every step of the way.

From the perspectives of both sales enablement and buyer centricity, the structure of vendor organisations needs to evolve to one where all functional activities are integrated and aligned to deliver superior value to their buyers. Remember, product-centric organisations are organised around functional silos defined by product categories, while buyer-centric organisations are structured around their buyers, with teams focused on buyer segment centres, and roles focusing on the buyer experience.[288]

Aligning resources with the new buyer journey

Most sales teams are structured based on internal sales processes and activities. However, the focus should be on how we can best serve our buyers—delivering the information, services and support they need when they need it—rather than on internally dictated quotas or revenue targets.

As the cornerstone of Deep Selling is having Deep buyer understanding, the logical place to start with team structure is the buyer journey.

As we discussed in chapter 7, the modern buyer journey no longer ends when a buyer makes a purchase. In fact, there are several additional stages to the buyer journey, starting with ensuring buyer success, which then leads to buyers becoming advocates, or raving fans.

When it comes to sales effectiveness, the most effective sales structure for both acquisition and retention will be one that mirrors this journey, delivering buyers the information and experience they want, through the channels they want, when they want it.

To achieve this, we recommend considering structure in terms of the core functions required throughout the journey: generating awareness and demand, identifying quality leads, nurturing those leads, conversion and customer success.

It's a waste of resources to allow traditional sales individuals to continue trying to manage the entire buyer journey, and entire sales process, independently. By dividing the buyer journey into functional buckets, vendors can ensure that each individual's skills are used to the best of their ability, and buyers have an exceptional experience from beginning to end.

Seventy-nine per cent of buyers expect consistent interactions across departments, with their top frustration being disconnected experiences.[289] To deliver a holistic experience, your organisation needs to consider the complete journey, rather than responsibilities that sit in each siloed team.

Core functions

If we consider structure in terms of core functions throughout the buyer journey, we can extrapolate the following (as illustrated in figure 8.1, overleaf):

- *Awareness:* demand generation is the core function. In most organisations, this sits with marketing, and responsibilities include building brand awareness and generating leads.
- *Consideration:* lead nurturing and qualification are the core functions. They sit with marketing and sales development. Marketing can nurture leads with content, while sales development qualifies and nurtures leads through building relationships and providing insights.
- *Purchase:* this is where core sales functions sit; or account executives, who are responsible for converting qualified leads into buyers.
- *Success, loyalty, advocacy:* this is the customer success function, where customer success managers ensure buyers get the most value from their products after purchase, identify opportunities to provide more value through other products and services, and solicit referrals. Customer support also sits in this bucket, answering day-to-day user questions and finding solutions to questions and complaints.

As you can see, this functional breakdown demonstrates that the end-to-end buyer journey reaches beyond the core sales team, even though a traditional field salesperson might have been involved in all of these areas in the past. In Deep-Selling organisations, a holistic buyer journey should span marketing, sales, customer success and customer support.

It also impacts other parts of the organisation:

- *Product development:* product development becomes a circular process, where customer success and customer support provide

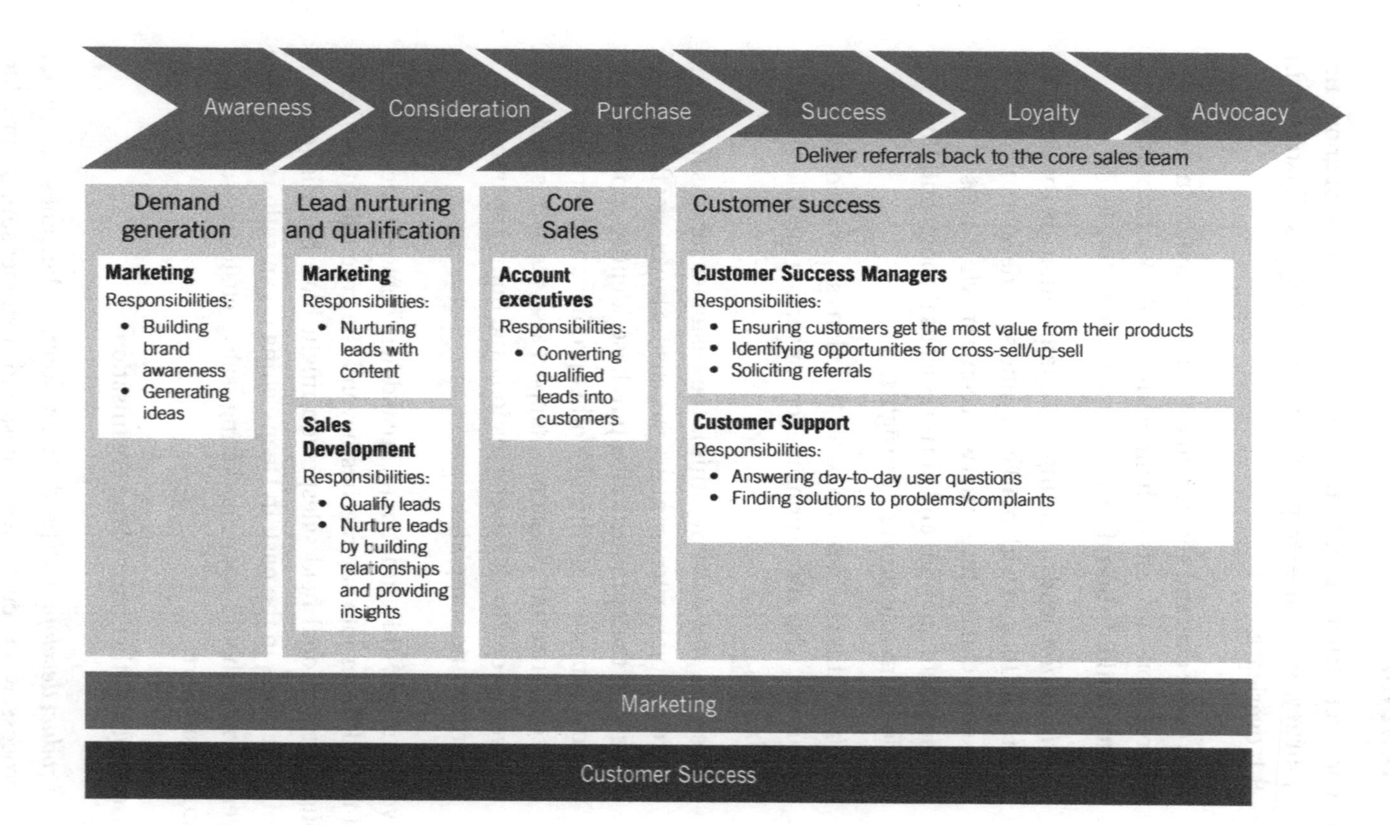

Figure 8.1: responsibilities for each sales function

feedback on product utilisation, effectiveness and value delivered to buyers; marketing provides insight on interest in marketing campaigns, which could highlight blue-ocean areas for investment; and finance feeds into product development by highlighting products that generate the highest ROI through average order value, lifetime buyer value, repeat orders and referral data.

- *Finance and HR:* these operations teams are responsible for measuring performance and incentivising success in this model.
- *Analytics:* because Deep Selling is data-driven, reports provided by analytics on product usage, value realisation, buyer relationship quality and more will also feed into product development and performance measurement.

Implementing a sales and marketing structure like this:

- ensures that the sales process is driven by the buyer journey and not the other way around
- creates value at every step of the buyer journey
- nurtures and grows buyer relationships without anything that might resemble push selling
- ensures that buyers are guided through a delightful buyer journey with the content, insights and support they most need at each stage
- encourages further collaboration and sharing of resources between sales and marketing (which is essential, given the larger role marketing plays in the buyer journey with the rise of marketing automation technologies, social media and content marketing)
- creates a more predictable, sustainable supply of leads for the sales development team to qualify

- ensures account executives are spending their time engaging with qualified leads, rather than wasting time on leads who are unlikely to convert
- ensures buyers aren't dropped or forgotten about after the purchase — that is, there's a dedicated team that ensures they are getting the best value, thereby increasing retention and referrals.

Let's take a deeper dive into each of the four functions.

Function 1: demand generation

It is often challenging to discuss the demand generation function with sales leaders, simply because most of the responsibilities seem to rest outside the traditional sales role. Prospecting was once all about churning through mountains of dirt in order to find a gold nugget, an approach that is now dangerously short-sighted because it ignores potential passive buyers.

According to Chet Holmes, author of *The ultimate sales machine*, only 3 per cent of your target addressable market is open to a vendor message at any given point in time (these are the active buyers who are already looking for a solution to a problem).[290] Therefore, 97 per cent of that target addressable market is passive, meaning that they are in a status quo window and unaware of any need or problem. Technology allows vendors to nurture the passive buyers while focusing on the active buyers, and this creates a massive competitive advantage for those vendors that no longer treat demand generation as a 'dirt sifting' exercise.

Quite often, in years gone by, vendor organisations have had a metaphorical Chinese Wall between the sales and marketing departments, with very little collaboration and cooperation between the two functions (see figure 8.2). In some cases, the dysfunction could best be described as adversarial. Marketing would complain that 'the sales team doesn't close the leads we give them', and sales would bemoan the fact that 'the brand isn't known, the brochures are no good and the leads aren't qualified'.

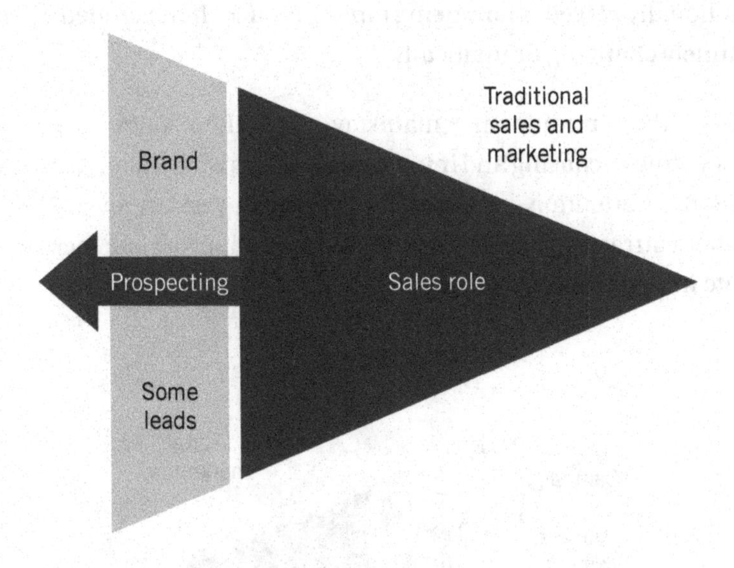

Figure 8.2: the traditional sales role

With the increasing trend towards self-service and automation, however, we have a very different breakdown of the duties, where the marketing role has been encroaching on areas that were once the domain of the sales role.

Demand creation, lead generation and prospecting in general have been forced to become much more sophisticated due to changing buyer behaviour and the new tech that drives this. Content and automated marketing, inbound and outbound programs, and, more recently, AI-powered chatbots are all designed to help create buying-stage-appropriate messaging, and improve the development, management and nurturing of those all-important leads.

Top-of-the-funnel and pipeline development is gradually going the way of marketing professionals, and more and more of this function will be automated in the years to come as AI and predictive analytics continue to paint clearer pictures of buyer tastes and preferences, along with buyer intent data. This means that the role that the salesperson has traditionally played is now being rapidly eroded. If not eroded, then it's definitely changing dramatically.

While the traditional mainstay of the sales role was prospecting — chasing and interrupting buyers with a blanket message to get their attention — the days of chasing buyers are over. Now, it's all about attracting buyers with buying stage-appropriate messages to create inbound leads (as illustrated in figure 8.3).

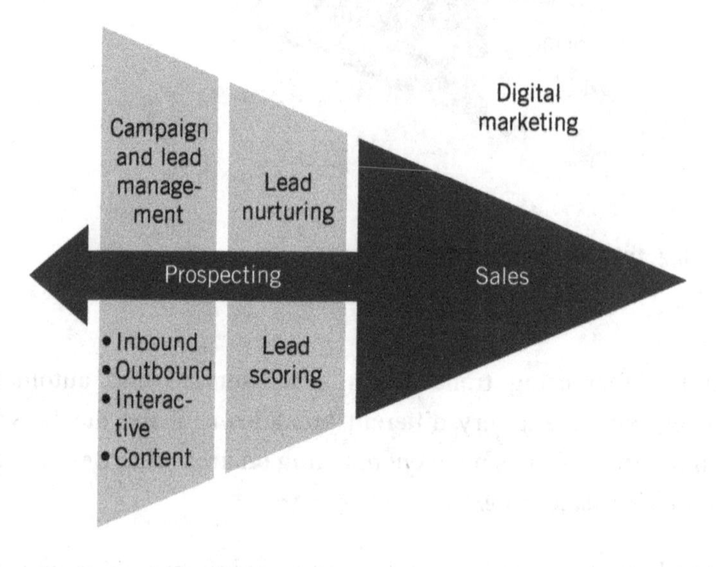

Figure 8.3: the modern sales role

With this in mind, it's important to consider the skills required across a vendor organisation, rather than simply focusing on sales or marketing. For a vendor to get the attention of the buyer, there needs to be alignment between the two to create a cohesive buyer journey. With the diminishing role of outside salespeople and the increased role of marketing technologies that allow both automation and scaled-up engagements, the future model is one where the two traditional sales and marketing functions will become a single team (see figure 8.4).

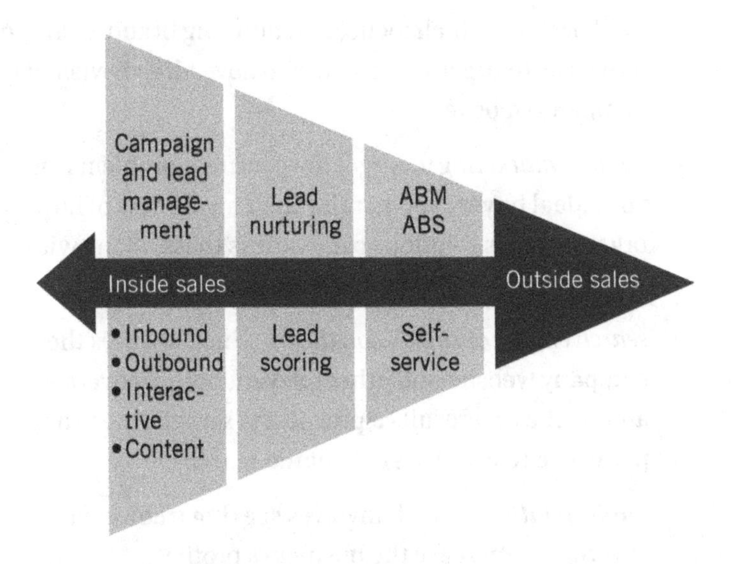

Figure 8.4: the one-team approach

These new buyer-facing teams will comprise a combination of traditional sales types and specialist marketing people, and a range of product-management experts.

These teams will also be highly integrated and made up of an increasing proportion of specialists, all of whom will work together to create a seamless buyer journey rather than generalists, who simply escort the buyer through the entire journey themselves.

In the demand generation function:

- *marketing* will create the vendor's brand and promote this to the target audience through the following activities:
  - *traditional advertising* (depending on budget), which focuses on building brand awareness
  - *online advertising*, including social media ads, display advertising and search engine advertising (also known as

SEM or PPC), which focuses on building brand awareness as well as retargeting people who have already visited the company website

- *content marketing* to target the common problems facing your ideal buyers and to raise their awareness of how the organisation's solutions can address these, along with gated content to start generating leads
- *search engine optimisation (SEO)*, which ensures the company website and other relevant online coverage is among the first results a prospect is served when they perform a relevant search engine search
- *public relations*, which involves seeking traditional media coverage to increase the business's profile

- *analytics* will focus on:
  - gaining a deeper understanding of the market based on its behaviour
  - providing feedback to marketing and sales to develop more targeted campaigns
  - segmenting the database for appropriate lead nurturing.

Function 2: lead nurturing and qualification

Once leads have been identified, the second function focuses on qualification and nurturing programs. This function involves a mix of marketing and traditional sales skills:

- *Marketing* delivers relevant content and advertising to a vendor's databases, segmented into each of the chosen target markets. This will include:
  - *email nurturing campaigns* answering the most common questions asked by prospective buyers, moving them through the consideration thought process and closer to purchase

  - *social media advertising* retargeting the existing database to increase buyer awareness, to direct buyers to more content and to position the vendor brand as top of mind
  - *display advertising* retargeting those who have visited the vendor website to point them back to the website, as well as to keep the vendor brand front of mind.

- *Marketing analytics* provide reporting on the effectiveness of different campaigns and advertising, including lead scoring based on levels of interaction with campaigns.
- *The sales development team* assists marketing with content *amplification*, which helps establish them as industry/market specialists, building relationships with leads and qualifying them for the core sales team. This might include:
  - publishing thought leadership content to help establish the individual reps as subject-matter experts, as well as the vendor as a leader in the market. This provides reps the ability to offer specialised insight to leads
  - personally connecting with leads who match the ideal buyer persona and building a relationship
  - qualifying leads provided by marketing based on lead scoring, the technical fit between the product offering and the buyer's needs, their level of seniority in the buyer business, the understanding of the buyer's vendor stack, and whether the buyer matches the ideal buyer persona defined in chapter 7.
- *Market response* focuses on qualifying *inbound* leads — namely those that reach out to the vendor through their website or phone, specifically enquiring about a product or service. For every 400 leads per month that require human attention, a company needs at least one market response representative.[291]

By qualifying leads early in the sales cycle, the lead nurturing and qualification function ensures that the leads that are most likely to convert are the ones passed on to the core sales function. This then makes way for higher close rates by both inside and outside salespeople, as they are only focusing on qualified opportunities.

Note that the lead generation function also includes account-based marketing (ABM), where the focus of sales and marketing campaigns is narrowed to target a specific account. If a vendor organisation wanted to target a large prospect — think IBM, Walmart or JP Morgan — that organisation has a large enough buyer base that it could be the target for a unique campaign.

The benefit of these campaigns is that the sales and marketing approach can be so targeted that it better cuts through the noise, with 80 per cent of account-based marketers saying that ABM outperforms all other marketing investments.[292]

This further highlights that the traditional 'shotgun' approach to sales is no longer effective in the buyer-led era, and teams therefore need to be structured accordingly.

Function 3: core sales

As Aaron Ross and Marylou Tyler argue in their book *Predictable revenue,*

> *an important step towards turning your sales organisation into a sales machine [is] letting your Account Executives (the sales reps closing business) focus on what they do best: work active sales cycles and close.*[293]

With marketing and sales development representatives focused on generating and qualifying leads, account executives are free to focus on moving qualified opportunities from the consideration stage of the buyer journey to close.

In most vendor organisations, the account executive roles start by being a mix of outside and inside sales — or the traditional, face-to-face salesperson versus a salesperson who conducts the sales process remotely. However, with new technology and changing buyer preferences, all but the highest value opportunities will be closed via an inside-sales model in the coming years.

When inside sales forces are properly utilised, they reduce the cost of sales by 40 to 90 per cent relative to field sales. Meanwhile, revenues are maintained, if not grown.[294] To put dollar amounts on those percentages, a single outside sales call costs between USD215 and USD400; an inside sales call costs USD25 to USD75.[295]

Inside salespeople can review buyer information on the company CRM, conduct meetings over the phone, Skype or web-conferencing while emailing additional information in videos or PDFs, and can easily automate follow-up activities. Continued advancements in CRM and sales engagement platforms are making the role of inside sales so much more effective and scalable and, in many cases, giving buyers the efficient service they want:

- Account executives will establish themselves as industry/market specialists, continuing to build relationships with leads by publishing and sharing thought leadership content.
- Account executives will create conversion pathways and manage the buyer transition from consideration to purchase, including:
  - *presenting product demos* via web conference or in-person meetings, with downloadable resources provided after the demo
  - *providing additional information* to continue establishing themselves as trusted advisers, including market forecasts, case studies from similar buyers, white papers and more
  - *delivering ROI forecasts* based on a buyer's unique needs, goals and business demographics
  - *following up after interactions* and opening further opportunities to discuss the business's needs

- *developing customisations as required to meet the buyer's needs,* including liaising with the product development team to clarify buyer requirements and confirm customisation options
- *handing the new buyer over to customer success,* and ensuring a smooth transition by outlining what they can expect next.

Note that there is some overlap between functions 2 and 3 when it comes to establishing salespeople as industry experts and building relationships with prospects. The key difference is their focus: function 2 focuses on engaging, qualification and nurturing, while function 3 focuses on further qualifying and creating conversion pathways.

Function 4: customer success

As we discussed in part 1, the traditional sales model was one where salespeople were encouraged to always be closing. This approach, which prioritises short-term revenue over long-term buyer success, is incompatible with the new world in which we find ourselves: one where buyers have more information, options and power than ever before, and where vendor business models rely on ongoing, subscription-based revenue rather than big, upfront sales.

In this world, Deep-Selling organisations need to focus on lifetime buyer value.

This is where customer success comes in.

Every successful organisation on the planet should begin with the overarching objective of creating an ongoing and delightful experience for each buyer — that is, one that generates the greatest lifetime value and most repeat purchases. Moreover, vendors need to create such an amazing ongoing buying experience that buyers become advocates who will refer them to other potential buyers.

Customer success is the function at a company responsible for managing the ongoing relationship between a vendor and its buyers. The goal of customer success is simply to create the most valuable outcomes throughout the buyer lifecycle in order to make the buyer as successful as possible which, in turn, improves lifetime buyer value. Customer success is enabled by:

- *customer success managers* (CSMs): this strategic role focuses on helping buyers achieve the best results with their new products or services. Each new buyer should have a dedicated CSM for a minimum onboarding period, if not ongoing. Their responsibilities include:
  - onboarding buyers, including demonstrating product features, taking buyers through their unique customisations and end-user training
  - helping buyers get optimal value from the product, including strategy calls about needs, priorities and objectives, as well as sharing useful content about how similar businesses are using the product, as well as information about different product features
  - monitoring product utilisation, usually in conjunction with an analytics function, to determine which features are/are not being used and why, and whether there are any missed opportunities
  - identifying opportunities for cross-sell/up-sell by being aware of the buyer's needs and how they will best be met
  - reporting on success in conjunction with the analytics team, so buyers can see how the product has improved their business results
  - turning buyers into advocates by soliciting case studies, testimonials and referrals for the core sales team

  - identifying opportunities to reduce buyer spend. This creates enormous goodwill, which in turn positively impacts retention, loyalty, advocacy and lifetime buyer value.

- *customer support:* this covers the general help desk/support function, where a buyer can quickly get the help they need to address any issues when their CSM might not be available. This is not a replacement for the CSM role, but an additional benefit. This covers:

  - answering product questions
  - troubleshooting problems
  - directing problems to the appropriate business unit for solving
  - keeping buyers informed of progress on issues
  - communicating with CSMs so the entire support team is in the loop.

The sales enablement layer

The *2022 State of Sales Enablement Report* found that 80 per cent of organisations surveyed had had a sales enablement process in place for more than two years, and those organisations experienced a 7 per cent increase in sales win rates over organisations that had had sales enablement processes in place for less than two years.[296]

The same report found that organisations with an established sales enablement function were 57 per cent more likely to experience high buyer engagement, and 92 per cent of respondents believed that having a dedicated sales enablement team improved sales performance.[297]

With the four core functions in place (demand generation, lead nurturing and qualification, core sales and customer success), your organisation is addressing all the key stages of the modern buyer journey.

To further improve results, the next step is establishing a standalone sales enablement function:

> *A strategic, collaborative discipline designed to increase sales results and productivity by providing integrated content, training, and coaching services for salespeople and frontline sales managers along the entire buyer journey, powered by technology.*[298]

In other words, sales enablement is the process of providing a vendor organisation with information, content and tools that help salespeople sell more effectively. However, it isn't simply about the sales team: it's about empowering the sales team to give buyers what they want, so all sales enablement changes should be considered with the buyer in mind.

Sales enablement is key to vendor organisations that are planning to scale, as it provides the entire sales force with the knowledge, tools and resources they need to succeed.

To establish a sales enablement program, consider the following topics.

Who will own sales enablement?

We recommend making sales enablement a shared marketing and sales function for two reasons.

First, the two areas must collaborate on creating resources for the program. Sales development representatives, account executives and customer success managers all have direct contact with your buyers and understand their needs, while marketing has the skill sets required to make great content with that knowledge (these skills include copywriting, graphic design, videography and more).

Second, sharing this knowledge helps ensure a consistent approach is taken across the wider organisation when it comes to understanding your buyers and how products and value propositions are communicated outside the organisation. Having both areas involved also helps establish a broader culture of sales enablement across the organisation, rather than it just being a hub within sales itself.

Set clear objectives for the program

While the overall objective of sales enablement is to help salespeople sell more effectively, this is a mammoth task that can be attacked from several angles. In fact, the steps you are taking to become a Deep-Selling organisation would naturally sit in this function.

However, given that some of these actions may be pretty hefty (like investing in new technology or restructuring the team) it can be helpful to have some smaller initiatives running at the same time. This gives the team the opportunity to experience some quick wins, and helps demonstrate the value of the function to the wider organisation.

Here are some quick wins to consider:

- *Providing content to support the sales process,* including training materials for salespeople as well as information to share with prospects and buyers throughout the buyer journey
- *Analysing the best practices of top performers* and using these to define processes and inform training going forward
- *Training and development,* including sales best practices for the modern buyer journey and building specialised knowledge to deliver valuable insights.

A larger project, and part of increasing your Deep-Selling maturity, is establishing a sales technology stack to facilitate lead management, nurturing and customer success.

Most vendors have room for improvement in all areas. The key is defining priorities, rather than trying to tackle everything at once. These priorities should focus on three areas:

1. What are the most pressing problems currently facing the sales team?
2. What are the quick wins that can be implemented with little investment?
3. What are the *big* wins that will take more time and investment, but will make a big difference?

Simply start by solving the most pressing problems that are preventing salespeople from performing their roles as well as they could. Then, address any quick wins—that is, tools and techniques that can be implemented with little time or investment required. Once those two areas have been addressed, any remaining initiatives can be prioritised based on what will deliver the greatest return to the organisation.

Regardless of your chosen activities, note that the buyer experience should be the foundation of any sales enablement activities, as the goal is not only increasing sales success, but ensuring a better experience for your buyers.

Continuous improvement

Sales enablement isn't something an organisation can do once. It is an ongoing effort. As the B2B landscape is in a constant state of flux, so are sales best practices and buyer expectations. Vendors need to stay on top of this by constantly monitoring their progress and investing in ongoing training and development.

With this in mind, we recommend establishing a quarterly review of sales enablement efforts, including:

- the level of uptake of sales enablement tools and initiatives across the sales team

- reasons for the level of uptake: what are team members engaging with, and what aren't they engaging with? Why is this the case?
- How is this impacting sales enablement results?
- What are the priorities to further improve results in the next quarter?

At the end of the day, sales enablement is supposed to make your salespeople more effective in how they sell, and there should be measurable business outcomes to justify the ROI. When done well, though, this should be easily provable, with CSO Insights finding that 'having a sales enablement function leads to two-digit improvements for quota attainment and win rates for forecast deals compared to those organisations without enablement'.[299]

Assessing your team's skill composition

How can you ensure your organisation has the right composition of team skills? For instance, how can you ensure you have some great presenters? How about some good social sellers? What about people who are good at writing proposals? Do you have others who can create video content?

The simplest approach is creating a skills matrix like the one in figure 8.5 listing the essential skills required across the core functions of the buyer journey and charting which team members have which skills. By doing so, you can get a bird's-eye view of the skills mix within any team and identify areas that are over-resourced as well as areas that require additional development or people.

Name	Skills and experience	Product knowledge	Prospecting	Networking	Building rapport	Creating buyer consensus	Active listening	Social selling	Content creation	Communication	Lead qualification	Objection handling	Presentation skills	Closing techniques	Onboarding	Customer support	Up-sell and cross-sell	Time management	Management	Coaching

White	No experience or knowledge
Red	Little experience or knowledge
Yellow	Reasonable experience or knowledge
Green	Considerable experience or knowledge

Figure 8.5: skills matrix template

To create a skills matrix, start by defining the skills required to support buyers along the buyer journey. These might include:

- product knowledge
- prospecting
- networking
- building rapport
- creating buyer consensus
- active listening
- social selling
- content creation
- communication
- lead qualification
- objection handling
- presentation skills
- closing techniques
- onboarding
- customer support
- up-selling and cross-selling
- time management
- management
- coaching.

As you will have observed, we recommend building sales teams that mirror the buyer journey, covering the areas of demand generation, lead nurturing and qualification, core sales and customer success. In a vendor organisation that is large enough to support separate functions, it is worthwhile considering the unique skill sets required for each function, as these will vary. In this case, you will also need to collaborate with the leaders of the other teams involved in this journey, to ensure you have a complete view of the required skills.

Smaller organisations with cross-functional teams can consider how the relevant skills apply to the team in general.

Once you have identified the required skill sets, the next step is to assess existing team members for their ability in each skill. For easy reference, we recommend a four-tiered approach, with each level of capability being represented by a different colour:

- no capability (white)
- basic capability (red)
- intermediate capability (yellow)
- advanced capability (green).

Using the skills matrix, you can then plot out each team member and mark their level of skill. This will give you and lateral team leaders an at-a-glance view of skills that are well covered by the existing team (the green areas), skills with some coverage (the yellow areas), and skills that need development or resourcing (the red and white areas).

From this point, you can identify the best people for each of the functional buckets you've defined, based on their current skill sets. This could lead to some interesting conversations. Some team members might be excited for the opportunity to grow into a new role (consider a marketing professional who has great presentation and networking skills who would like to do a secondment in the core sales team). On the other hand, some team members might not have skills that are appropriate for their current position but might not be interested in moving teams. In this case, there is an opportunity for training and development if they are interested in growing in the role. If not, it's worth looking at their results and considering whether they are a good fit for the organisation.

This also gives you and other leaders a clear picture of the gaps that need to be filled, either by further training and development or by hiring new resources.

An important note here is that you don't want to train your people to be all-rounders. This is an old-world, traditional sales approach and is ineffective in the new sales and buying landscape, and it fails to leverage the specialised skills in your team.

In our experience, most salespeople possess one or two core strengths that they build their career around. Some salespeople are great presenters. Some are great prospectors. Others are excellent at relationship building and networking. To use older language: some are hunters, and others are farmers. Some are great collaborators with high levels of emotional intelligence, while others are analytical types with high IQs. So why not leverage these strengths?

Instead of trying to create all-rounders, encourage your people to home in on those core strengths, and focus on ensuring you have skills coverage across the team, rather than in a single person.

Fighting the age of attrition

You have embarked on one of the most confronting stages of developing Deep-Selling maturity, as phases 2 and 3 require the most significant changes to the way your organisation has been running: changes that reach beyond the sales team.

While challenging, it is critical for vendor organisations to rethink their people strategy in the age of attrition. It is worth noting that 50.5 million people in the United States quit their jobs in 2022, beating the previous record of 47.8 million in 2021, and annual turnover among salespeople alone has hit 50 per cent.[300,301]

Aligning the team to the buyer journey means employees across sales, marketing, customer support and customer success are empowered to provide even more value. Providing more value means more satisfied, loyal and successful buyers, which will lead to increased spend and referrals. This creates a positive feedback loop, where salespeople are meeting their targets and are therefore more motivated to do better, which will help fight against the high levels of attrition within the profession.

This approach also creates the opportunity for new incentive structures to better reward all buyer-facing staff members (we will discuss this in detail in chapter 10).

CHAPTER 9
EVOLVE YOUR SALES EXECUTION MODEL

The traditional sales execution model starts when a prospect becomes aware of a vendor organisation or its products, usually by seeing an ad, some social content or the company website (see figure 9.1, overleaf). The prospect takes an action such as completing a quote request or downloading a free resource, and becomes a lead. The lead receives a call from a sales development representative (SDR), and this is where things start to go wrong.

The SDR typically relies on brute force, push selling in their rush to produce short-term revenue, and during this call there is no consideration for:

- the buyer experience, including modern buyer preferences for a personalised, data-driven, omnichannel journey

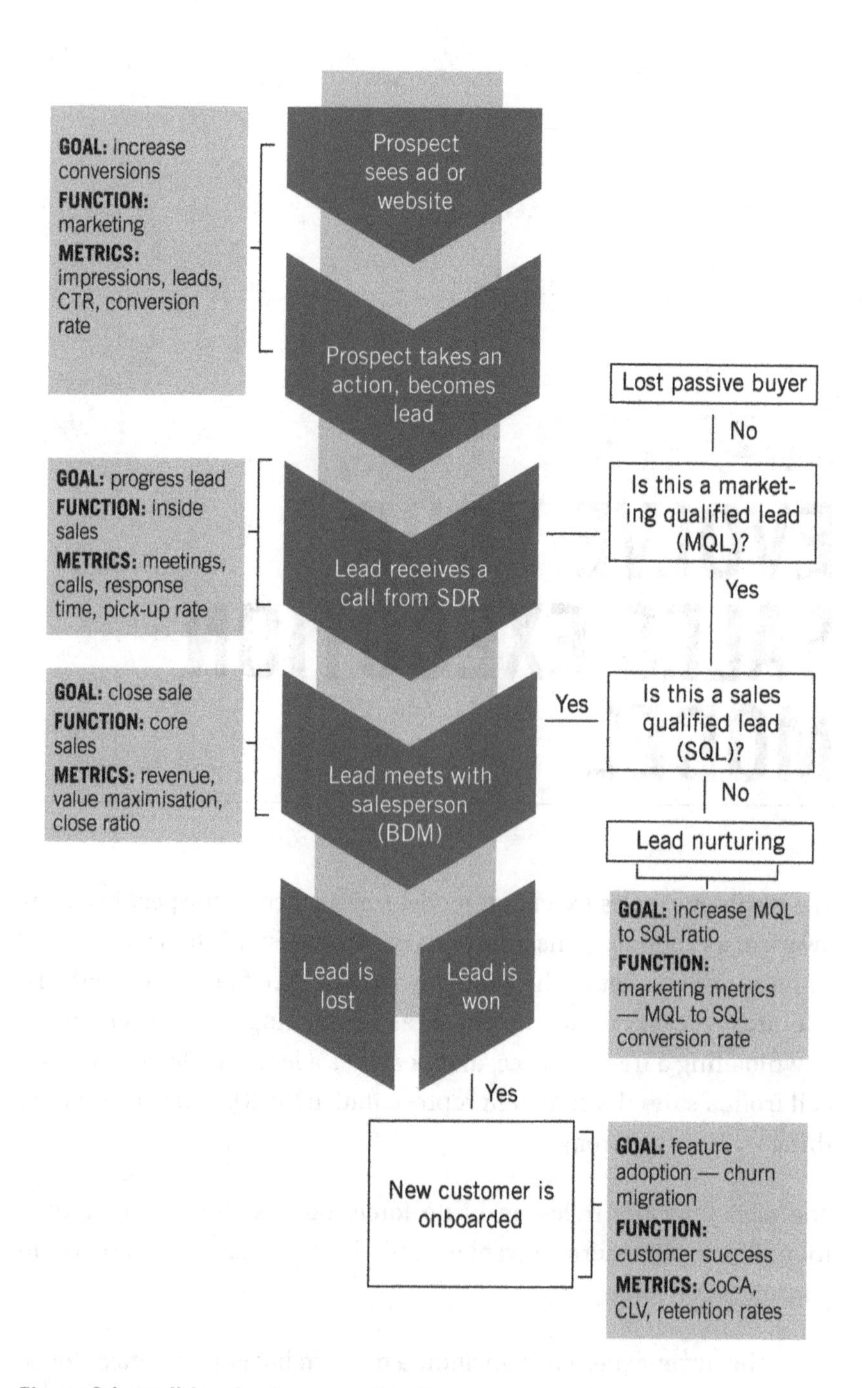

Figure 9.1: traditional sales execution flow

- the indecision that arises from fragmented buyer groups information overload and fear of messing up, or
- long-term buyer success and/or lifetime buyer value

... and the problems with this approach don't stop with sales!

As discussed in chapter 8, the sales execution process sits across multiple organisational functions, including marketing, inside sales, core sales, customer success and customer support. The challenge in most organisations is that each of these teams have different KPIs and ways of measuring success.

For marketing, the priority is increasing conversions and the ratio of marketing-qualified leads (MQLs) to sales-qualified leads (SQLs). For inside sales, the priority is pushing their leads to the next stage, while the focus of core sales is closing the deal. Customer success is then targeted with increasing feature adoption and reducing buyer churn.

With no overarching ownership of the buyer journey and no alignment on metrics, is it any wonder buyers are growing increasingly frustrated and sales teams are struggling to get results?

While chapter 8 started to address these issues by establishing cross-functional teams, this is just one piece of the puzzle. If those teams aren't also given new ways of working, they will continue doing what they've been doing, and will likely continue to work in existing silos.

The secret with all process design is to begin with the desired output in mind. What should the process produce? In this case, we want the sales approach to produce sales performance improvement: put simply, more buyers, more value provided to those buyers, greater lifetime buyer value and more sustainable long-term revenue growth. In other words, the sales process must understand, align with, adapt to and support the buyer journey.

Ultimately, the right sales model will not only help vendors win more deals; it will help them win bigger deals faster and more frequently.

Effective buyer outreach

Before considering the best way to engage with your ideal buyers, it is important to look at how your organisation is reaching them. Most organisations focus on outbound, inbound or a combination of the two.

Outbound is traditional sales outreach: pounding the pavement, making calls, reaching out over LinkedIn, playing the numbers game until you hit your quota. As we shared in part 1, this approach is ineffective. Modern B2B buyers are struggling with information overload from overly enthusiastic salespeople and are now blocking unsolicited and intrusive sales calls and emails.

Inbound, or inside sales, has been made possible over the past couple of decades due to advancements in technology. However, while it once stood as a beacon of hope for sales professionals — one that empowered them to use their time more effectively by sharing content in a one-to-many approach as well as cutting the time required for physical travel between meetings — it is becoming increasingly difficult to make a mark due to the explosion of content now available at every buyer's fingertips. Generative AI has only exacerbated the problem, with content creation now being easier than ever, and buyers struggling to keep up.

But if outbound is dead, and inbound is withering on the vine, where does that leave vendor organisations?

Leverage nearbound for Deep-Selling success

Nearbound is being described as a new way of sourcing business opportunities. However, nearbound is in effect a new term for an old concept known more broadly as 'partner ecosystems' or 'channel partners' — that is, partners that a vendor organisation uses to reach its target buyers.

Early iterations of some nearbound concepts can be traced back to post-war Japan. *Keiretsu* is a Japanese term that originated during the post-World War II period. Its development was influenced by the need to rebuild and strengthen the Japanese economy. The concept evolved from the earlier *zaibatsu* system, which were large, family-controlled vertical monopolies that dominated pre-war Japan.[302]

The Allied occupation forces, led by the United States, aimed to dismantle the *zaibatsu* to decentralise economic power and promote democracy, leading to the companies being dissolved and their assets being redistributed. However, many former *zaibatsu* companies restructured themselves into smaller, interconnected groups, and the modern *keiretsu* system began to take shape as companies formed horizontal and vertical alliances to regain economic strength and stability. These alliances included cross-shareholding, shared directorships and close business cooperation.

Nearbound, as the modern-day evolution of *keiretsu,* refers to leveraging relationships with partners who are in close proximity to your target buyers to generate leads and drive sales. Unlike traditional outbound or inbound strategies, nearbound focuses on leveraging the established trust and credibility of any party that is known to your target buyers, leading to faster and more successful sales conversions.

Key benefits of nearbound partner sales include:

- *increased reach:* nearbound models help vendor organisations extend their reach into markets that they can't address with a direct sales model
- *trust and credibility:* if the partner is already well known by a target market, the vendor doesn't need to establish their brand presence. The credibility of the existing brand will bolster the unknown one

- *collaborative marketing and sales:* nearbound strategies often involve joint marketing efforts, co-branded materials, and shared resources to attract and convert leads
- *localised knowledge:* partners typically have a deeper understanding of local markets, buyer needs and cultural nuances, which can help tailor sales approaches more effectively
- *cost efficiency:* utilising nearbound strategies can drive the same revenue as five or six salespeople at a fraction of the cost. It can also be easier and cheaper to bring on new partners than to make a new hire, with a much shorter onboarding period
- *scalability:* building a network of partners can help scale your sales efforts more rapidly and efficiently than trying to grow an internal sales team
- *test and learn:* partners can help vendors experiment with new buyer bases, products, packages, promotions and marketing campaigns in a low-stakes environment.

Adopting this approach can significantly drive growth, as leveraging the strengths, resources and networks of multiple organisations effectively extends your reach. This can also enhance organisational stability, resource sharing and market competitiveness. By fostering long-term, trust-based relationships, sharing resources and knowledge, and creating financial interdependencies, organisations can build a strong, resilient network that benefits all members.

As Mark Zuckerberg once said, 'Nothing influences like a recommendation from a trusted friend'.[303]

Notwithstanding the obvious benefits, some organisations pay scant regard to partner ecosystems, preferring to go it alone. These risk-averse doubters often see partners as interfering with their own direct sales execution efforts. Others view partners as potential competition, but this is short-sighted and happens only when the partner ecosystem is not being managed effectively.

This is understandable, given that the model comes with risks such as:

- *loss of control:* the moment a vendor starts working with a partner, they no longer have direct control over the sales process and can't take the reins if a partner is managing a deal poorly. It can also be hard to manage partners when making changes to sales strategy, messaging or products
- *sales execution:* vendor organisations sometimes complain that multi-product channel partners don't position their product well enough or often enough. Some partners might also carry hundreds of vendor products. How do you ensure that your product is 'front of mind'?
- *lower profits:* partners will take a cut from all revenue they generate, eating into vendor profit margins
- *brand risk:* if the partner has a poor reputation, it could damage your brand
- *potential competition:* it's important to carefully manage the parameters around which sales the partner makes, and which ones your own sales force make. If this isn't clear, it can lead to the sales forces competing for the same opportunities
- *slow feedback:* because market feedback will come via the partner, it will be slower to come back to you and may not always be accurate (note that this risk can be mitigated with new technologies)
- *cost of sale:* vendors that fail to adequately train and maintain their partner relationships often end up running the sales pursuit and carrying the cost of the sale because the partner simply identifies the leads and then brings the vendor in to run the sale. Revenue share in these cases can then be inequitable.

Despite the inherent challenges, considering channel coordination, partner policies, communication approaches, integrated systems and incentives upfront can help navigate the complexities and unlock the full potential of combining direct and indirect sales channels.

By implementing a nearbound strategy, you can effectively create pull through a channel partner model, driving demand for your products and ensuring that both your company and your partners benefit from increased sales and market reach.

Technologies to drive nearbound models

We are now witnessing the emergence of a range of tech players who are focused on enhancing and optimising channel partnerships by providing a collaborative, data-sharing ecosystem.

Crossbeam is one example of a platform designed to help organisations manage their partnerships more effectively by enabling secure data integration, collaboration and shared insights. Simply, users can search for partners on Crossbeam's existing partner network (which had over 19000 companies at the time of writing) and can securely share their CRM data with the platform, at which point Crossbeam will identify overlapping accounts. Partners can then benefit from Deeper buyer insights based on the pooled data. Vendors can use this data to generate more pipeline, or act on buying signals in real time.[304]

Platforms such as Crossbeam can help partners better align goals and strategies, leading to coordinated sales and marketing efforts. They can generate more revenue opportunities by proactively identifying overlapping accounts, and improve efficiency by qualifying leads more accurately, allowing teams to focus on the most high-value activities, and automating processes relating to account mapping and data sharing. They can also strengthen the relationship between partners, with transparent data sharing and collaboration ensuring that both parties see the mutual benefits of the partnership.

Most importantly, Crossbeam and similar tools give vendor organisations the ability to make data-driven decisions, with deeper buyer insights based on shared data and performance metrics to track the success of partnerships and strategies.

Crossbeam is just one of many platforms that are now addressing various elements of nearbound:

- *PartnerStack* provides a platform for managing and scaling partner programs, including features for tracking leads, payments and performance analytics.
- *Allbound* offers a partner relationship management (PRM) platform that helps companies build and manage their channel partner programs, including features for partner onboarding, enablement and collaboration.
- *Impartner* is a comprehensive PRM platform that helps companies manage all aspects of their partner ecosystem, including partner recruitment, enablement and analytics.
- *WorkSpan* is a collaborative platform specifically designed for managing joint go-to-market initiatives between companies, including features for partner planning, execution and performance tracking.
- *Channeltivity* offers a PRM solution focused on helping companies build and manage channel partner programs, including features for lead distribution, deal registration and partner portal management.
- *LogicBay* provides a PRM designed to help manufacturers and distributors manage their partner networks, including features for partner training, certification and performance tracking.

And we can't forget LinkedIn Sales Navigator, which we shared in chapter 7 as a tool to help develop deeper buyer understanding.

When it comes to nearbound strategies, LinkedIn Sales Navigator helps sellers discover hidden allies—that is, influential individuals within an organisation who may not have obvious titles or roles, but who can significantly impact decision making.[305] Sales Navigator helps salespeople identify these individuals through some incredibly powerful advanced search filters and insights.

The ability to uncover any hidden allies and determine the *best path in* provides salespeople with a strategic advantage, enabling them to connect with key influencers, build trust quickly and navigate the sales process more effectively.

The sales model continuum

After effectively reaching your buyer, the next factor to consider is the best way to engage with them, or the most appropriate sales model.

There is a continuum of sales approaches available to any vendor organisation, based on where the perceived value of the transaction takes place.

The old-world, vendor-push era focused on value in exchange, where the value of a product or service is exchanged at the time of purchase. By contrast, the new-world, buyer-led era focuses on *value in use*, where the true value is received by the buyer when they are *using* the product or service, not at the point of purchase.

Clayton Christensen's 'Jobs to be Done' framework argues that your buyer doesn't buy a drill; they buy a hole. Old-world businesses are focused on selling drills, while new-world ones focus on selling holes.[306]

Consider Michelin, the second-largest tyre manufacturer in the world.[307] Michelin understand that their buyers aren't interested in tyres but care more about the kilometres that the tyres facilitate. With this deep understanding of their buyers' needs, Michelin have been innovating their business model for more than two decades to ensure their buyers are receiving the most value.

This process started when they expanded their offering in 2000 with Michelin Fleet Solutions (MFS), with the idea being that since their tyres were priced at a premium, they could create a value-added service for large vehicle fleet operators. Instead of making their buyers bear a large, upfront cost for their tyres (as well as the replacement cost), MFS shared the risk by charging a monthly fee.[308] Unfortunately, MFS didn't perform to expectations, with low profitability, but the company still believed there was value in a servitised model.

In 2013, they leveraged IoT technologies to create EFFIFUEL, an ecosystem that used sensors inside vehicles to collect data such as tyre pressure, fuel consumption, speed, temperature and location, which Michelin's experts could then analyse to provide recommendations for improving fuel economy. Once again recognising that their buyers care about kilometres, Michelin focused on how those kilometres could be travelled as efficiently and economically as possible and unlocked significant savings for their buyers as a result—namely,

> *a reduction in fuel consumption of 2.5 litres per 100 kilometres represents annual savings of EUR3200 for long-haul transport travelling over 120 000 km (at least 2.1 per cent reduction in total cost of ownership and 8 tonnes in CO^2 emissions).*[309]

This approach means that Michelin needs to focus more on the quality and performance that their tyres deliver in practice, and less on the initial upfront price of their tyres. In other words, they are prioritising value in use over value in exchange.

When vendor organisations focus on value in exchange, revenue is tied to the sale, usually requiring a large, upfront purchase. Their only option for growing over time is finding new buyers to make more purchases, or releasing new products.

When organisations focus on value in use, revenue grows because buyers receive value from the products they invest in and are therefore more likely to go deeper with those same products by adding users, increasing features and renewing subscriptions. When these organisations introduce new products, existing buyers are more likely to use those new products due to the value they have already experienced.

Prioritising value in use naturally ties into buyer success and long-term revenue. But it starts with the vendor organisation, and individual salespeople, understanding that the sale isn't about making a transaction — it's about selling the value that the buyer will receive in future. The buyer then purchases that future value, which makes it easier for the organisation to manage that post-purchase experience as well.

So how can you determine the appropriate sales execution model for your buyers and your product?

The core sales models sit on a continuum like the one illustrated in figure 9.2, ranging from transactional selling through to value-based selling, and the value provided to the buyer increases as a vendor moves up the curve.

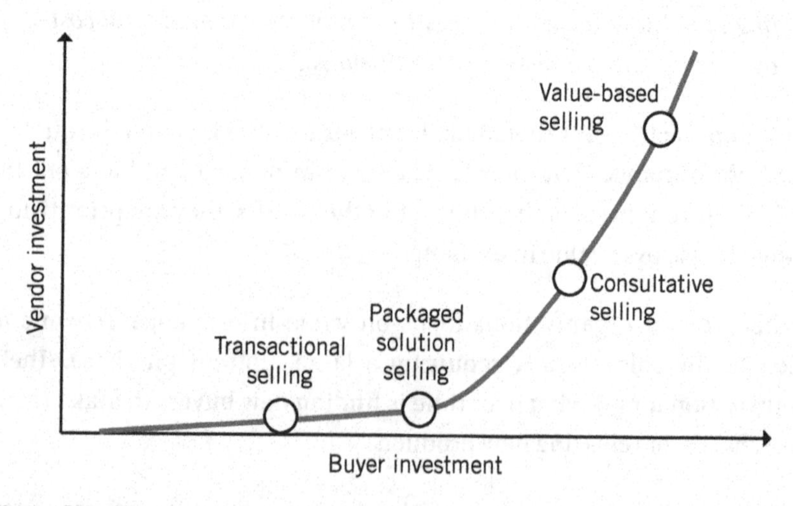

Figure 9.2: the sales model continuum

Let's take a closer look at each of the four selling models.

1 Transactional selling

The transactional selling model involves products where there is a low investment from both the buyer and the vendor. These products are typically out-of-the-box ones with no customisation required, meaning the buyer doesn't need any direct interaction with the vendor to make a purchasing decision. In many cases, they will process an order online. At this end of the spectrum, each sale is seen as a separate transaction and the buyer rarely has any interest in developing an ongoing relationship with the vendor.

Interestingly, while transactional selling is not what we would consider to be a true Deep-Selling model, vendor organisations with this model can still leverage new technologies to develop a more buyer-centric (or Deeper) approach. If we return to the tech-stack audit from chapter 6, organisations with a Shallow level of tech-stack maturity simply won't have the tools to deliver transactional sales in the way their buyers expect, and they are limited to basic tools such as static web content and transactions being processed via phone and email with manual invoicing.

As organisations increase their tech-stack maturity, their ability to deliver to buyer expectations increases exponentially, with Emerging organisations offering e-commerce stores, Exploring organisations offering omnichannel buyer lifecycle management and chatbots, and Deep organisations owning their own digital marketplaces and having AI-driven functionality. In short, the right tech stack can empower even a vendor with a transactional selling approach to deliver a delightful buyer experience.

These organisations are the ones that are downsizing their traditional sales forces. The reason for this is simple: in transactional sales, buyers are price conscious and keen to see ROI. They also don't differentiate between the vendors providing these products, as the products are highly commoditised. Consequently, there is little value in the added expense of a traditional sales force on either side of the value equation:

for the buyer, a traditional sales force will only make the end product more expensive, and for the vendor, this cost will eat into profit margins.

The transactional approach is in alignment with the way modern buyers want to buy, which is why many of the world's leading tech companies are taking this approach.

Consider Atlassian, an Australian company that develops popular project-management and chat apps such as Jira and HipChat. Atlassian doesn't run on sales quotas and end-of-quarter discounts. In fact, the company doesn't even have a sales team!

Instead, what Atlassian focuses on is developing great products, offering free trials and allowing their products to spread by word of mouth, social content marketing and network effects, whereby a good or service becomes more valuable when more people use it.

Free trials are not new. They are the good-old puppy-dog close. Give someone a puppy to play with, and they won't want to give it back. The difference here is that these savvy technology companies are now finally aligning to the fact that the balance of power has shifted to knowledgeable and demanding buyers. So, why not give those buyers what they want?

The bottom line is that it's working: Atlassian's total revenue was more than USD3.5 billion in the 2023 financial year, without a single sales employee, serving more than 250 000 buyers.[310] According to previous research, Atlassian's sales and marketing costs account for a measly 19 per cent of their budget. Talk about a high-margin model!

Other tech companies, such as Dropbox and Slack, are taking a hybrid approach to sales by relying on grass-roots pitches to land initial users, then setting up sales calls once those users grow to a critical mass. And tech behemoths such as Tesla and Apple are following suit by reducing the focus on expensive salespeople to help drive uptake and market penetration.

2 Packaged solution selling

As the name suggests, the packaged solution selling model involves selling a packaged solution to a buyer. Because the solution doesn't change, the sales model is fairly simple. If a salesperson is involved, they will usually be following a script or following a guided selling model.

Guided selling is one example that clearly demonstrates the influence technology is having on the role salespeople play in the buyer-led era. Guided selling simplifies and automates both the gathering and the interpretation of all the knowledge required to analyse a buyer's needs, determine the solution and make a recommendation to fulfil those needs.

A common example is the retail store where each salesperson is holding a tablet. A buyer approaches the salesperson and they run through a sequence of steps on the program, allowing them to ask the buyer the right questions to ascertain their needs, answer any questions and make an appropriate product recommendation.

In this scenario, the salesperson is simply the facilitator. As long as they follow the steps, they don't need unique skills or specialist knowledge to make a sale. The guided selling program can filter the information to determine what's most relevant to the buyer.

In a purely digital format, the same result can be achieved with chatbots. While the newest generation of chatbots are leveraging generative AI, this technology isn't even necessary to get reliable results when selling packaged solutions. Because these sales conversations often rely on scripts and there are a limited set of features available, a chatbot can be programmed with the same questions a salesperson would ask the prospect and can produce a solution based on a simple decision tree. If the bot is confronted with anything out of the box, it's only then that the sale is referred to a live agent.

A typical characteristic of packaged solution selling is that when a buyer chooses to purchase the same solution again, they won't need any input from a salesperson. In other words, once their solution is packaged, most buyers are comfortable reverting to a transactional model, assuming their requirements don't change.

3 Consultative selling

As we've discussed at length, with the increasing commoditisation of products, availability of information online and proliferation of self-serve options, many buyers no longer see the need to engage with vendor salespeople and actively avoid them.

However, there are exceptions, which relate to the complexity of the product or service being considered, the complexity of the buying environment or both. This is illustrated in figure 9.3.

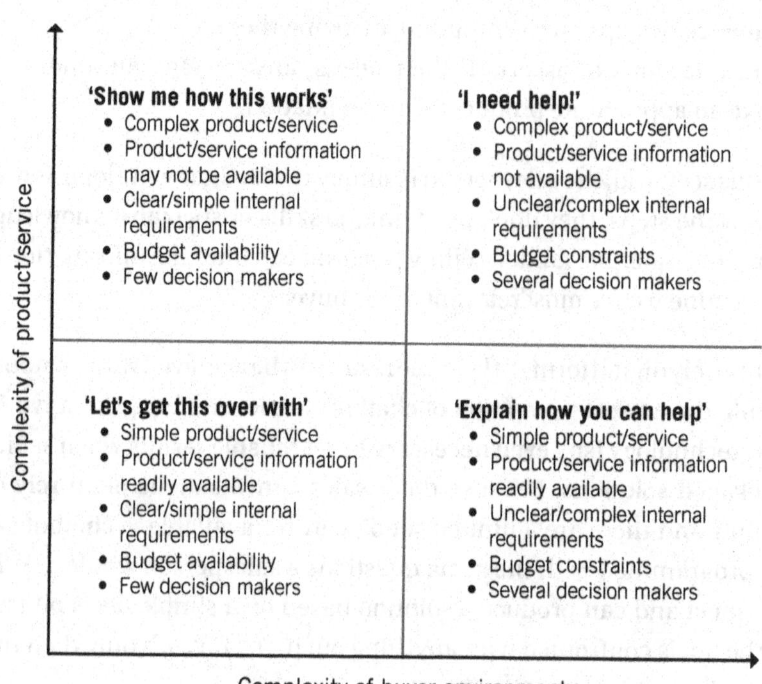

Complexity of product/service
'Show me how this works'
• Complex product/service
• Product/service information may not be available
• Clear/simple internal requirements
• Budget availability
• Few decision makers
'I need help!'
• Complex product/service
• Product/service information not available
• Unclear/complex internal requirements
• Budget constraints
• Several decision makers
'Let's get this over with'
• Simple product/service
• Product/service information readily available
• Clear/simple internal requirements
• Budget availability
• Few decision makers
'Explain how you can help'
• Simple product/service
• Product/service information readily available
• Unclear/complex internal requirements
• Budget constraints
• Several decision makers
Complexity of buyer environment

Figure 9.3: the four buyer quadrants

When both the product and the buying environment are simple, by the time a buyer contacts a vendor, they are often ready to place an order. For this reason, they will want to complete the transaction as easily as possible.

When the product is simple but the buying environment is complex due to budget constraints or multiple decision makers, the buyer will need to address these environmental barriers before making a purchase. On the other hand, when the reverse is true (the buying environment is simple and the product is complex), the buyer will need to spend more time learning about the product itself before making a decision.

Finally, when both the buying environment and the product are complex, the buyer is unlikely to make a purchase decision on their own and will need input from a vendor salesperson to do so.

In the final three scenarios, the buyer will require specialist salespeople who have a thorough understanding of the buyer's industry and company dynamics as well as strong product knowledge. Only this knowledge will allow them to act in the consultative role.

The consultative selling approach involves the salesperson gaining a strong understanding of a buyer's problems and needs and recommending the best solution to fix them. Because the solution is often tailored to the buyer's needs, a great deal of consultation will be involved throughout the sales process to determine the buyer's requirements, hence the name of the model.

4 Value-based selling

The growth of consultative selling and value-based selling is the reason why we firmly believe this is the best time to be in sales — not *despite* the challenges we discussed in part 1, but *because* of them.

In the past, sales was a vocation that was difficult to be proud of, and a career that was not respected. The role of the salesperson was one that was associated with self-serving behaviour and snake-oil salesmen, a role for unqualified peddlers, smooth-talkers and charismatic quota-crushers.

It used to be all about churning through the numbers: aggressive sales tactics, interrupting buyers, pushing and pitching your product.

All that has changed.

Consultative selling is first and foremost about *solving*, not selling. This involves developing a deep understanding of your buyer, as discussed in chapter 7. It requires vendor organisations to meet buyers where they now reside (online), and to provide seamless, omnichannel experiences. It requires vendor organisations and sales teams to attract buyers instead of chasing them.

In this new world, salespeople must genuinely analyse buyer problems, demonstrating credibility and building trust as industry experts with Deep subject-matter knowledge. Salespeople must forensically dissect the data to go beyond surface-level solutions.

Value-based selling, then, takes this a step further, moving beyond simply solving problems to *creating value*.

Any elite sales professional understands that the average buyer doesn't always know what their problem is, which is why problem solving has given way to value creation. This puts salespeople in the position of collaborating with the buyer to help them figure out what isn't working and suggest solutions the buyer may have never considered.

This goes beyond creating value for the buyer alone, as in many cases you are helping them create value for *their* buyers. Consider a B2B vendor organisation working with a B2C buyer: how can updating your buyer's systems or enhancing their products offer more value to *their* end users?

This puts sales professionals in the position of being trusted advisers.

Taking this approach with a genuine buyer-first mindset means salespeople will never need to 'sell' again. The sale is just something that happens when salespeople are immersed in helping buyers create value.

This is the very definition of 'going Deep'.

Value-based selling is the most specialised selling model, and usually requires both the buyer and the vendor to make a significant investment to develop the solution as they work together as strategic partners. Should the deal close, the relationship that forms following a value-based selling approach will usually have high levels of commitment and trust, with buyers remaining loyal for years (assuming the vendor delivers the promised value, of course).

How to choose the right sales model

When considering these selling models from the buyer's perspective, the value to the buyer goes up as vendors move along the sales model continuum. In a transactional relationship, the buyer might not even deeply consider the long-term value of their purchases. However, as they engage in more consultative and value-based interactions with vendors, the value created 'in use' becomes more important.

The best sales model for any vendor organisation will be informed by several factors. However, the most important ones are the requirements of your buyers and the product or service being sold.

For more complex products, or for vendors who build innovative, custom solutions, a value-based or consultative approach might be appropriate (particularly in the high-tech space where there could be up to 23 stakeholders involved in any buying decision).[311]

In cases where there is a suite of packaged products available, an inside salesforce following a guided or scripted approach will be able to meet most buyers' needs, though it would also be worth considering developing a self-service model, since this is how modern buyers prefer to buy.

For simple, low-cost products that are seen as commodities in today's marketplace (many subscription-based software programs are the perfect example of this), a transactional selling model might be best suited. It allows modern buyers to buy the way they want and reduces unnecessary costs from a vendor perspective.

The key takeaway here is that, while we are building Deep-Selling excellence in your organisation, consultative and value-based execution models are not always necessary to achieve this.

Deep-Selling excellence leverages people, technology, metrics and strategy to create value for buyers. This involves an organisation-level commitment to provide technology and resources to enable Deep-Selling execution, and a commitment from individual salespeople to adhere to Deep-Selling principles when interacting with buyers.

We have already introduced the benefits of taking this approach—namely, that it enables a firm to understand how its buyers want to be interacted with. It informs when and how salespeople should interact with buyers and it accepts that buyer preferences might change over time. In this way, Deep Selling fosters deeper relationships with your buyers and increases trust as you co-create value over the long term.

In the context of a sales execution model, Deep Selling requires the sales organisation to identify how each buyer wants to interact, and to adapt its sales model to suit each buyer's needs. For example, if a buyer wants a transactional relationship, a Deep-Selling organisation will facilitate it through a mix of self-service and simplified vendor touchpoints. If a buyer needs a more customised approach, the vendor organisation will use a more consultative or value-based model.

Therefore, Deep Selling goes beyond the definition of a sales model. Instead, Deep Selling is an overarching sales methodology that guides a sales organisation to understand how its buyers want to be sold to at any point in time and adapts the sales model to meet those needs, both in real time and based on solid buyer data.

If you identified that your buyers have Shallow needs, then the best way to go Deep is to offer them a simple way to transact with you, rather than working to develop a custom solution. Ultimately, Deep-Selling organisations put their buyers' wants and needs front and centre, and your sales execution model will be informed by that.

Deep sellers don't waste time accelerating old and outdated prospecting habits, and they don't waste time trying to warm up cold leads. Deep sellers focus their attention on likely leads, and then use data and insights to direct their actions towards those accounts. These actions have a much higher return.

Approaches to value-based selling

For organisations that are keen to transition to a value-based selling approach, the most common question is how to achieve this.

Like selling approaches in general, value-based selling also sits on a continuum, depending on the level of change appropriate for and/or desired by your organisation. These approaches have been adapted from the article *Three ways to sell value in B2B markets* by Joona Keränen, Harri Terho and Antti Saurama, which we highly recommend reading for a deeper look at value-based selling.[312]

The first approach to value-based selling is leading with benefits. This is an evolution from the traditional, product-centric approach to sales that focuses on product features, and instead highlights buyer benefits with estimates around the expected value a buyer will receive when using the product. Pricing is based on expected value in use and the vendor is responsible for providing resources that will support the buyer in realising that value. The responsibility for value creation still sits with the buyer.

The next approach looks at buyer process optimisation. Instead of selling a product, this sales approach focuses on enabling improvements in processes within the buyer organisation, which will then lead to measurable benefits such as increased productivity and cost reduction. Vendors are able to charge premium pricing based on the expected value of these process improvements, and after the sale that value is co-created between the buyer and the vendor.

To achieve this value co-creation, the vendor will actively consult with the buyer. The buyer is then responsible for providing the business inputs the vendor requires to consult effectively, along with implementing process adaptations as recommended by the vendor. The vendor will need access to internal metrics from the buyer to ensure the buyer is realising the value that was promised.

The final approach is when the vendor commits to buyer performance outcomes. In the previous approaches, pricing was based on estimated value; in this model prices are based on realised value in use. This is the highest risk model for vendor organisations, as they are taking full responsibility for improved performance. Consequently, for this model to work it is reliant on buyers outsourcing some business processes to the vendor.

For buyers who are in need of a complex, customised solution, the approach of committing to results is the most buyer centric, as it aligns vendor revenue directly to buyer outcomes. However, it is the most challenging one to implement due to the changes required on both the vendor and the buyer sides of the equation.

The various value-based selling approaches are summarised in table 9.1.

Table 9.1: value-based selling approaches[313]

		Value-based selling		
	Product-centric selling	**Lead with benefits**	**Buyer process optimisation**	**Commitment to results**
Sales focus	Sell products that meet buyer-specified needs	Sell benefits instead of product features	Sell process improvements instead of product improvements	Sell realised performance outcomes instead of potential value
Value focus	Estimated value-in-use not explicitly expressed	Estimated value-in-use of the offering	Estimated value-in-use of the process improvements	Realised value-in-use in the buyer processes
Pricing logic	Cost/competition based	Premium pricing based on estimated value in use	Premium pricing based on estimated value in use	Premium pricing based on realised value in use
Seller role	Providing resources for buyer value creation	Providing optimised resources for buyer value creation	Facilitating buyer's value-creation processes	Taking responsibility and bearing the risk for buyer's value-creation processes
Buyer role	Fully responsible for value creation	Responsible for value creation	Co-create value with selling party	Co-create value with selling party

(continued)

Table 9.1: value-based selling approaches (*cont'd*)

	Product-centric selling	Value-based selling		
		Lead with benefits	Buyer process optimisation	Commitment to results
Buyer adaptations	None	Minimal product-usage adaptations	Process adaptations	Governance and business process adaptations
Suitable buying approach	Price-focused product buying	Total cost focus in buying	Long-term business value in buying	Long-term business value in buying
Requirements	Cost advantage	Product excellence and value communication	Process expertise and value facilitation	Performance optimisation and value realisation
Challenges	Commoditisation	Product imitation	Continuous improvement and contract renewal	Risk assessment and variable control

Choose the right value-based selling model

To determine the best model for your organisation, Keränen, Terho and Saurama recommend a four-step process.

1. *Work with your strengths.* Is your organisation's strength in building exceptional products, expertise in process optimisation or delivering buyer performance improvements? This will tell you whether you can deliver monetary value by focusing on improving your products, enhancing your buyer's processes or guaranteeing performance.
2. *Identify existing value creation opportunities.* What are the key profit drivers in your buyers' business models? These might include costs, revenues or tied-up capital, and opportunities for improvement in any of these areas can point you in the direction of the best value-based selling model for your business: benefits-based selling relies on cost savings, buyer process optimisation can lead to enhanced revenue generation, while committing to results can help release tied-up capital.
3. *Analyse the required internal adaptations.* Value-based selling can be an organisation-level exercise that requires the commitment of multiple departments. It is important to analyse the magnitude of change and identify potential sources of internal resistance.
   - Benefits-based selling is largely a mindset shift, as salespeople will still use product expertise, but need to shift their focus from product features to quantifiable benefits. Buyer-process optimisation, on the other hand, requires your sales force to develop Deep consulting capabilities in order to co-create value with buyers.
   - Committing to buyer results requires significant structural and governance changes, and these will extend beyond your sales team. For instance, to guarantee performance, a vendor needs to be able to manage buyer processes, which

could include assigning team members to the buyer's organisation or establishing joint buyer–vendor teams.

4 *Find buyers who are willing to buy value.* Not all buyers are willing to buy value, particularly when it comes to those with simple needs who are comfortable using out-of-the-box solutions. For these buyers, there is no point developing a new business model based on process improvement or guaranteed results — this isn't what they are looking for, and they will find a simpler (and cheaper) offering instead.

To determine if it makes sense for your organisation to look at the process-optimisation or guaranteed-results approach, start by targeting buyers who are capable of realising long-term, organisation-wide benefits that go above and beyond immediate cost savings, and then further segment to those with strong buying centres that are open to supporting these changes (unfortunately, it doesn't matter how much potential value is on the table for a buying organisation if their buying centre is too inflexible to accept a new approach).

Building your sales playbook

Now that we have looked at the different sales execution models, and you have assessed which one is most appropriate for your organisation and your buyers, how does this translate into a sales playbook?

We started this chapter with the objective of establishing a sales approach that would produce sales performance improvement: more buyers, more value provided to those buyers, greater lifetime buyer value and more sustainable long-term revenue growth. However, much of this discussion has been theoretical.

The goal of this exercise is to document your new sales model — one that focuses on attracting buyers, not chasing them — and condense it into a one-page playbook for repeatable wins. Your playbook will list the key stages of your go-to-market model, clarify who does what, and document what is achieved at each stage in the process.

Depending on your sales model, you might have a zero-touch, light-touch or heavy-touch playbook:

- The zero-touch playbook is one where there is no human involvement. The buyer journey is completely automated and the buyer is able to complete transactions independently. To facilitate this, products must be easily understood, easily consumed and easily supported — think of tech companies such as Atlassian, Mailchimp and Twilio. Vendor organisations that have self-serve journeys spend about 25 per cent of revenues on sales and marketing, versus 50 per cent for the average enterprise startups.[314]
- In a light-touch playbook, much of the manual work that was performed by the traditional field salesperson has been replaced by automated technologies. At the awareness stage of the buyer journey, digital marketing takes care of most lead generation and prospecting. At the consideration stage, buyers can sign up for a free trial of a new tool, and usage data from this trial becomes part of the sales evaluation process. It is only after the buyer is qualified (based on their trial usage data) that an inside salesperson will close the deal.

  Businesses with light-touch playbooks often offer packaged solutions, which means the role of the salesperson is largely to help the buyer decide which package is right for them. This accelerates the speed at which buyers can start experiencing value (as they don't need to wait for a custom solution), while also reducing the effort and cost to the vendor organisation. Examples of companies with this model include Slack, Cloudera and Splunk.[315]
- The heavy-touch playbook is the traditional, enterprise go-to-market model, where a person is required to lead most

steps in the process. Marketing generates leads, which are then qualified by a salesperson after multiple in-person meetings. This approach usually has more steps, more people involved, longer time frames and a higher acquisition cost than the light- or zero-touch approaches.

While we are now in the buyer-led era of automation and AI, and we know an increasing number of buyers don't want to interact with salespeople, a heavy-touch playbook isn't necessarily a bad thing. In fact, the consultative and value-based selling approaches tend to be heavy touch due to the level of consultation required to solve buyer problems and deliver value in use. The key consideration is that *your playbook should be reflective of the value being delivered*: no-one wants to have multiple in-person meetings or Zoom calls with a salesperson for a transaction they could complete themselves online. If that salesperson is acting as a trusted adviser, and providing genuine value, it is a different story.

Let's look at the steps for building your sales playbook.

1 Condense the buyer journey map into key touchpoints

Start with the buyer journey mapping exercise you completed in chapter 7. Then, with your sales execution model in mind, consider the following:

- How do your internal processes need to change to deliver the experience your buyers want and expect?
- If you are taking a consultative or value-based selling approach, how do these processes need to change to deliver more value to your buyers?
- How do these process changes align with the new buyer journey?

- What are the touchpoints for your buyers and your team, and where do they intersect?

These touchpoints are key. Both your buyers and your own team will undertake a range of activities concurrently. On the buyer side, they will be gathering requirements, researching solutions, requesting quotes and more. On the vendor side, your team will be running marketing campaigns, preparing documentation, customising solutions and more. To keep things simple, your playbook will just look at the moments when your buyer engages with your organisation.

This means while the ideal buyer experience you mapped out in chapter 7 is likely highly complex, with dozens of activities, responsible people and deliverables, your sales playbook will be much simpler. This transition is illustrated in figure 9.4 (overleaf).

Once you have a working process flow, sense-check this with the sales and marketing teams (and perhaps product as well, if your organisation offers free trials as part of your sales funnel). Note that, depending on your organisation's offering (and your buyers), you might have different flows for different products.

Like your sales execution models, these will be informed by the complexity of the product and the complexity of the buying environment. The simpler your offering and the simpler the buying environment, the lighter touch your playbook should be, whereas more complex products and environments will require a more consultative approach and a heavier touch playbook.

2 Add objectives, content and owners

Once you have outlined each of the sales flows for your organisation, the next task is to identify the objectives of each step, the key information that needs to be shared at each step and which team owns each step.

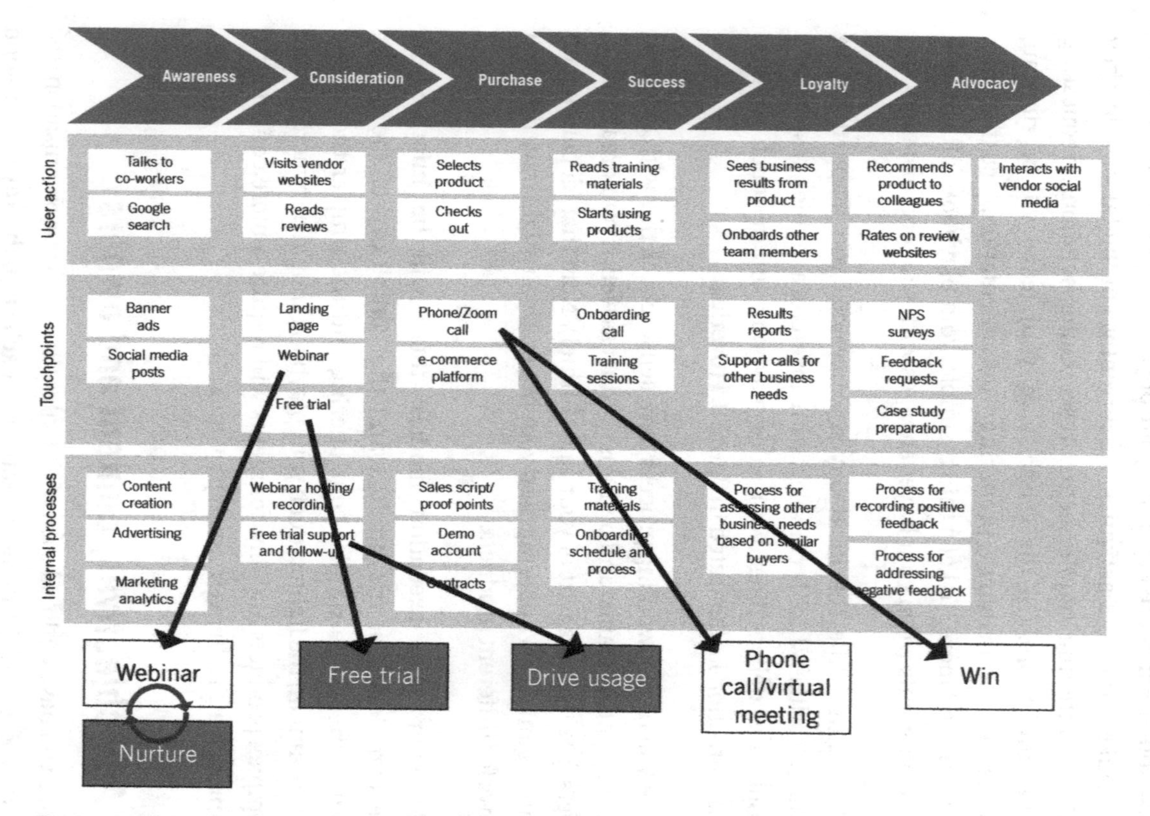

Figure 9.4: from buyer experience map to sales playbook

Understanding these factors is the foundation of a repeatable sales playbook, as each team involved is clear on its responsibilities. The challenge is getting this onto one page, as there is much more work happening in the background than what can be covered in a simple diagram (see figure 9.5, overleaf).

While it can be frustrating for professionals to condense their role in the process into a couple of bullet points, it is an essential part of the process. This act of distillation helps uncover what is most important to your organisation and your buyers, and it ensures every individual is prioritising those elements when performing their part of the process, which contributes to organisational alignment and a cohesive buyer experience.

This brevity also makes the sales playbook a valuable internal tool for onboarding, training and communicating to stakeholders who only need an overview of the process, rather than the detail that is required for those working in sales and marketing on a day-to-day basis.

To determine these elements, ask representatives from sales and marketing the following:

- *Objective:* What should be achieved in this step in the flow?
- *Content:* What information should be shared?
- *Owner:* Who owns this step in the process?

This is a discussion that is best had in a workshop setting, as it means everyone involved can see where there is misalignment and come to a consensus about the best way forward. If there are instances where team members are trying to squeeze too many things into a certain stage, ask them, 'If you could only achieve one of these things, what would it be?'

This question then paves the way for a robust discussion around what is really important and gives team members the opportunity to

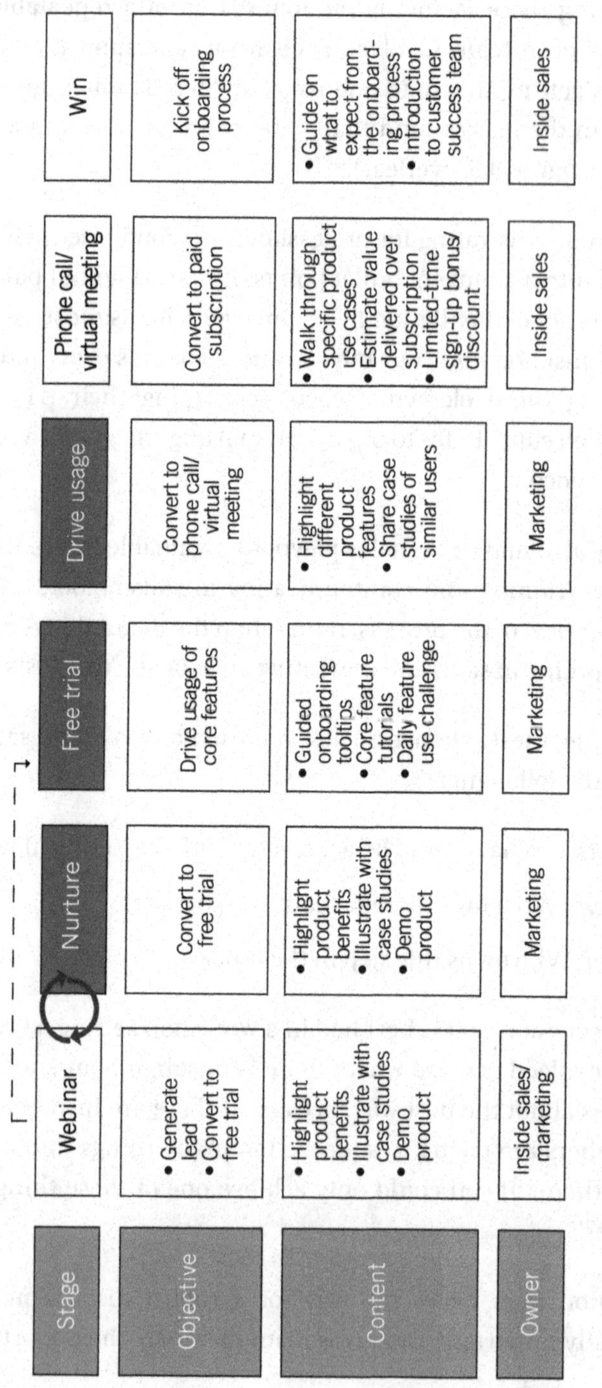

Figure 9.5: sales playbook with activities, objectives, content and owners

ask questions as well as defend their points of view. By the end of the discussion, everyone should have a clear understanding of both what is important and why it matters.

3 Identify the tools required to succeed

The final step is identifying which tools are required for each step in the playbook to achieve its objective and communicate the information required. These tools will encompass the various digital tools we listed in the tech-stack audit in chapter 6, and will also consist of collateral and resources required for buyers to get the information they need, and for salespeople to effectively communicate. These typically include presentations, downloadable PDFs, marketing and training videos, legal agreements, onboarding guides and more.

Consider the examples in table 9.2.

Table 9.2: sales playbook tools

Activity	Tools required for success
Building buyer awareness	• Website • Advertising • Active social media presence and content publishing • Gated content for lead generation • Email nurture sequences • Outreach templates for salespeople
Webinar	• Presentation • Webinar hosting software with email capture • Webinar reminder emails • Share recording link post webinar • Post-webinar nurture sequence

(continued)

Table 9.2: sales playbook tools (*cont'd*)

Activity	Tools required for success
Free trial	• Tutorial videos/articles • Email nurture sequence highlighting new features • Chatbots populated with answers to common questions
Demo	• Software setup with dummy account similar to prospect • ROI calculators
Client meetings	• Meeting schedulers • Presentation • Supporting documentation • Video conferencing and recording (if remote)
Close	• Online legal agreements/contracts • e-commerce functionality (for transactional selling and packaged solutions) • Onboarding resources and training videos

The list of tools required will depend on the playbook. Like the previous exercise, where the team was forced to focus on the main objective and content for each stage in the flow, this flow forces them to be decisive about which tools to invest in and which resources to develop. If a resource doesn't support a key stage of the playbook, then it is not a priority.

Once you have completed this exercise, you should have a one-page sales playbook that lists the key touchpoints in your sales process, the objectives and owners of each step and key content to be shared, and the tools required for each step to be completed successfully. See figure 9.6 for an example of a completed sales playbook.

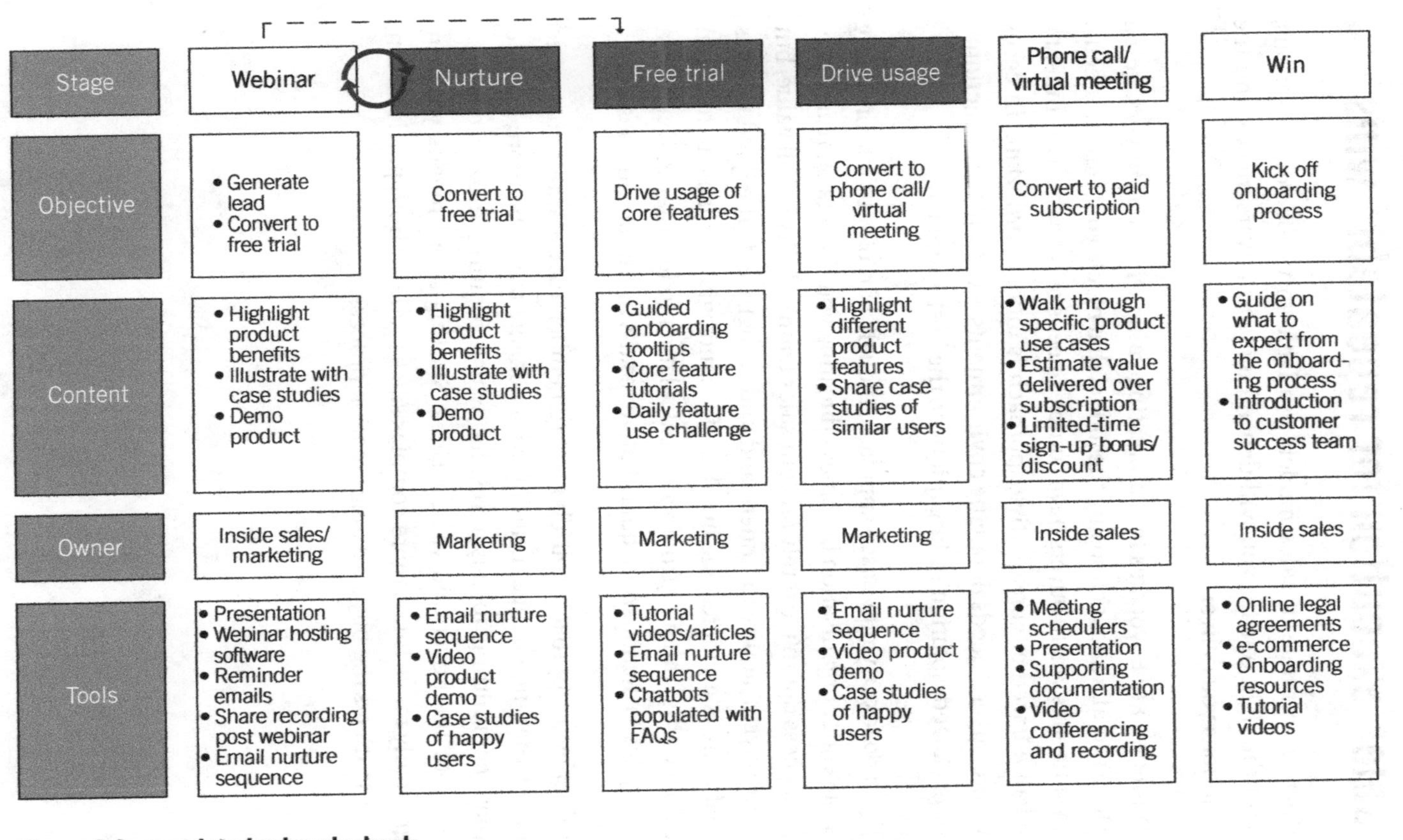

Figure 9.6: completed sales playbook

Sales execution for repeatable wins

There is a range of sales models available to vendor organisations, and the right one for you will depend on your buyers' needs and the solutions you deliver.

While we are advocates for co-creating value with your buyers, going Deep is really about choosing the model that meets your buyers' needs. In situations where buyers have complex needs or buying environments, a value-based or consultative approach is more appropriate. In cases where buyers' needs or buying environments are simple, transactional or packaged, solution selling might be the best approach.

If you *do* take a value-based approach, though, part of your responsibility as a vendor organisation becomes educating your buyers on true value, as success doesn't just rely on your sales team's ability to sell value, but your buyers' ability to understand and recognise it. The good news is that there is an increasing number of technologies available to help you achieve this, ranging from value calculators to leveraging Deep data analytics to demonstrate quantitative results in similar businesses.

Whichever approach you choose, remember that a small change is better than no change. Leading with benefits might be more feasible than committing to buyer results, which requires drastic changes on both the buyer and vendor sides. Starting small means you can gradually move into a more complex sales model as both parties learn how it affects the buyers' value creation process.

PHASE 3
EXPLORING TO DEEP

The final phase of this roadmap looks at embedding and routinising a Deep-Selling culture to move your organisation from Exploring to Deep on the Deep-Selling maturity model.

As a Deep-Selling organisation, you can expect to see the following results in each of the Deep-Selling elements:

- *People:*
  - Your people enthusiastically support a buyer-centric culture and are rewarded based on the ongoing success of your buyers.
  - Employees are well trained on processes and are committed and engaged to your organisation's sales execution model.
  - Regular benchmarking ensures performance issues are addressed as they occur, and the overall performance of buyer-facing teams continues to improve and deliver more value to your buyers.
- *Metrics:*
  - Your organisation has redefined success in the context of Deep Selling and buyer success, with new metrics that are implemented across the organisation.
  - Higher buyer success metrics correlate with improved traditional financial metrics.
  - All departments support a buyer-centric culture and are digitally mature.

- *Technology:*
  - The organisational tech stack supports and enables data-led sales activities.
  - The tech stack accurately measures buyer health and success and identifies opportunities to go deeper.
- *Strategy:*
  - Effective processes and measures have been established and drive buyer success and value outcomes.
  - A balanced scorecard has been developed to measure progress on an ongoing basis and to embed the organisational change.

This phase in the journey consists of two steps:

1. *Create a buyer-obsessed, high-performance culture.* In chapter 10, you will redefine what success means to your organisation, digging deep into measuring buyer heath. These metrics will be used as KPIs for the sales team, and compensation approaches will be revisited to drive Deep-Selling behaviours.
2. *Embed Deep Selling with a balanced scorecard.* Chapter 11 will bring all your previous work together into a balanced scorecard that will empower you and your leadership team to measure your organisation's progress and routinise the changes required to maintain Deep-Selling maturity.

Let's go deeper!

CHAPTER 10
CREATE A BUYER-OBSESSED, HIGH-PERFORMANCE CULTURE

In the 1980s, the focus in enterprise organisations was business process innovation. These businesses worked closely with consultancy firms to determine how processes could be optimised and made more effective.

Despite large investments of time, budget and human resources, within a decade, many of these organisations realised that the majority of those activities were ineffective. The reason is that there is only so much that can be achieved with process optimisation alone. Often, there are improvements, but these improvements are incremental, and these incremental gains rarely stick. The investment is not worth the return.

Culture eats strategy for breakfast

Real change happens on the cultural level.

We can see this in the countless surveys, case studies and research papers available that demonstrate the importance of culture in business.

PricewaterhouseCoopers found that organisations with a distinctive culture are 48 per cent more likely to have better business outcomes, and this is backed up by research from McKinsey, which found that companies with top-quartile cultures posted shareholder returns 60 per cent higher than median companies, and *200 per cent* higher than those in the bottom quartile.[316,317]

From a people perspective, 94 per cent of executives and 88 per cent of employees believe a distinct workplace culture is important to business success.[318] Culture also attracts top performers, with 35 per cent of workers in the United States saying they wouldn't take a job that was a perfect fit if the organisational culture clashed with their values, and 71 per cent citing workplace culture as a reason for looking for a new role.[319,320]

Gallup reported that the top 20 per cent of candidates choose organisations with a strong culture, and organisations that keep those employees report 41 per cent less absenteeism, 59 per cent less turnover, 17 per cent higher productivity and 21 per cent higher profitability.[321] This is supported by research from Columbia University, which found turnover in organisations with strong cultures is just 13.9 per cent, in contrast with companies with weak company cultures, where the turnover was 48.4 per cent.[322]

For all its importance, though, there is often confusion around what culture actually means. It remains an element that is understood on an instinctual level but is notoriously difficult to define.

According to *Forbes*, culture is 'the shared values, belief systems, attitudes, and the set of assumptions that people in a workplace share'.[323] Put more simply by Gallup, culture is 'how we do things around here'.[324]

We define culture as the behaviour that an organisation is willing to tolerate. In short, it doesn't matter what an organisation's professed vision, values or strategy say if the organisation tolerates, or even encourages, behaviour that runs contrary to the stated vision, values or strategy.

Consider the Wells Fargo cross-selling scandal, which was widely reported in the mid 2010s. Wells Fargo, a global financial services company with more than 70 million customers, had a range of internal publications advising employees on appropriate behaviour, including the *Wells Fargo Code of Ethics* and the *Wells Fargo Team Member Handbook*.[325] These threatened employees who engaged in 'the manipulation and/or misrepresentation of sales or referrals ... in an attempt to receive compensation or to meet sales goals' with immediate termination.[326] Yet, the extreme internal pressure to achieve sales quotas led to the opposite behaviour.

The sales culture was driven by 'morning huddles' to discuss sales goals with hourly check-ins by managers to see if bankers were on track. The daily target in 2008 was to sell eight products a day, which increased to 8.5 in 2010. After hours 'call nights' were scheduled for bankers who were having trouble meeting their goals. As one investigator wrote in 2004, 'Whether real or perceived, team members ... feel they cannot make sales goals without gaming the system ... The incentive to cheat is based on the fear of losing their jobs'.[327]

Yesenia Guitron, a personal banker hired at the St Helena branch in California in March 2008, was interviewed about her experience in *Vanity Fair*. She shared that she raised concerns more than 100 times, including making calls to the Wells Fargo EthicsLine. Thirty-seven times she provided records to support her complaints.[328]

In theory, Guitron's behaviour aligned with Wells Fargo's code of ethics. How did the organisation respond to her actions? First, they made it harder to meet her sales goals. Then, in January 2010, she was fired.[329]

Culture is the behaviour an organisation tolerates. This means it is impossible to put a strategy in place without addressing organisational culture: if an organisation's leaders say that the organisation is buyer centric, yet they continue to accept and reward product-centric behaviours, then the organisation isn't truly buyer centric.

Buyer centricity is at the core of Deep-Selling success. So, what does a buyer-centric culture look like?

In buyer-centric organisations, every decision begins with the buyer and opportunities to create more value for them. Employees are buyer advocates. And there is an organisation-wide belief that buyer loyalty is the key to long-term financial success.[330]

This culture shift requires leadership commitment to buyer centricity, a long-term vision and commitment to the change, success measures and incentives that encourage the change; and structures, processes and systems to support the change.

While achieving culture change is difficult, it is possible. In phase 2 of the Deep-Selling roadmap, we discussed several of the requirements for a buyer-centric culture shift, including developing Deep buyer insights and reviewing the structures, processes and systems required to support the change.

The next step is changing behaviour. To address this, we will redefine success for a buyer-centric organisation, including how to measure success and how to incentivise buyer-centric behaviours.

Redefining success for buyer centricity

High-performance cultures are built around clear objectives. Leaders cannot expect any team, let alone a sales team, to achieve high performance if there is not total clarity around what they are expected to achieve.

In fact, one of the biggest reasons that sales-team engagement is as low as 19 per cent is because employees are often being measured in a way that is not congruent with an organisation's stated vision, values and strategy.[331]

As we discussed in part I, the business model of most vendor organisations has shifted from being product focused to selling their offerings as a service. This shift means there is an urgent need for sales models to evolve as well.

The old-world, product-centric model focused on push selling with a short-term focus. Salespeople would pitch as many prospects as possible with the expectation that one of those prospects would convert in a large, upfront purchase. At that point, the salesperson would move on to the next pitch, with little concern for the long-term success of the previous buyer.

Measuring the success of this approach looks at the number of sales, the size of those sales, and revenue resulting from those sales, which feeds into the higher level objectives of the C-suite and board: increasing share price or growing market share.

For sales teams, this is all condensed into quotas.

Yet, as we've already discussed, the majority of B2B salespeople are failing to meet their quota.

Often, this isn't because the salespeople are traditionally poor performers. Instead, it's a combination of two factors.

The first is the changing B2B context, whereby skills that used to be effective no longer are. With evolving buyer tastes and preferences, the rise in e-commerce and self-service technologies, the increased commoditisation of most product categories and buyers' easy access to information, we have entered a new era. These changes have culminated in a shift in power, where the pendulum has swung from vendors to buyers and is not coming back. This is the Age of the Buyer, which means a shift in sales methods, benchmarks, compensation and performance management is required.

In this age, sales teams must shift from the typical, vendor-push model of chasing buyers to a buyer-pull model, where the focus is attracting buyers. Buyers will no longer accept having their busy days interrupted by a stranger with a blanket sales message. Buyers are sick of being pushed, harassed, cajoled and manipulated by salespeople who have a vested interest in hitting their quotas.

Instead, buyers across every industry now want to pull their preferred vendors through the buying journey. This precipitates the timely dissemination and synthesis of information, allowing decision making to occur when the buyer is ready, and not when it's the end of the month or quarter for the vendor salesperson.

In the Age of the Buyer, vendor business models are service oriented, not product oriented. The salesperson provides much more value upfront and when their prospect converts, it is to a subscription-based model instead of making a large, upfront purchase. Many software-as-a-service (SaaS) organisations that we have worked with don't break even until buyers have been with them for 18 months, when considering the investment involved in onboarding, software implementation and helping their buyers achieve maximum productivity. This model means that salespeople and vendor businesses *must* have a vested interest in the ongoing success of their buyers.

The second problem with quotas goes beyond the changing sales and buying landscape, and is simply that, in many vendor organisations, management sets quotas that are unattainable.

Management often sets quotas knowing they are impossible to achieve, based on an arbitrary growth uplift from the previous year's quota as opposed to actual results. In some cases, quotas are used to facilitate a low-friction exit process for a salesperson who is out of favour. This approach not only neglects to acknowledge changes in the B2B landscape, but it damages the vendor organisation and the careers of its salespeople.

On one hand, we find ourselves with vendor organisations that are saying they want to be more buyer centric, and on the other, they are still using the same outdated metrics to measure success.

If we come back to the idea that culture is the behaviour an organisation is willing to accept, then this approach will continue to encourage old behaviours—push selling, playing the numbers game, the focus on closing—and not long-term buyer success.

Making revenue quotas the key objective for sales performance makes it almost impossible to cultivate a buyer-obsessed, high-performance culture. Individual quotas run counter to being buyer centric, as they invariably promote a dog-eat-dog culture, poor performance and high attrition. While unrealistic quotas are often intended to reduce the overall cost burden of the business, what this approach fails to consider is the damage that a constant revolving door of salespeople is doing to its culture, buyers and brand reputation.

As you will have gathered from the previous steps on sales structure and execution, Deep Selling requires a totally different type of salesperson and a re-evaluation of what constitutes success for vendors and their sales teams. In this new context, success is no longer about vendors maximising revenue attainment. Instead, sales leaders and vendor organisations need to shift their focus to one of delivering value to their buyers.

Buyer experience and success therefore become the foundation of all modern sales objectives, benchmarks, compensation structures and performance management guidelines, and are the fuel that will drive a high-performance culture.

Identifying new success metrics

It bears repeating: sales quotas in isolation make it impossible to create a high-performance sales culture in the buyer-led era. Quotas put salespeople at odds with the buyer's needs and result in them having a vested interest in closing the sale — whether or not that sale is in the buyer's best interest. This is contrary to the Deep-Selling approach and, consequently, makes it harder for salespeople to achieve high performance.

In fact, this outdated practice results in many of today's salespeople not focusing on the quota itself, but instead on surviving by not being in the bottom 10 to 15 per cent of performers. In other words, core performers benchmark themselves against the lowest performers, rather than aspiring to be elite performers.

This is the opposite of a high-performance culture.

So, if quotas are ineffective, how do we measure success?

There are two components to buyer-centric measurement and management:

1. How to reward teams for acquiring new buyers
2. How to reward teams for developing and retaining existing buyers.

1 Buyer acquisition metrics

To achieve high performance, acquisition metrics need to go beyond the number of sales being made in each reporting period. Instead, vendor organisations also need to consider:

- How well do prospects align with the organisation's ideal buyer persona (as defined in chapter 7)?
- How efficiently are prospects moving through the pipeline, and how well are they converting?
- How well defined are the buyer's needs?
- How well has the salesperson addressed and communicated value in use rather than value in exchange?

These questions help sales leaders and senior management understand not only how many sales are being made, but also process efficiency and the quality of the deals coming in. This information can then be used to identify weak points in the process, which can be addressed to improve results. In other words, understanding these elements is far more meaningful than solely focusing on headline sales numbers.

To answer the above questions, consider the buyer acquisition metrics summarised in table 10.1.

Table 10.1: buyer acquisition metrics

	Measure	Data collection	Objective/ subjective	Data source
Enquiries/ Inbound lead volume	Number of leads coming in through all channels	Monthly/ Quarterly	Objective	CRM/ Marketing analytics
Cost per lead	What is the average cost of obtaining a lead?	Ongoing	Objective	CRM/ Marketing analytics

(continued)

Table 10.1: buyer acquisition metrics (*cont'd*)

	Measure	Data collection	Objective/ subjective	Data source
Conversion rate	Visitor to MQL MQL to SQL SQL to sale	Ongoing	Objective	CRM/ Marketing analytics/ Sales team
Average sales cycle time	Visitor to MQL MQL to SQL SQL to buyer Overall sales cycle time	Ongoing	Objective	CRM/ Marketing analytics/ Sales team
Average order value	What is the average order value across all products/ subscriptions?	Monthly/ Quarterly	Objective	Sales team/ Financial dashboards
Cost of acquisition	What is the total average cost to acquire a buyer?	Ongoing	Objective	Sales team/ Financial dashboards

2 Buyer health metrics

As discussed in part I, retention is key to any organisation's success, with 15 per cent of an organisation's most loyal buyers accounting for anywhere between 55 per cent and 70 per cent of total revenue.[332] This is why it is crucial for vendor organisations to move beyond acquisition metrics as a measure for success, and instead focus on long-term buyer health.

Buyer health is a simple and effective measure that can be used to supplement traditional sales measures such as revenue, profit, growth and market share. Buyer health comprises data points that track the quality of the buyer relationship, the level of product usage and the value realised by the buyer.

Tracking buyer health has a range of benefits that go beyond what can be achieved with traditional financial and acquisition metrics alone. First, a key component of Deep Selling is using data to drive Deep buyer understanding and inform effective selling behaviours. Buyer health measures leverage the flow of available information to provide vendor organisations with a real-time assessment of buyer relationships. Second, buyer health measures combine traditional relationship marketing metrics such as buyer satisfaction with other data sources, which can then be combined to provide a single, comprehensive metric that can be used as a leading indicator of probable buyer churn. Third, a clear measure of buyer health gives both executives and Customer Success Managers the ability to gauge the pulse of their buyer relationships. Customer success managers can then use this information to better manage these relationships.[333]

To start measuring buyer health, consider the measures in table 10.2 (overleaf, adapted from the paper 'Customer Success Management, Customer Health, and Retention in B2B Industries' by Bryan Hochstein, Clay M Voorhees, Alexander B Pratt, Deva Rangarajan, Duane M Nagel and Vijay Mehrotra).[334]

As an organisation, you can decide which metrics are the most relevant for gauging buyer relationship quality, product usage and buyer value realisation, and you can combine these to create an overarching buyer health measure.

Transform new metrics into KPIs

Buyer acquisition metrics and buyer health metrics all provide valuable information to sales leaders and executives at vendor organisations. To bring the discussion back to culture, though, how can these be used to drive buyer-centric behaviour?

Simply, these metrics should be used as the key performance indicators (KPIs) on which salespeople are measured and, importantly, rewarded.

Table 10.2: buyer health metrics

	Measure	Data collection	Objective/ Subjective	Data source
Buyer relationship quality				
Buyer satisfaction	How satisfied are you with vendor XYZ?	Quarterly/Annually/ Following support calls	Subjective	Buyer/User
Trust	I trust vendor XYZ	Quarterly/Annually	Subjective	Buyer/User
Commitment	I am willing to go the extra mile to remain a buyer of vendor XYZ	Quarterly/Annually	Subjective	Buyer/User
Net Promoter Score	How likely is it that you would recommend vendor XYZ to a friend or colleague?	Quarterly/Annually	Subjective	Buyer/User
Referenceability	I am willing to serve as a referee for vendor XYZ during the sales process	Quarterly/Annually	Objective	Buyer/User
Number of referrals from existing buyers	Total number of referrals obtained	Quarterly/Annually	Objective	CRM
Number of repeat buyers	Total number of buyers who have renewed their subscription/ purchased again	Per renewal period	Objective	CRM

Percentage of repeat buyers	What percentage of buyers have renewed their subscription/ purchased again?	Ongoing	Objective	CRM
Average buyer tenure	How long do buyers remain with vendor XYZ?	Ongoing	Objective	CRM
Lifetime buyer value	What is the average value of a buyer over their lifetime?	Ongoing	Objective	CRM
Buyer product usage				
Product usage	Clickstream data New feature adoption Equipment usage (number of users) Equipment usage (frequency)	Ongoing	Objective	Passive collection from product
Product support	Number of support tickets Number of bug reports Number of feature requests	Ongoing	Objective	CRM
New product requests	New feature request of existing product New adoption of vendor's existing products		Objective	CRM Sales/Support teams

(continued)

Table 10.2: buyer health metrics (*cont'd*)

	Measure	Data collection	Objective/ Subjective	Data source
Buyer value realisation				
Achievement of goals	Setting and assessing buyer's usage goals	Ongoing/Monthly/ Annually	Objective	Customer success Manager and buyer
Reduced costs	Buyer realisation of savings from product use	Ongoing/Monthly/ Annually	Objective	Customer success Manager and buyer
Increased productivity	Tracking changes in end-user productivity	Ongoing/Monthly/ Annually	Objective	Comparison of product use data to identify efficiency trends
Product-related value	Tracking tasks unique to the product that bring value to the buyer	Ongoing	Objective	Product usage data/ Buyer feedback/ Sales and support teams
Downstream customer value	Tracking value realisation of the buyer's customers	Ongoing	Objective	Buyer's CRM, Buyer surveys/Sales and support teams

From the previous discussion, we have four key result areas:

1 Buyer acquisition
2 Buyer relationship quality
3 Product feature usage
4 Buyer value realisation.

The measures in each of these areas then become KPIs for team members and could be recorded as shown in table 10.3.

Table 10.3: KPIs template

Key result area	Key Performance Indicator (KPI)	Weight of KPI	Target	Actual	Score
Buyer acquisition	Enquiries/Inbound lead volume				
	Cost per lead				
	Conversion rate: Visitor to MQL				
	Conversion rate: MQL to SQL				
	Conversion rate: SQL to sale				
	Average sales cycle time				
	Average order value				
	Cost of acquisition				
Buyer relationship quality	Buyer satisfaction				
	Buyer trust				
	Net promoter score				
	Referenceability				
	Number of referrals to other buyers				
	Number of repeat buyers				
	Percentage of repeat buyers				
	Average buyer tenure				
	Lifetime buyer value				

(continued)

Table 10.3: KPIs template (*cont'd*)

Key result area	Key Performance Indicator (KPI)	Weight of KPI	Target	Actual	Score
Product feature usage	New activations				
	New feature adoption				
	Level of ongoing use				
	Number of support tickets				
	Number of bug reports				
	Number of feature requests				
	Adoption of new products				
Buyer value realisation	Achievement of buyer goals				
	Increased buyer productivity				
	Reduced buyer costs				
	Product-related value				
	Increased downstream customer value				
		100		Total	

Setting the benchmark for sales performance

You have now identified the metrics you will need to track in order to achieve Deep-Selling excellence. These should be a combination of buyer acquisition, buyer health and traditional financial metrics. In chapter 11, we will share how you can track all of these in a simple balanced scorecard.

Next, we are going to look at how to use those metrics to drive sales performance by following three steps.

1 Define success

Choosing the metrics you want to track is only the first piece of the performance puzzle. The next piece is setting targets for those metrics.

What numbers define success in your organisation? What is your target inbound lead volume, cost per lead and conversion rate? What is your target NPS, percentage of repeat versus new buyers and level of product usage? What results would you expect a successful buyer to experience from using your products?

Many organisations set arbitrary targets that are simply an increase on the previous year's targets, not recognising whether they are achievable, or even desirable. Instead, you want targets that will contribute to bottom-line financial metrics (higher revenue, profit and market share), but that are also achievable for your team in the current B2B context.

First, you want to get a clear picture of your organisation's current performance by reviewing the relevant data sources for each of the measures discussed earlier. These sources will encompass both internal systems and data from your buyers, including:

- CRM
- marketing analytics
- finance dashboards
- the payroll system
- the expense reporting system
- the HR system
- the sales management team
- customer success managers
- records of customer support interactions
- product usage data
- buyer feedback
- NPS surveys
- your buyer's CRM (for tracking downstream customer value).

Having a clear understanding of your starting point will tell you what's feasible in the next performance period. If your team is closing 40 deals a quarter with a 50 per cent retention rate, hitting 100 deals and an 80 per cent retention rate in the following quarter wouldn't be likely without significantly increasing the size of the team.

However, keep in mind that improving your current results is only one part of the puzzle. If your sales force is underperforming, it is entirely possible that just aiming for an improvement on existing numbers will mean they are still falling short. To put it in more concrete terms, if your team is getting 10 per cent of the results they should be getting, even doubling those results means they are still only achieving 20 per cent of what they should be.

What constitutes good performance, then?

Beyond understanding the team's current level of performance, you will want to understand industry benchmarks for your metrics in order to gain a competitive edge. Fortunately, in the information age we have access to more of this data than ever before. Just some sources for researching industry benchmarks include:

- Google search
- trade associations
- university publications
- market research
- research firms such as the Sales Benchmark Index.

For instance, Forrester Research found that typical B2B retention rates are between 76 per cent and 81 per cent, while HubSpot found that the average sales close rate was 29 per cent.[335,336] How does your organisation compare?

The final element to consider when setting targets is your organisation's financial metrics. How many sales need to be made to break even, and to turn a profit? How long does a buyer need to remain with your organisation to cover the cost of the sale? What is the acquisition cost of different buyer types, and how would the number change if you drove more sales in different areas? (For example, if your team focused on referrals and upselling to existing buyers, what numbers would they need to achieve to break even, given that the acquisition cost is much lower than when converting a new buyer?)

The discussion around what is required for your organisation to be in the black is one that will go beyond the sales team, but it is one worth having, because it could highlight underlying business model issues. For instance, if the only way for the organisation to break even is for the sales team to achieve targets that are several times the industry average (and several times what they are currently achieving), perhaps there is scope for the business model to change.

It is only by considering your team's current performance, industry benchmarks for sales performance and the break-even requirements of your organisation that you can set targets that will be achievable and that will drive results.

Note that, depending on how far your team is from where it needs to be, you might need a roadmap to transition to the new targets, where the targets increase slightly every month or every quarter until they are where they need to be.

2 Create a success profile

After defining the targets required for the team as a whole, you want to look at individual performance within the team.

To do this, use the KPI template in table 10.3 refined with the metrics you have decided to track with appropriate weighting for each KPI based on their position. You want to then score each member of the team based on their contribution to current results (the focus is current results for the moment because you want to establish a baseline for their performance — future KPI management will be measured against targets).

Once you have scored each member of the team, you can see how the points are distributed. In most cases, this will create a bell curve such as the one illustrated in figure 10.1, with the majority of salespeople achieving results somewhere in the middle, a minority of high performers to the right, and a minority of underperformers to the left.

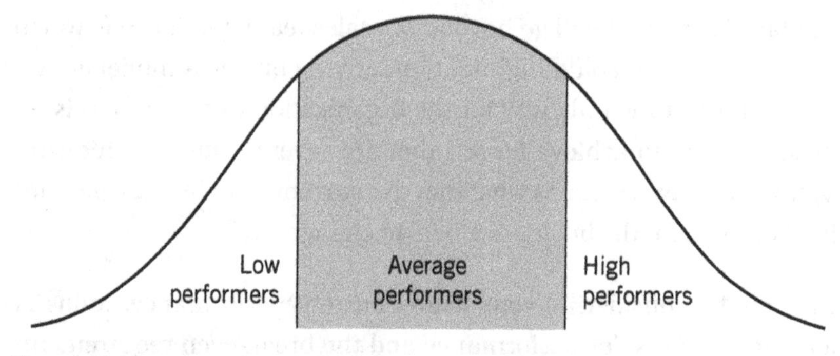

Figure 10.1: an example team benchmarking bell curve

Plotting data points like this allows vendor organisations to pinpoint the top performers in each area, and potentially identify a handful of elite performers whose results are strong across all metrics. By identifying these people, you can then identify trends shared by the most successful sales individuals, as well as any weaknesses shared by those who are underperforming.

This information can be used to create a success profile, which holistically captures the qualities of individual team members — their knowledge, experience, competencies and personal attributes — and defines what enables them to succeed in their roles.

Note that this success profile will draw heavily on the skills matrix you completed in figure 8.5, as having each member of the team focus on where their skills lie is a prerequisite to creating a high-performance culture.

3 Performance improvement

After identifying the knowledge, experience, competencies and personal attributes common in the top performers (as well as those common in underperformers), the next step is to develop a plan to improve performance across all sales functions. How do you bring the low performers up? Shift the middle performers to high performers? And how do you then push the high performers even higher?

In many vendor organisations, sales team performance is a grey area when it comes to assessments and benchmarking, with many teams limping along with substandard performance because the high performers overachieve on their quotas by enough to compensate for the underperformers. While the team may still hit its numbers, that doesn't mean the team is optimised.

The most effective teams nearly always find a way to maximise individual strengths while simultaneously limiting or covering individual weaknesses. To achieve this, start with the following questions:

- Which salespeople have upside in their performance?
- Which salespeople likely have downside in their performance?
- Which salespeople are big talent in a small territory?
- Which salespeople are small talent in a big territory?
- Who are the obvious low performers who require action?
- Who has high talent but needs a new role?
- Who has big potential but requires a bigger territory or role?
- Who is a high flight risk that you do not want to lose?
- Who is playing a strong cultural role?
- Who needs to play a stronger cultural role in the team?
- Who is having a negative cultural impact on the team?
- Who has headroom for growth/improvement, and who is at their limit?

It is only when you answer these questions that you can manage the range of performance in the team. This will involve:

- taking steps to improve the performance of the underperformers
- cutting those poor performers who don't improve after performance management
- identifying which average performers can be coached into high performance
- challenging the top performers by increasing their capacity.

The end goal is reducing the range and then moving the entire range up, or shifting the middle to the right (see figure 10.2).

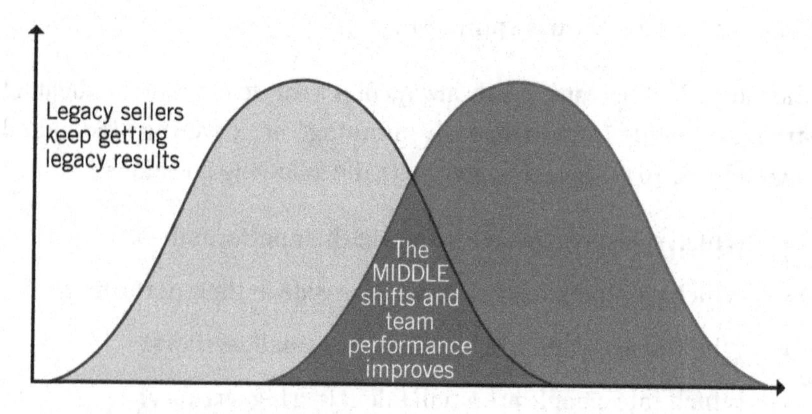

Figure 10.2: improving the bell curve

The final step in team benchmarking is to establish an approach for continuous improvement. Benchmarking is not a one-off exercise to analyse performance only to be put aside due to day-to-day pressures. Instead, team benchmarking should be a regular activity: one where data is drawn on a quarterly basis to monitor improvements and identify areas that could be further refined.

By continually benchmarking the sales team and identifying areas for improvement, vendor businesses can secure a competitive advantage and sales performance improvement.

Rewarding success with the right incentives

A 10-year study of more than 200 established management practices across 160 companies found that in 90 per cent of the companies that outperformed their peers, pay was tightly linked to performance. However, this was the case in only 15 per cent of underperformers.[337] This is the next piece of the culture puzzle.

You have redefined what success means to your organisation and how it will be measured. You have also evaluated the current team and have put a performance improvement plan in place. Now you will look at driving culture change by how success is rewarded. This means reviewing the traditional commission-based salary structure for salespeople.

While commissions are one of the most common incentive structures for salespeople, unfortunately they do not drive buyer-centric behaviour. Instead, commissions encourage salespeople to focus on vendor success over buyer success, with the emphasis being on closing the deal over providing long-term value. These models encourage a culture of quota-smashing lone wolves who treat the buyer as an adversary to be conquered, rather than a partner they can work with to co-create value.

This is the point when many executives in vendor organisations (particularly those with a traditional, field sales background) will object, saying that sales teams need to have commissions: how else will you motivate them?

In reality, commissions are not the be-all and end-all of sales-team motivation, and a growing number of organisations are seeing spectacular results with commission-free models.

Take Monday.com, a SaaS company that Graham interviewed for the SalesTribe podcast.[338] Monday.com pays no commission on short-term revenue attainment because their business model focuses on long-term revenue generated by software subscriptions. Additionally, they don't want their people driving bad sales — ones where the buyer is given something they don't need. Their focus is finding alignment between the company, the buyer and the salesperson's interest. To achieve this, they offer their salespeople equity in the company. This means salespeople think and act like owners and are interested in the long-term success of both their buyers and Monday.com.

How is this model working for them? Their sales group consists of more than 100 people, and in the past three years not one of them has chosen to leave. Whereas salespeople on commissions often stop once they hit their quota, Monday.com's team continue fighting for every opportunity even after hitting their monthly and quarterly targets because of their belief in what the company does.

This feeds into stellar financial performance, with Monday.com experiencing 94 per cent growth year-on-year with an IPO in June 2021 that valued the company at just under USD7 billion. Their share price opened at USD155 and had reached USD389 less than six months later, bringing the company's valuation to USD17 billion.

All without commissions.

Quotas, like commissions, are also an outdated, ineffective approach when it comes to motivating salespeople, not to mention that this approach is completely at odds with the modern vendor's objective of buyer success.

Let's return to Wells Fargo. In 2013, the *Los Angeles Times* revealed the extreme pressure put on bank managers and individual bankers to meet aggressive quotas. Employees were tasked with selling at least four financial products to 80 per cent of their customers, but top executives reportedly pushed employees to average eight products per household and branch managers were expected to commit to hitting 120 per cent of the daily quotas. Long-term quotas included a requirement that tellers generated at least 100 sales for financial services per quarter.

To meet these quotas, employees opened accounts that customers didn't need, opened duplicate accounts without customers' knowledge, ordered credit cards without customers' permission and forged signatures on paperwork. Some employees asked family members to open ghost accounts, and others enrolled unhoused people in financial products.[339]

Between 2011 and 2015, it was found that Wells Fargo employees had opened more than 1.5 million deposit accounts and 565 000 credit card accounts that may not have been authorised.[340]

Employees reportedly stayed late and worked weekends, and anyone falling short after two months was fired. According to one branch manager, 'If you do not make your goal, you are severely chastised and embarrassed in front of 60-plus managers in your area by the community banking president.'[341]

Beyond being unethical and illegal, this behaviour led to appalling customer experiences, with some customers being charged fees on accounts they didn't know they had, and even receiving calls from collection agencies to collect on these unpaid fees.[342]

This was a costly mistake for Wells Fargo as well, with the bank being fined USD185 million in September 2016 for creating unauthorised accounts between 2011 and 2016.[343] In April 2017, the company reported that credit card applications were down by 42 per cent and new cheque account openings were down 35 per cent year-on-year. Later that year, the bank set aside USD3.25 billion for future litigation expenses.[344]

While this is an extreme example, it clearly illustrates the issues with quotas and commissions. The fixation on hitting quotas encourages salespeople to focus on short-term revenue, which is at odds with finding buyers who will get value from a solution over the long term. This leads to lower lifetime buyer value and negatively impacts long-term overall revenue.

This approach is also very dangerous when buyers expect to be taken on a long-term journey. Treating sales as a win/lose game increases the chances of post purchase dissonance, where buyers feel like they have been misled by a salesperson who has over-promised and then under-delivered. If one side of a business transaction is the losing side, then it's only a matter of time before the 'winning' side loses those buyers.

Ultimately, vendor organisations cannot afford to continue taking this risk.

What is the solution, then? We will start by looking into what really motivates salespeople, which will then inform new approaches to compensation.

What really motivates salespeople?

While financial incentives can provide some motivation for salespeople, the truth is that financial incentives are only one part of the puzzle. In fact, many researchers have found that intrinsic rewards are more motivating than extrinsic ones.

Simply, extrinsic motivation relies on rewards that are external to the work or task being performed. These might include rewards such as commissions and bonuses, extra holiday leave, getting sent on a conference or a trip, receiving benefits such as a company car and phone, and even being recognised in front of the team.

Intrinsic motivation, on the other hand, is the satisfaction provided by performing the work itself. This could be the enjoyment a sales individual gets from crafting a great piece of online content, from helping a prospect identify their needs, from the challenge of finding the right solution for a prospect, from having coaching and training, and more.

While much of the discussion on culture and motivation over the past decade has focused on intrinsic motivation, various meta-analyses of scientific literature have revealed that both forms of incentive have value and both can be incorporated into effective incentive structures.[345]

What is more important to keep in mind is that different people are motivated by different things. Take a 2014 incentives study that investigated whether salespeople had universal reward preferences, broadly basing the preferences investigated on those in the Four Drives Theory of Motivation, which lists the four drives as: to acquire, to bond, to defend and to learn.

Most sales compensation programs focus on the drive to acquire new buyers with commissions rewarded at the time of sale. Interestingly, it was found that of the older, more experienced salespeople with longer tenure (read: traditional, field salespeople, consisting of the Baby Boomer and Gen X cohorts), there was an 85 per cent preference for monetary rewards with the drive to acquire.

A second group, which was focused on customer service (read: younger and from the Millennial cohort), had shorter tenures. There was an almost equal split between those who preferred to bond and belong (29 per cent) and those who preferred to acquire (33 per cent). While both groups had the same compensation, it was much less motivating for the second group.

As a sales leader, you can perform a similar assessment to discover the motivation preferences of your own sales force.

When it comes to how incentives lead to motivation, we can see this in the motivation model created by Professor Victor Vroom of Yale University, shown in figure 10.3 (overleaf).

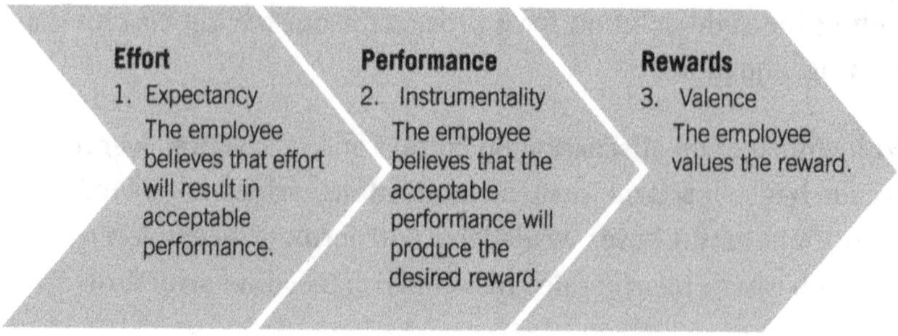

Effort
1. Expectancy
The employee believes that effort will result in acceptable performance.

Performance
2. Instrumentality
The employee believes that the acceptable performance will produce the desired reward.

Rewards
3. Valence
The employee values the reward.

Figure 10.3: Victor Vroom's motivational model

In brief, a person decides how much effort to expend based on the expectation that the effort will translate into acceptable performance. If the performance is acceptable, they must believe that it will turn into rewards. Finally, the person must value those rewards.

So, when it comes to effective sales compensation and incentives, the key factors to consider are:

- What constitutes good performance that should be rewarded? (As we've mentioned, this should focus on long-term buyer success, rather than immediate sales revenue.)
- How can vendor organisations communicate the relationship between performance and rewards?
- Which rewards do sales individuals most value?

Keeping these points in mind, we can argue that effectively motivating any sales force will involve a combination of intrinsic and long-term extrinsic rewards, rather than a fixation on commissions paid for short-term results.

By ensuring the role itself is rewarding (leading to intrinsic motivation) and remodelling any other rewards based on the long-term success of buyers (leading to extrinsic motivation), as well as ensuring that those rewards are valued by the individual salespeople, vendor businesses and sales leaders can help their teams hit the motivational sweet spot.

Sales compensation recommendations

From here, our recommendations are:

- *Base KPIs and performance metrics on buyer health.* Buyer success outcomes, retention rates, loyalty and that all-important buyer advocacy are what make vendor organisations sustainable, so it follows that we must shift the mindset, culture and KPIs to those that create genuine buyer alignment.
- *Don't abandon existing incentives (yet).* This might sound contrary to the previous point, but if your people already have the expectations of receiving commissions for certain behaviours, it will take a significant cultural shift to remove them. Extrinsic motivation can be powerful when combined with intrinsic motivation, so we recommend creating a plan to shift from the current performance structure to the ideal state. This gives salespeople time to adjust their thinking and see the benefits of the new model, and allows you to increase the desired incentives while reducing the existing incentives (that are encouraging the old vendor-push model) gradually.
- *Improve intrinsic motivations for the sales team.* If your sales team is entirely motivated by commissions, it's time to take a hard look at the intrinsic motivators offered by their roles. Extrinsic incentives cannot continue filling the gap between job satisfaction and performance, especially as Baby Boomers move into retirement and a greater proportion of the workplace is comprised of Millennials and Gen Z.
- *Look at your sales leaders.* If you work at an organisation where there is a layer of sales leaders in between you and the people on the ground, review how those leaders approach managing their teams. If you are the sole sales leader, it is time to reflect on your own role. If the sales incentive plan is the sole source of motivation among the sales team (a symptom of this is usually when the plan includes dozens of metrics and tries to reward

every element of the role), leaders might be overly relying on incentives rather than actively mentoring, motivating and coaching the team. A sales compensation plan will not make up for poor management.

- *Take a holistic approach.* Focusing on just intrinsic or just extrinsic rewards leaves salespeople unfulfilled and increases attrition. Extrinsic rewards might keep top performers motivated in the short term, but soon they will look for a more fulfilling role elsewhere. Meanwhile, if the focus is solely on intrinsic rewards, top performers will ultimately pursue better compensation elsewhere.
- *Consider a team-based approach.* When considering team structure in relation to the buyer journey, it's also important to consider the concept of compensation across the various buyer-facing functions, rather than just in core sales roles. How can KPIs and rewards be fairly split across the buyer journey? A simple starting point is to share incentives equitably across the team: every role plays a part in converting a prospect; therefore, every member should be rewarded.

How vendor organisations are redefining success and rewards

Sales quotas and commissions are completely at odds with buyer success. If you truly want to create a Deep-Selling organisation, this is impossible while continuing to use revenue attainment as a way to measure and reward sales performance. As we've discussed, revenue quotas and commission payments drive salespeople to be anything but buyer centric, and instead encourage salespeople to treat the buyer as an adversary to be conquered.

Instead, look to companies around the globe that are introducing innovative new models for measuring and rewarding success, which has a rolling impact on culture.

We have already shared the example of Monday.com, which has experienced 94 per cent growth year-on-year and grown its sales team to more than 100 people with no-one quitting in the past three years, all on a commission-free model.

Similarly, there are no commissions or quotas for salespeople at SaaS company Culture Amp and 'the results have been astounding'. Revenue has grown by 15 times, conversion rates and sales efficiency are higher than at similar companies, they win deals against team competitors who are commission driven, and the team is happy to work very hard for sustained periods.[346]

Behaviour drives culture, and the right incentives can drive the right behaviour, so it is time to throw out the old compensation models and find one that will drive the behaviour you (and your buyers) want.

CHAPTER 11
EMBED DEEP SELLING WITH A BALANCED SCORECARD

Financial metrics have defined business success throughout the history of enterprise, with the earliest evidence of accounting language coming from Mesopotamian civilisations between 8000 and 5000 BCE! Modern bookkeeping then emerged in the 1400s when businesses used ledgers to track income and expenses.[347]

However, financial metrics truly started being used as a sign of business health in the 1800s, when corporations began publishing balance sheets as a way of attracting investors.[348] This gave investors a simple way to assess a business's ability to turn a profit, and to gauge the likelihood that it would continue to make a profit in future and thereby deliver a return on their investment.

Even though executives, boards and investors have used financial metrics as the measure for success for centuries, relying on these numbers alone has several limitations.

The first is that these numbers aren't always reliable. As shared in the *Harvard Business Review* article 'Where Financial Reporting Still Falls Short', there are no universal standards for accounting measures, which means a profit in one measure could be a loss in another. Consider Twitter, which reported a loss of USD0.96 per share in 2014 using one measure, but a profit of USD0.34 using another. Similarly, in 2015 Amazon reported earnings of USD0.37 per share using one measure, and USD4.14 per share using another.[349]

What gets measured gets managed

The lack of universal standards makes it difficult to compare the performance of like organisations, and this is further compounded with unofficial earnings measures. EBITDA (earnings before interest, taxes, depreciation and amortisation) is commonly used in the high-tech space, yet isn't an official accounting measure.

Similarly, 'fair value accounting' is a method for assessing an organisation's assets by calculating the difference between the price originally paid for an asset and the amount that asset could be sold for today, yet because there is no standard for 'fair value', the measure is subjective and, once again, makes it difficult to benchmark similar organisations against each other.

And these are all problems that occur when organisations are acting in good faith: numbers can all be manipulated to appear more attractive to boards and investors, and the discrepancies inherent in accounting measures make this even easier to achieve.

Beyond the reliability of financial metrics, there is a secondary concern when it comes to their impact on innovation and continuous improvement. When financial metrics become the top priority of an organisation, leaders and frontline staff will often focus on achieving those metrics in any way they can, regardless of whether this is in their buyers' best interests.

Returning to the discussion on culture, a single-minded focus on financial metrics results in salespeople pushing buyers into large purchases without considering their long-term success. At an organisational level, a revenue metric could lead to a focus on finding the simplest way to boost revenue, which is likely to be just increasing prices instead of innovating to find new ways to deliver more value.

If financial metrics look good, it can also lead to organisations resting on their laurels. After all, why bother innovating if you are already getting the results you want?

In short, financial metrics alone aren't enough for long-term Deep-Selling success.

In the 1980s, many executives recognised the inefficacies of this approach and started prioritising operational measures instead. The logic was that if organisations improved operational measures such as cycle times and defect rates, financial results would follow.[350]

In reality, this didn't prove to be the case. Between 1987 and 1990, an electronics company listed on the New York Stock Exchange optimised its operations, reducing outgoing defects from 500 parts per million to 50, improving on-time delivery from 70 to 96 per cent and increasing yield from 26 per cent to 51 per cent. Yet, despite making these operational changes, the company's stock price plummeted to a third of its value and other financial results saw little improvement.[351]

What was going wrong? When operational improvements fail to lead to financial benefits, it usually comes down to one of two problems.

Either the organisation is failing to capitalise on the improvements it has made, or the organisation has made incorrect assumptions about the value of the operational improvements that need revisiting.

This is why neither financial nor operational metrics alone is the answer. Focusing solely on one set of metrics is like being a pilot at the controls of a plane and only looking at the altitude. In order to pilot the plane successfully, you need to be watching airspeed, fuel gauge and dozens of other measures. It is only when every measure is in balance that the plane will successfully reach its destination.

Yet, so many executives at vendor organisations still focus on financial or operational metrics to the exclusion of everything else. This creates a drive for shareholder returns at all costs, and ultimately leaves organisations blind to the other metrics required to achieve sustainable results.

Measuring multiple metrics allows you to bring together distinct parts of the organisation. Without this common ground, different departments can easily become siloed, which can generate internal competition for resources.

Considering multiple metrics also helps organisations optimise for performance. When organisations attempt to improve one set of metrics in isolation, not only does it increase internal silos and competition, but it can have a negative impact on overall performance. Considering seemingly disparate measures together means leaders can assess whether improvement in one area is being achieved at the expense of another. An organisation might want to reduce time to market and could achieve this by only releasing products that are similar to their existing products, meaning they are achieving an operational metric, but they are achieving it at the cost of truly innovating.

Like piloting a plane, to successfully pilot an organisation, you need to look at multiple data points to understand how the organisation is performing.

The challenge is finding a simple way to capture the most important metrics in a single view for effective communication with senior leadership, the board, shareholders and other influential stakeholders.

This is where the balanced scorecard comes in.

Introducing the balanced scorecard

The balanced scorecard is a concept developed by Robert Kaplan and David Norton, published in the *Harvard Business Review* in 1992. At the time, Kaplan and Norton were working with organisations struggling to find measures that would drive performance — often either focusing solely on financial metrics or operational ones.[352]

They argued that leaders should not have to choose between metrics, as no single measure could provide clear performance targets or highlight critical areas. Instead, leaders needed a way to capture multiple metrics at a glance.

The balanced scorecard achieves this by giving leaders an overview of key business measures in several areas at once. In Kaplan and Norton's model, the scorecard included financial measures, customer measures, internal business measures, and innovation and learning measures.

Having a single-page scorecard helped reduce information overload by limiting the number of metrics used. A common issue, particularly in large organisations, is that leaders are tempted to add new metrics every time one becomes relevant (in the previous chapter alone, we introduced 24 metrics to consider in relation to buyer acquisition and buyer health!). By limiting themselves to just two to four metrics per area, those reading the scorecard don't get overwhelmed. It also forces the organisation to prioritise: which of your metrics are the most important to driving success? If someone suggests a new metric, is it significant enough to replace an existing one?

This single-page view also helps achieve the objectives we mentioned earlier — bringing together different parts of the organisation to ensure all teams are working towards the same objectives, and allowing leaders to see whether optimisations in one area are detrimental to another.

There was a reason why 'visibility of metrics' was one of the criteria we asked you to consider in the buyer-centricity audits in chapter 6: monitoring and measuring buyer outcomes in a format that is visible to the entire organisation helps drive buyer-centric behaviour. The balanced scorecard is the mechanism through which you achieve this.

What should be included in the balanced scorecard?

The Deep-Selling balanced scorecard builds on the original model proposed by Kaplan and Norton, focusing on the metrics that are most important for Deep-Selling excellence. These include:

- *financial metrics:* these are the traditional metrics that organisations prioritise, measure and reward. These might include revenue, profit, gross margin, market share and more.
- *sales metrics:* these metrics drive traditional sales performance and are seen in most product-centric organisations. Some examples include cost of acquisition, pipeline conversion rate, average order value, lifetime buyer value, and so on.
- *buyer metrics:* these metrics focus on buyer health, as discussed in chapter 10. They include buyer relationship quality, product usage and buyer value realisation. Very few organisations focus on these metrics, but they are essential to developing Deep-Selling maturity.
- *transformation metrics:* These metrics measure an organisation's progress towards Deep-Selling excellence in terms of buyer centricity and digitalisation. To measure this, you can return to the audits in chapter 6 on buyer centricity, digital readiness and tech-stack maturity.

A Deep-Selling balanced scorecard such as the one presented in figure 11.1 brings together all the elements we have covered in the previous chapters and gives you a clear, transparent view to monitor your progress towards becoming a Deep-Selling organisation over time.

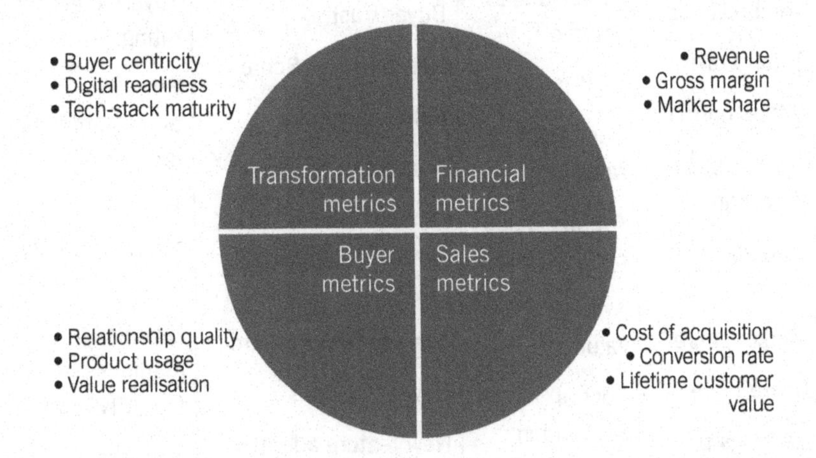

Figure 11.1: a Deep-Selling balanced scorecard

Optimising the balanced scorecard for your organisation

While the four quadrants of the Deep-Selling balanced scorecard remain consistent for any organisation developing its Deep-Selling maturity, the specific metrics that you track will depend on what is most relevant for your organisation.

Just some of the metrics you might consider in each quadrant are listed in table 11.1 (overleaf).

Table 11.1: potential balanced scorecard metrics

Financial metrics	Sales metrics	Buyer metrics	Transformation metrics
Sales volume	Enquiries/ Inbound lead volume	Buyer satisfaction	People buyer-centricity rating
Total revenue	Cost per lead	Buyer trust	Strategy buyer-centricity rating
Total profit	Conversion rate	Net Promoter Score	Metrics buyer-centricity rating
Gross margin	Average sales cycle time	Referenceability	Digital readiness/ Maturity level
Operating cash flow ratio	Average order value	Number of referrals	Tech-stack maturity level
Working capital	Cost of acquisition	Number and percentage of repeat buyers	Deep-selling maturity level
Market share	Lifetime buyer value	Average buyer tenure	
Share price	Sales growth rate	New activations	
Earnings per share		New feature adoption	
		Level of ongoing use	
		Number of support tickets	
		Number of bug reports	
		Number of feature requests	
		Adoption of new products	
		Achievement of buyer goals	
		Increased buyer productivity	
		Reduced buyer costs	
		Product-related value	
		Increased downstream customer value	

Importantly, these metrics are indicative of what *can* be measured, not what *should* be measured. To create a single-page scorecard, you will need to commit to between two and four metrics per quadrant. While the organisation will continue to track other metrics within team-specific dashboards, which leaders can then view for deeper insight, the purpose of this exercise is to develop an at-a-glance view of your organisation's performance.

When it comes to choosing the metrics for your scorecard, some elements to consider are:

- your organisation's size and level of maturity
- the complexity of your products
- your target market
- your acquisition/retention breakdown
- your sales model.

These factors will influence which metrics are most important for you.

Let's consider organisational maturity as an example. The startup phase of an organisation is usually the most difficult one, with the priority being to prove their concept, test their products and become known within their niche. At this stage, the focus is on survival, and industry participants often have to seed the market to find those all-important early adopters. Startups will invest any profits into the business to help it generate enough momentum to reach the growth stage.

With this in mind, they might focus on the following metrics:

- *Financial metrics:* sales volume, total revenue, operating cash flow
- *Sales metrics:* enquiries/inbound lead volume, conversion rate, average sales cycle time

- *Buyer metrics:* new activations, adoption of new products, number of referrals to other buyers
- *Transformation metrics:* buyer-centricity level, digital readiness/ maturity level.

By contrast, mature organisations are those that have experienced a period of strong, consistent growth that has started to level out. While growth continues, it is at a slower rate than before, often falling from triple digits to single digits.

Some organisations will disrupt the lifecycle through product innovation or launching internal startups to create new growth, and these products or organisational branches will likely focus on similar metrics to those listed above.

Organisations that continue to focus on their existing products and markets will prioritise growing and retaining their existing buyers, meaning their balanced scorecard will focus more on buyer health than acquisition, with a focus on:

- *Financial metrics:* total revenue, market share, earnings per share
- *Sales metrics:* lifetime buyer value, average buyer tenure
- *Buyer metrics:* buyer trust, number and percentage of repeat buyers, achievement of buyer goals
- *Transformation metrics:* Deep-Selling maturity level.

This process may take some iteration. We recommend working with leaders across your organisation to determine the most important measures as a starting point and, in cases where you can't reach a consensus on the top two to four metrics per quadrant, create sample scorecards with different metrics using historical data to gauge which are the most useful for tracking organisational health and informing future actions. If the historical data still isn't enough to reach a consensus, you could create a dashboard with balanced scorecard variations for the next quarter and revisit it after seeing how they perform in the real business environment.

How the balanced scorecard reimagines performance measurement

The balanced scorecard puts vision and strategy at the centre, focusing on the way an organisation wants to evolve and trusting that its people will adopt the necessary behaviours to achieve that vision.[353]

In this way, you routinise and embed the journey towards Deep-Selling maturity in your organisation.

CONCLUSION: YOU CAN NO LONGER SURVIVE IN THE SHALLOWS

In our early careers in the mid 1990s and early 2000s, the Shallows were full of fish. With the water at our ankles, we could dangle the bait of our employer's latest high-tech solution, and the fish would swim to us, hungry for a bite.

Even landing whales was relatively easy, with buyers willing to fork out millions of dollars upfront with no vendor risk. To continue the metaphor, these whales were practically beaching themselves in their eagerness to implement the next solution that could give them an edge.

As we have discussed at length, with changing buyer dynamics, new technologies and more competitive markets, the Shallows are where everyone fishes. It is a crowded red ocean of bloody competition.

Market maturity and globalisation have led to the saturation of high-tech solutions. Business buyers have more options to choose from and vendor organisations are competing on both a local and international level, leading to increased commoditisation and price pressures due to the lower cost of international labour and materials.

Buyers have access to more information than ever before due to the growth in digital technologies and they are able to shop the global marketplace for the best deal. This leads to higher expectations and puts the power of the buyer-vendor relationship in their hands.

At the same time, buying environments are more complex, with up to 23 decision makers taking part in the purchase of high-tech solutions.[354] Increased access to information is also leading to information overwhelm, and the fear of messing up means between 40 and 60 per cent of purchasing journeys end in a 'no decision' outcome.[355]

And the ever-increasing pace of technological development, particularly the most recent boom around generative AI, is further accelerating these changes.

Is it any wonder so many vendor sales teams are struggling? Most vendor organisations are understandably holding tight to the old-world, product-centric focus. This is what their leaders have always known, and it is how they are used to driving and measuring results. Yet, this approach is unsustainable: sales teams are becoming less effective with each passing year, with more than three-quarters of salespeople not hitting their targets in the fourth quarter of 2022 and attrition rates as high as 50 per cent.[356,357]

Lower sales results combined with falling tenure, longer sales cycles and longer onboarding times means sales teams are becoming even more expensive in real terms, with the total cost of a salesforce going up while the revenue they generate declines.

You can no longer survive in the Shallows. Instead, vendor organisations and sales teams need to evolve. It is time to go Deep.

The opportunity of going Deep

Despite all these challenges, we fundamentally believe this is a time of great opportunity for vendor organisations, sales leaders and sales professionals. There is no need for you to sit at the edge of a pier with a fishing rod and pray for a whale, or even a large tuna, to get close.

Instead, you have the opportunity to go deeper, and this book has given you the roadmap. After following this journey, you will:

- understand the current state of your organisation and have used this understanding to make a compelling case for change
- develop *Deep* buyer understanding, including ideal and minimum buyer personas and an ideal buyer experience map
- know how to adapt your team structure to meet your buyers' needs
- understand the best sales execution model for your buyers and your products
- transform how your organisation defines and measures success, establishing the foundations for a buyer-obsessed, high-performance culture
- embed and routinise the change using the Deep-Selling balanced scorecard.

With this roadmap, your sales team and the wider organisation can adapt to the new world of sales: one where you can defend and champion the journey to achieve Deep-Selling excellence, where your team knows how to build Deep relationships and trust with your buyers and achieve results with your buyers' best interests at heart, and where your buyers view your team and organisation as trusted advisers who can help their own organisation achieve their business goals.

As your buyers achieve their business goals, they will become more loyal, with higher levels of trust and satisfaction. They will use your products more frequently, with deeper penetration across their organisation and more activated features. They will become advocates for your organisation, referring more buyers your way. And these behaviours will drive those bottom-line metrics—higher average order values, lifetime buyer value and lower acquisition costs—which means more revenue with higher margins.

Ultimately, going Deep empowers you and your organisation to deliver the value your buyers want in the way they want it, and this generates sustainable, long-term success.

Going Deep is a significant change for most vendor organisations, and changes such as this are challenging and generate resistance. But when you do it—when you get to those Deep waters—you will discover *that* is where the big fish are, and the wider market pressures of competition and commoditisation cease to be important.

You choose the limit

Finally, remember that the level of change—how Deep you go—is up to you and your organisation. There is no reason to stop once an initial wave of change has successfully been implemented, and it is always possible to look for more opportunities to optimise.

As we shared at the beginning of this journey, this is our goal with the process: it is intended to be cyclical, so you can continue going deeper. Once you develop one persona, you can refine it as you get more information. As you increase collaboration between marketing, sales, customer success and customer support, you could trial cross-functional squads that collaborate to deliver superior experiences for strategic buyers. If you started measuring new metrics before changing compensation plans, seeing positive results in those metrics could lead to endorsement for a new approach to compensation.

The changes occurring in the buying and sales landscape are not going anywhere. Technology will continue to evolve, buyer needs and wants will continue to develop, and the pressure for buyers to make the best decision will continue to grow as competition intensifies across B2B sectors.

The most important thing is making a start: get off the pier and into a boat. Even if you can only sail around the bay, you are still moving away from the shore. In more concrete terms, any move that increases your level of buyer centricity, your digital readiness and your tech-stack maturity—that is, the areas that define your Deep-Selling maturity—is a move in the right direction.

And once you've set sail, you can start heading towards the ocean.

◆ ◆ ◆

To continue your organisation's path to Deep-Selling excellence, visit www.deepselling.com, or follow the QR code below, for the latest resources.

ACKNOWLEDGEMENTS

We would like to acknowledge the significant contribution of many people in our personal and professional circles who contributed to the content in this book. The knowledge contained herein is based on years of research into the effects, consequences, antecedents and impacts of technology on the evolution and transformation of the sales function.

While much of the primary research which went into this publication is our own—based heavily on an award-winning thesis which has received accolades including 'the best B2B thesis in Industrial Marketing Management 2024'—it also contains findings and insights from many others in the academic community, including: Dr Joona Keranen (Ass. Professor, RMIT University, Melbourne, Australia), Dr Olga Kokshagina (Ass. Professor, EDHEC, Paris, France), Prof. Deva Rengarajan (Professor IESEG School of Management, Paris, France) and many others in the wider academic community. While we lean heavily on academic concepts developed by these and other leading sales and marketing researchers, the book is written with a managerial focus. It is meant for sales and management practitioners who we hope will benefit from years of academic work and apply these concepts in the real world. We hope we have managed to do justice to the extensive work of the academic community throughout this book which aims to demystify the challenges facing sales and management professionals, considering the transformation of the profession.

We would also like to recognise the contribution of Brent Adamson—one of the world's foremost experts in sales and customer management strategy, and author of The *Challenger Sale* and *The Challenger Customer.* Our many conversations with Brent, who wrote the foreword for this book, helped to shape the focus and content in this publication. In addition to working with Brent on the development of AI-based sales platform, www.Qoos.ai, Brent is a friend, mentor, sounding board and voice of reason for all that is sales, sales management and customer management. In a world full of infinite noise, Brent is the signal.

We would also like to acknowledge the extensive skills and expertise of Jacqui Pretty, without whom this publication would never exist. Jacqui's ability to compile, comprehend, compress and construct the structure of this book from the hundreds of resources we brought to the table was amazing. We are both in awe of your capability and we thank you for your hard work throughout the writing process.

To our professional networks who are very important to us both—thank you for your ongoing support. We are passionate about helping to deliver value to our networks and we believe that this book is another very positive step in that direction. We hope to delve deeper into the concepts and opportunities contained in this book with each of you individually.

And, finally, to our families; thank you for your ongoing support. We do this for you and, while at times our business pursuits take us further away, know that you are, and will always remain, our primary focus.

Mark and Graham

NOTES

1. Matthew Dixon and Ted McKenna. *The Jolt Effect: How high performers overcome customer indecision* (New York: Portfolio/Penguin, 2022), xiv.
2. Barry Trailer, Jim Dickie, Tamara Schenk, Anne Petrik et al. *Drawing Back the Bow: 2016 CSO Insights Sales Best Practices Study* (Littleton, CO: CSO Insights, 2016), 22.
3. *Sales Development: Models, Metrics, and Compensation Research* (The Bridge Group, 2023), 20, 24.
4. Bravado. 'Bravado on LinkedIn: #REVENUERECAP2023.' LinkedIn, 28 February, 2023. https://www.linkedin.com/posts/wearebravado_revenuerecap2023-data-sales-activity-7036419292455727104-twsl/.
5. Jonathan Hughes, David Chapnick, Isaac Block and Saptak Ray. 'What Is Customer-Centricity, and Why Does It Matter?' *California Management Review*, 26 September, 2021. https://cmr.berkeley.edu/2021/09/what-is-customer-centricity-and-why-does-it-matter/.
6. Maxie Schmidt-Subramanian and Samuel Stern. 'How to Make the Case That CX Transformation Is Both Important and Urgent.' Forrester Research Inc. 17 August 2017. https://www.forrester.com/blogs/make-the-case-that-cx-transformation-is-both-important-and-urgent/.
7. 'Customer Centricity.' Gallup.com, 27 March, 2024. https://www.gallup.com/workplace/311870/customer-centricity.aspx.
8. Brooke Landon and Jillesa Gebhardt. 'Report: How a Customer Centric Culture Ties to Happier Employees.' SurveyMonkey. Accessed 10 May, 2024. https://www.surveymonkey.com/resources/report-customer-centric-culture-happier-employees/.

9. 'Internet and Social Media Users in the World 2024.' Statista, 7 May, 2024. https://www.statista.com/statistics/617136/digital-population-worldwide/.
10. 'IOT Connected Devices Worldwide 2019–2030.' Statista, 27 July, 2023. https://www.statista.com/statistics/1183457/iot-connected-devices-worldwide/.
11. GSMA report: *The Mobile Economy 2024* (London: GSMA, 2024), 8.
12. 'Number of Worldwide Social Network Users 2028.' Statista, 17 May, 2024. https://www.statista.com/statistics/278414/number-of-worldwide-social-network-users/.
13. Ryan Mullins and Raj Agnihotri. 'Digital Selling: Organizational and Managerial Influences for Frontline Readiness and Effectiveness.' *Journal of the Academy of Marketing Science* 50, no. 4 (18 January, 2022): 800–21. https://doi.org/10.1007/s11747-021-00836-5.
14. Andris A Zoltners, Prabhakant Sinha, Dharmendra Sahay, Arun Shastri and Sally E Lorimer. 'Practical Insights for Sales Force Digitalization Success.' *Journal of Personal Selling & Sales Management* 41, no. 2 (3 April, 2021): 87–102. https://doi.org/10.1080/08853134.2021.1908144.
15. Heiko Fischer, Sven Seidenstricker and Jens Poeppelbuss. 'The Triggers and Consequences of Digital Sales: A Systematic Literature Review.' *Journal of Personal Selling & Sales Management* 43, no. 1 (5 August, 2022): 5–23. https://doi.org/10.1080/08853134.2022.2102029.
16. 'Social Selling: Definition, Benefits & Tips for Sales Leaders.' Linkedin.com. Accessed 20 May, 2024. https://business.linkedin.com/sales-solutions/social-selling.
17. Niladri Syam and Arun Sharma. 'Waiting for a Sales Renaissance in the Fourth Industrial Revolution: Machine Learning and Artificial Intelligence in Sales Research and Practice.' *Industrial Marketing Management* 69 (February 2018): 135–46. https://doi.org/10.1016/j.indmarman.2017.12.019. *The Future of Sales: Transformational Strategies for B2B Sales Organizations* (Gartner, 2020), 2.
18. Michelle D Steward, James A Narus, Michelle L Roehm and Wendy Ritz. 'From Transactions to Journeys and Beyond: The Evolution of B2B Buying Process Modeling.' *Industrial Marketing Management* 83 (November 2019): 288–300. https://doi.org/10.1016/j.indmarman.2019.05.002.
19. Denni Arli, Carlos Bauer and Robert W Palmatier. 'Relational Selling: Past, Present and Future.' *Industrial Marketing Management* 69 (February 2018): 169–84. https://doi.org/10.1016/j.indmarman.2017.07.018.
20. Jagjit Singh Srai and Harri Lorentz. 'Developing Design Principles for the Digitalisation of Purchasing and Supply Management.' *Journal of Purchasing and Supply Management* 25, no. 1 (January 2019): 78–98. https://doi.org/10.1016/j.pursup.2018.07.001.

21. Leeya Hendricks and Paul Matthyssens. 'Platform Ecosystem Development in an Institutionalized Business Market: The Case of the Asset Management Industry.' *Journal of Business & Industrial Marketing* 38, no. 2 (29 April, 2022): 395–413. https://doi.org/10.1108/jbim-10-2021-0484.
22. Jeannette Paschen, Jan Kietzmann and Tim Christian Kietzmann. 'Artificial Intelligence (AI) and Its Implications for Market Knowledge in B2B Marketing.' *Journal of Business & Industrial Marketing* 34, no. 7 (5 August, 2019): 1410–19. https://doi.org/10.1108/jbim-10-2018-0295.
23. Graham Hawkins. *Future of the Sales Profession: How to survive the big cull and become one of your industry's most sought after B2B sales professionals* (Cheltenham: Grammar Factory Pty, Limited, 2017), 78–98.
24. E K Strong. 'Theories of Selling.' *Journal of Applied Psychology* 9, no. 1 (March 1925): 75–86. https://doi.org/10.1037/h0070123.
25. Raymond W LaForge, Thomas N Ingram and David W Cravens. 'Strategic Alignment for Sales Organization Transformation.' *Journal of Strategic Marketing* 17, no. 3–4 (June 2009): 199–219. https://doi.org/10.1080/09652540903064662.
26. Walter A Friedman. 'John H Patterson and the Sales Strategy of the National Cash Register Company, 1884 to 1922.' *Business History Review* 72, no. 4 (1998): 552–84. https://doi.org/10.2307/3116622.
27. Patrick J Robinson, Charles W Faris and Yoram Wind. *Industrial Buying and Creative Marketing* (Boston: Allyn & Bacon) 1967.
28. Robinson, Faris and Wind. *Industrial Buying and Creative Marketing.*
29. Frederick E Webster and Yoram Wind. 'A General Model for Understanding Organizational Buying Behavior.' *Journal of Marketing* 36, no. 2 (April 1972): 12. https://doi.org/10.2307/1250972.
30. Walter A Friedman. 'John H. Patterson and the Sales Strategy of the National Cash Register Company, 1884 to 1922.' Working Knowledge (1 November, 1999): 552–84.
31. K E Kristian Möller. 'Research Strategies in Analyzing the Organizational Buying Process.' *Journal of Business Research* 13, no. 1 (February, 1985): 3–17. https://doi.org/10.1016/0148-2963(85)90010-4.
32. Gitesh Dhairyashilrao Chavan, Ranjan Chaudhuri and Wesley J Johnston. 'Industrial-Buying Research 1965–2015: Review and Analysis.' *Journal of Business & Industrial Marketing* 34, no. 1 (13 February, 2019): 205–29. https://doi.org/10.1108/jbim-02-2018-0077.
33. Gopalkrishnan R Iyer. 'Strategic Decision Making in Industrial Procurement: Implications for Buying Decision Approaches and Buyer-seller Relationships.' *Journal of Business & Industrial Marketing* 11, no. 3/4 (1 June 1996): 80–93. https://doi.org/10.1108/08858629610125487.

34. E Robert Dwyer, Paul H Schurr and Sejo Oh. 'Developing Buyer-Seller Relationships.' *Journal of Marketing* 51, no. 2 (April 1987): 112. https://doi.org/10.1177/002224298705100202.
35. Dwyer, Schurr and Oh. 'Developing Buyer-Seller Relationships.' 112.
36. R A DeCormier and D Jobber. 'The Counselor Selling Method: Concepts and Constructs.' *Journal of Personal Selling & Sales Management* 13 no. 4 (1993): 39–59.
37. N C Campbell and M T Cunningham. 'Customer Analysis for Strategy Development in Industrial Markets.' *Strategic Management Journal* 4, no. 4 (October 1983): 369–80. https://doi.org/10.1002/smj.4250040407.
38. Robert M Morgan and Shelby D Hunt. 'The Commitment-Trust Theory of Relationship Marketing.' *Journal of Marketing* 58, no. 3 (July 1994): 20. https://doi.org/10.2307/1252308.
39. James C Anderson, Hakan Hakansson and Jan Johanson. 'Dyadic Business Relationships within a Business Network Context.' *Journal of Marketing* 58, no. 4 (October 1994): 1. https://doi.org/10.2307/1251912.
40. Kim Harris and John Pike. 'Issues Concerning Adoption and Use of Sales Force Automation in the Agricultural Input Supply Sector.' *Agribusiness* 12, no. 4 (July 1996): 317–26. https://doi.org/10.1002/(SICI)1520-6297(199607/08)12:4%3C317::AID-AGR2%3E3.0.CO;2-1.
41. A Wedell and D Hempeck. 'Sales Force Automation—Here and Now.' *The Journal of Personal Selling & Sales Management* 7, no. 2 (1987): 11.
42. Ralph W Jackson, Lester A Neidell and Dale A Lunsford. 'An Empirical Investigation of the Differences in Goods and Services as Perceived by Organizational Buyers.' *Industrial Marketing Management* 24, no. 2 (March 1995): 99–108. https://doi.org/10.1016/0019-8501(94)00037-w.
43. Alke Töllner, Markus Blut and Hartmut H Holzmüller. 'Customer Solutions in the Capital Goods Industry: Examining the Impact of the Buying Center.' *Industrial Marketing Management* 40, no. 5 (July 2011): 712–22. https://doi.org/10.1016/j.indmarman.2011.06.001.
44. William C Moncrief and Greg W Marshall. 'The Evolution of the Seven Steps of Selling.' *Industrial Marketing Management* 34, no. 1 (January 2005): 13–22. https://doi.org/10.1016/j.indmarman.2004.06.001.
45. Arun Sharma. 'The Shift in Sales Organizations in Business-to-Business Services Markets.' *Journal of Services Marketing* 21, no. 5 (7 August, 2007): 326–33. https://doi.org/10.1108/08876040710773633.
46. Adam Rapp and Thomas L Baker. 'Introduction to the Special Issue on the Intersection of Professional Selling and Service.' *Journal of Personal Selling & Sales Management* 37, no. 1 (2 January, 2017): 4–10. https://doi.org/10.1080/08853134.2017.1292099.

47. Elina Jaakkola and Taru Hakanen. 'Value Co-Creation in Solution Networks.' *Industrial Marketing Management* 42, no. 1 (January 2013): 47–58. https://doi.org/10.1016/j.indmarman.2012.11.005.
48. W Anthony. 'B2B traffic on the rise in electronic commerce terms, business-to-business (B2B) transactions will surpass the value of business-to-consumer (B2C) transactions. By 2002, the business of B2B will be worth billions, and counting.' National Edition 1. *National Post (Toronto)*, 1999.
49. Garrido-Samaniego, Gutiérrez-Arranz and San José-Cabezudo. 'Assessing the Impact of E-Procurement on the Structure of the Buying Centre.' 135–43.
50. Adam Lindgreen, Joëlle Vanhamme, Erik M van Raaij and Wesley J Johnston. 'Go Configure: The Mix of Purchasing Practices to Choose for Your Supply Base.' *California Management Review* 55, no. 2 (January 2013): 72–96. https://doi.org/10.1525/cmr.2013.55.2.72.
51. José Garrido Samaniego, Ana M. Gutiérrez Arranz and Rebeca San José Cabezudo. 'Determinants of Internet Use in the Purchasing Process.' *Journal of Business & Industrial Marketing* 21, no. 3 (1 April, 2006): 164–74. https://doi.org/10.1108/08858620610662813.
52. R Bergmann and P Cunningham. 'Acquiring Customers' Requirements in Electronic Commerce.' *Artificial Intelligence Review* 18 (2002): 163–93. https://doi.org/10.1023/A:1020757322687.
53. Garrido-Samaniego, Gutiérrez-Arranz and San José-Cabezudo. 'Assessing the Impact of E-Procurement on the Structure of the Buying Centre.' 135–43.
54. Thomas R Eisenmann, Geoffrey Parker and Marshall W Van Alstyne. 'Platform Envelopment.' *Strategic Management Journal* 32 (2010): 1260–85. https://doi.org/10.2139/ssrn.1496336.
55. Walter A Friedman. 'John H Patterson and the Sales Strategy of the National Cash Register Company, 1884 to 1922.' *Working Knowledge* (1 November, 1999): 552–84.
56. R E Anderson. 'Personal Selling and Sales Management in the New Millennium.' 17–32.
57. S S Venkatraman. 'Anytime, anywhere: The flexible networking environment of wireless LANs.' *Journal of Systems Management* 45 no. 9 (September 1994): 6.
58. Greg W Marshall, William C Moncrief, John M Rudd and Nick Lee. 'Revolution in Sales: The Impact of Social Media and Related Technology on the Selling Environment.' *Journal of Personal Selling & Sales Management* 32, no. 3 (June 2012): 349–63. https://doi.org/10.2753/pss0885-3134320305.
59. James 'Mick' Andzulis, Nikolaos G Panagopoulos and Adam Rapp. 'A Review of Social Media and Implications for the Sales Process.' *Journal of Personal Selling & Sales Management* 32, no. 3 (June 2012): 305–16. https://doi.org/10.2753/pss0885-3134320302.

60. 'About Linkedin.' About LinkedIn. Accessed 30 May, 2024. https://about.linkedin.com/.
61. Michael Ahearne and Adam Rapp. 'The Role of Technology at the Interface between Salespeople and Consumers.' *Journal of Personal Selling & Sales Management* 30, no. 2 (March 2010): 111–20. https://doi.org/10.2753/pss0885-3134300202.
62. Brian C Williams and Christopher R Plouffe. 'Assessing the Evolution of Sales Knowledge: A 20-Year Content Analysis.' *Industrial Marketing Management* 36, no. 4 (May 2007): 408–19. https://doi.org/10.1016/j.indmarman.2005.11.003.
63. Caroline Emberson and John Storey. 'Buyer–Supplier Collaborative Relationships: Beyond the Normative Accounts.' *Journal of Purchasing and Supply Management* 12, no. 5 (September 2006): 236–45. https://doi.org/10.1016/j.pursup.2006.10.008.
64. D Ross Brennan, Peter W Turnbull and David T Wilson. 'Dyadic Adaptation in Business-to-Business Markets.' *European Journal of Marketing* 37, no. 11/12 (1 December, 2003): 1636–65. https://doi.org/10.1108/03090560310495393.
65. Jeong Eun Park, Juyoung Kim, Alan J Dubinsky and Hyunju Lee. 'How Does Sales Force Automation Influence Relationship Quality and Performance? The Mediating Roles of Learning and Selling Behaviors.' *Industrial Marketing Management* 39, no. 7 (October 2010): 1128–38. https://doi.org/10.1016/j.indmarman.2009.11.003.
66. Othman Boujena, Wesley J Johnston and Dwight R Merunka. 'The Benefits of Sales Force Automation: A Customer's Perspective.' *Journal of Personal Selling & Sales Management* 29, no. 2 (March 2009): 137–50. https://doi.org/10.2753/pss0885-3134290203.
67. Stephen L Vargo and Robert F Lusch. 'Evolving to a New Dominant Logic for Marketing.' *Journal of Marketing* 68, no. 1 (January 2004): 1–17. https://doi.org/10.1509/jmkg.68.1.1.24036.
68. Ronald Zallocco, Ellen Bolman Pullins and Michael L Mallin. 'A Re-examination of B2B Sales Performance.' *Journal of Business & Industrial Marketing* 24, no. 8 (9 October, 2009): 598–610. https://doi.org/10.1108/08858620910999466.
69. R E Anderson. 'Personal Selling and Sales Management in the New Millennium.' 17–32.
70. Jagjit Singh Srai and Harri Lorentz. 'Developing Design Principles for the Digitalisation of Purchasing and Supply Management.' Science Direct 25, no. 1, (January 2019): 78–98.
71. Niladri Syam and Arun Sharma. 'Waiting for a Sales Renaissance in the Fourth Industrial Revolution: Machine Learning and Artificial Intelligence in Sales Research and Practice.' Science Direct 69 (February 2018): 135–46.

72. Srai and Lorentz. 'Developing Design Principles for the Digitalisation of Purchasing and Supply Management.' 78–98.
73. Jagdip Singh et al. 'Sales Profession and Professionals in the Age of Digitization and Artificial Intelligence Technologies: Concepts, Priorities, and Questions.' *Journal of Personal Selling & Sales Management* 39, no. 1 (2 January, 2019): 2–22. https://doi.org/10.1080/08853134.2018.1557525.
74. Paschen, Kietzmann and Kietzmann. 'Artificial Intelligence (AI) and Its Implications for Market Knowledge in B2B Marketing.' 1410–19.
75. Syam and Sharma. 'Waiting for a Sales Renaissance in the Fourth Industrial Revolution: Machine Learning and Artificial Intelligence in Sales Research and Practice.' 135–46.
76. Srai and Lorentz. 'Developing Design Principles for the Digitalisation of Purchasing and Supply Management.' 78–98.
77. William C Moncrief. 'Are Sales as We Know It Dying . . . or Merely Transforming?' *Journal of Personal Selling & Sales Management* 37, no. 4 (2 October, 2017): 271–79. https://doi.org/10.1080/08853134.2017.1386110.
78. Srai and Lorentz. 'Developing Design Principles for the Digitalisation of Purchasing and Supply Management.' 78–98.
79. Garrido-Samaniego, Gutiérrez-Arranz and San José-Cabezudo. 'Assessing the Impact of E-Procurement on the Structure of the Buying Centre.' 135–43.
80. Verhoef, Kannan and Inman. 'From Multi-Channel Retailing to Omni-Channel Retailing.' 174–81.
81. H Min. 'Artificial intelligence in supply chain management: theory and applications.' *International Journal of Logistics* 13, no. 1 (March 2009): 13–39. https://doi.org/10.1080/13675560902736537.
82. Syam and Sharma. 'Waiting for a Sales Renaissance in the Fourth Industrial Revolution: Machine Learning and Artificial Intelligence in Sales Research and Practice.' 135–46.
83. Javier Marcos Cuevas. 'The Transformation of Professional Selling: Implications for Leading the Modern Sales Organization.' *Industrial Marketing Management* 69 (February 2018): 198–208. https://doi.org/10.1016/j.indmarman.2017.12.017.
84. Syam and Sharma. 'Waiting for a Sales Renaissance in the Fourth Industrial Revolution: Machine Learning and Artificial Intelligence in Sales Research and Practice.' 135–46.
85. Paschen, Kietzmann and Kietzmann. 'Artificial Intelligence (AI) and Its Implications for Market Knowledge in B2B Marketing.' 1410–19.
86. Spyros Makridakis. 'The Forthcoming Artificial Intelligence (AI) Revolution: Its Impact on Society and Firms.' *Futures: The Journal of Policy, Planning and Futures Studies* 90 (June 2017): 46–60. https://doi.org/10.1016/j.futures.2017.03.006.

87. Rocio Rodríguez, Göran Svensson and Erik Jens Mehl. 'Digitalization Process of Complex B2B Sales Processes—Enablers and Obstacles.' *Technology in Society* 62 (August 2020): 101324. https://doi.org/10.1016/j.techsoc.2020.101324.
88. Joakim Björkdahl. 'Strategies for Digitalization in Manufacturing Firms.' *California Management Review* 62, no. 4 (5 May, 2020): 17–36. https://doi.org/10.1177/0008125620920349.
89. Sami Rusthollkarhu, Sebastian Toukola, Leena Aarikka-Stenroos and Tommi Mahlamäki. 'Managing B2B Customer Journeys in Digital Era: Four Management Activities with Artificial Intelligence-Empowered Tools.' *Industrial Marketing Management* 104 (July 2022): 241–57. https://doi.org/10.1016/j.indmarman.2022.04.014.
90. Jagjit Singh Srai and Harri Lorentz. 'Developing Design Principles for the Digitalisation of Purchasing and Supply Management.' 78–98.
91. Riccardo Mogre, Adam Lindgreen and Martin Hingley. 'Tracing the Evolution of Purchasing Research: Future Trends and Directions for Purchasing Practices.' *Journal of Business & Industrial Marketing* 32, no. 2 (6 March, 2017): 251–57. https://doi.org/10.1108/jbim-01-2016-0004.
92. Shannon Cummins, James W Peltier and Andrea Dixon. 'Omni-Channel Research Framework in the Context of Personal Selling and Sales Management.' *Journal of Research in Interactive Marketing* 10, no. 1 (14 March, 2016): 2–16. https://doi.org/10.1108/jrim-12-2015-0094.
93. Daniela Corsaro and Valerio D'Amico. 'How the Digital Transformation from Covid-19 Affected the Relational Approaches in B2B.' *Journal of Business & Industrial Marketing* 37, no. 10 (2 June, 2022): 2095–115. https://doi.org/10.1108/jbim-05-2021-0266.
94. Liz Harrison, Ryan Gavin, Candace Lun Plotkin and Jennifer Stanley. 'How B2B Sales Have Changed during COVID-19.' McKinsey & Company, 14 July, 2020. https://www.mckinsey.com/capabilities/growth-marketing-and-sales/our-insights/how-b2b-sales-have-changed-during-covid-19.
95. Corsaro and D'Amico. 'How the Digital Transformation from Covid-19 Affected the Relational Approaches in B2B.' 2095–115.
96. Harrison, Gavin, Plotkin and Stanley. 'How B2B Sales Have Changed during COVID-19.'
97. Samantha Lock. 'What Is AI Chatbot Phenomenon CHATGPT and Could It Replace Humans?' *The Guardian*, 5 December, 2022. https://www.theguardian.com/technology/2022/dec/05/what-is-ai-chatbot-phenomenon-chatgpt-and-could-it-replace-humans.
98. Pablo Rivas and Liang Zhao. 'Marketing with CHATGPT: Navigating the Ethical Terrain of GPT-Based Chatbot Technology.' *AI* 4, no. 2 (10 April, 2023): 375–84. https://doi.org/10.3390/ai4020019.

99. Michael Bloch, Sven Blumberg and Jürgen Laartz. 'Delivering Large-Scale It Projects on Time, on Budget, and on Value.' McKinsey & Company, 1 October, 2012. https://www.mckinsey.com/capabilities/mckinsey-digital/our-insights/delivering-large-scale-it-projects-on-time-on-budget-and-on-value.
100. David Taber. 'What to Do When Your CRM Project Fails.' CIO, 18 September, 2017. https://www.cio.com/article/288664/what-to-do-when-your-crm-project-fails.html.
101. Ginika Anajulu. 'Case Study: 10 World's Famous CRM Implementation Failures.' CRMside, 14 May, 2024. https://crmside.com/crm-implementation-failures/.
102. Stefan Thomke. 'High-Tech Tools Won't Automatically Improve Your Operations.' *Harvard Business Review*, 15 April, 2024. https://hbr.org/2015/06/new-technology-wont-automatically-improve-your-operations.
103. '10 Fastest Cars in the World 2024.' CarWow, 10 May, 2024. https://www.carwow.co.uk/blog/fastest-cars-in-the-world.
104. Mark Micallef, Joona Keränen and Olga Kokshagina. 'Understanding the Consequences of Digital Technology Use in Sales: Multilevel Tensions inside Sales Organizations.' *Journal of Personal Selling & Sales Management* 44, no. 1 (27 January, 2023): 84–99. https://doi.org/10.1080/08853134.2022.2159422.
105. Krystal Hu. 'CHATGPT Sets Record for Fastest-Growing User Base—Analyst Note | Reuters.' Reuters, 3 February, 2023. https://www.reuters.com/technology/chatgpt-sets-record-fastest-growing-user-base-analyst-note-2023-02-01/.
106. Aisha Malik. 'OpenAI's CHATGPT Now Has 100 Million Weekly Active Users.' TechCrunch, 6 November, 2023. https://techcrunch.com/2023/11/06/openais-chatgpt-now-has-100-million-weekly-active-users/.
107. *State of AI, Global | 2023 recap* (CB Insights, 2023).
108. 'Gartner Poll Finds 45% of Executives Say CHATGPT Has Prompted an Increase in AI Investment.' Gartner, 3 May, 2023. https://www.gartner.com/en/newsroom/press-releases/2023-05-03-gartner-poll-finds-45-percent-of-executives-say-chatgpt-has-prompted-an-increase-in-ai-investment.
109. Michael Chui et al. 'The State of AI in 2023: Generative AI's Breakout Year.' McKinsey & Company, 1 August, 2023. https://www.mckinsey.com/capabilities/quantumblack/our-insights/the-state-of-ai-in-2023-generative-ais-breakout-year.
110. Introducing ChatGPT enterprise. Accessed 20 April, 2024. https://openai.com/index/introducing-chatgpt-enterprise.
111. Smarter Selling with AI: New data on How the Sales Process Is Changing (HubSpot, CXD Studio), 19.
112. State of Sales, Third Edition (Salesforce Research, 2018), 17.

113. *Accelerating Sales and Marketing Efforts Through Artificial Intelligence* (Harvard Business School Publishing: 2019), 1.
114. Livia Rainsberger. *AI: The new intelligence in sales,* (Wiesbaden, Germany: Springer, 2022), 2.
115. Alan Turing. 'Computing Machinery and Intelligence', *Mind* LIX no. 236 (October 1950): 433–60, doi:10.1093/mind/LIX.236.433, ISSN 0026-4423.
116. Gio Wiederhold, John McCarthy and Ed Feigenbaum. 'Memorial Resolution: Arthur L Samuel' *Stanford University Historical Society* (1990). https://web.archive.org/web/20110526195107/http://histsoc.stanford.edu/pdfmem/SamuelA.pdf.
117. Rainsberger. *AI: The new intelligence in sales*, 8.
118. Matthew Hutson. *The 7 Laws of Magical Thinking: How Irrational Beliefs Keep Us Happy, Healthy, and Sane.* (New York: Penguin Group, 2013) 165–81.
119. Rainsberger. *AI: The new intelligence in sales*, 7–8.
120. 'Automation and Anxiety.' *The Economist*, 23 June, 2016. https://www.economist.com/special-report/2016/06/23/automation-and-anxiety.
121. Joanne Elgart Jennings. '3 White Collar Jobs That Robots Are Already Mastering.' PBS, 22 May, 2015. http://www.pbs.org/newshour/updates/3-white-collar-jobs-robots-can-already-better/.
122. Nurfilzah Rohaidi. 'IBM's Watson Detected Rare Leukemia in Just 10 Minutes.' *Asian Scientist Magazine*, 15 August, 2016. http://www.asianscientist.com/2016/08/topnews/ibm-watson-rare-leukemia-university-tokyo-artificial-intelligence/.
123. Maria Valdivieso de Uster. 'The 7 Biggest Trends Upending Sales Today.' Salesforce.com, 10 May, 2024. https://web.archive.org/web/20220121081120/https://www.salesforce.com/resources/articles/biggest-sales-trends/.
124. *Accelerating Sales and Marketing Efforts Through Artificial Intelligence*, 1.
125. *Smarter Selling with AI*, 7.
126. *Accelerating Sales and Marketing Efforts Through Artificial Intelligence*, 4.
127. Paschen, Kietzmann and Kietzmann. 'Artificial Intelligence (AI) and Its Implications for Market Knowledge in B2B Marketing.' 1410–19.
128. *Accelerating Sales and Marketing Efforts Through Artificial Intelligence*, 6.
129. *Smarter Selling with AI*, 12.
130. *Smarter Selling with AI*, 12.
131. Michael Chui, Nicolaus Henke and Mehdi Miremadi. 'Most of AI's Business Uses Will Be in Two Areas.' McKinsey & Company, 7 March, 2019. https://www.mckinsey.com/capabilities/quantumblack/our-insights/most-of-ais-business-uses-will-be-in-two-areas.
132. Annette Jump. *Emerging Tech Roundup: ChatGPT Hype Fuels Urgency for Advancing Conversational AI and Generative AI* (Gartner Research, 2023), 1.

133. *2024 generative AI predictions report* (CB Insights, 2024), 5–7.
134. *2024 generative AI predictions report*, 37.
135. Vibha Sathesh Kumar. 'Gen Z in the Workplace: How Should Companies Adapt?' *Imagine*, 16 November, 2023. https://imagine.jhu.edu/blog/2023/04/18/gen-z-in-the-workplace-how-should-companies-adapt/.
136. Matt Smith and Tom Hedges. *Meet the Millennials: Social media, entertainment and purchase journey trends* (GlobalWebIndex, 2023), 6, 20.
137. 'What Is Gen Z?' McKinsey & Company, 20 March, 2023. https://www.mckinsey.com/featured-insights/mckinsey-explainers/what-is-gen-z.
138. Hannah Fry. 'A 'Failure to Launch': Why Young People Are Having Less Sex.' *Los Angeles Times*, 3 August, 2023. https://www.latimes.com/california/story/2023-08-03/young-adults-less-sex-gen-z-millennials-generations-parents-grandparents.
139. *2024 generative AI predictions report*, 56.
140. Viji Diane Kannan and Peter J Veazie. 'US Trends in Social Isolation, Social Engagement, and Companionship—Nationally and by Age, Sex, Race/Ethnicity, Family Income, and Work Hours, 2003–2020.' SSM—Population Health 21 (March 2023): 101331. https://doi.org/10.1016/j.ssmph.2022.101331.
141. 'Character.Ai Traffic Analytics, Ranking & Audience.' similarweb. Accessed 2 May, 2024. https://www.similarweb.com/website/character.ai/.
142. Arun Arora, Liz Harrison, Candace Lun Plotkin, Max Magni and Jennifer Stanley. 'Rebalancing Works: Omnichannel Is More Effective Than Traditional Sales Models Alone,' McKinsey & Company, 23 February, 2022.
143. Garrido-Samaniego, Gutiérrez-Arranz and San José-Cabezudo. 'Assessing the Impact of E-Procurement on the Structure of the Buying Centre.' 135–43.
144. Min. 'Artificial Intelligence in Supply Chain Management: Theory and Applications.' 13–39.
145. Jagjit Singh Srai and Harri Lorentz. 'Developing Design Principles for the Digitalisation of Purchasing and Supply Management.' 78–98.
146. 'How B2B Sales Can Benefit from Social Selling.' *Harvard Business Review*, 14 November, 2016. https://hbr.org/2016/11/84-of-b2b-sales-start-with-a-referral-not-a-salesperson.
147. Andy Hoar. *Death of a (B2B) Salesman* (Cambridge, MA: Forrester Research Inc. 2015), 3.
148. *State of Sales*, Fifth Edition, 10.
149. *State of Amazon 2016* (BloomReach, 2016) 2.
150. Hoar. *Death of a (B2B) Salesman*, 5.
151. Hoar. *Death of a (B2B) Salesman*, 2.
152. Hoar. *Death of a (B2B) Salesman*, 2.
153. Guilherme Cruz et al. *Future of B2B sales: The big reframe* (New York: McKinsey & Company, 2022), 15.

154. *The Growing Buyer-Seller Gap: Results of the 2018 Buyer Preferences Study* (Littleton, CO: CSO Insights, 2018), 7.
155. 'The New B2B Buying Process.' Gartner. Accessed 24 April, 2024. https://www.gartner.com.au/en/sales/insights/b2b-buying-journey.
156. Steward, Narus, Roehm and Ritz. 'From Transactions to Journeys and Beyond: The Evolution of B2B Buying Process Modeling.' 288–300.
157. Cruz et al. *Future of B2B sales*, 6.
158. *Revolutionizing Customer Service in Manufacturing: Research insights from nearly 300 manufacturing service leaders worldwide* (Salesforce, 2016), 15.
159. Eric Almquist, Jamie Cleghorn and Lori Sherer. 'What B2B Buyers Really Care About.' *Harvard Business Review*, 5 April, 2018. https://hbr.org/2018/03/the-b2b-elements-of-value.
160. *State of the Connected Customer*, Sixth edition. (Salesforce, 2023), 15.
161 Cruz et al. *Future of B2B sales*, 6.
162. Cruz et al. *Future of B2B sales*, 6.
163. Lucia Rahilly. 'Customer Experience: New Capabilities, New Audiences, New Opportunities.' McKinsey & Company, Volume 2 (June 2017).
164. *State of the Connected Customer*, Sixth edition, 14.
165. Cruz et al. *Future of B2B sales*, 6.
166. Arnau Bages-Amat, Liz Harrison, Dennis Spillecke and Jennifer Stanley. 'These Eight Charts Show How COVID-19 Has Changed B2B Sales Forever.' McKinsey & Company, 14 October, 2020. https://www.mckinsey.com/capabilities/growth-marketing-and-sales/our-insights/these-eight-charts-show-how-covid-19-has-changed-b2b-sales-forever.
167. *State of the Connected Customer*, Sixth edition, 12.
168. 'Omnichannel Marketing: Deliver Consistent, Personalized High-quality Customer Experience across Channels.' IBM. 8 March, 2015. https://www.ibm.com/blogs/insights-on-business/ibmix/omnichannel-marketing-new-vocabulary/.
169. Cruz et al. *Future of B2B sales*, 6.
170. Matt LoDolce and Jordan Brackenbury. 'Gartner Survey Finds Aligning Commercial Functions as Sales Leaders' Top Priority for 2023.' Gartner, 7 March, 2023. https://www.gartner.com/en/newsroom/press-releases/2023-03-07-gartner-survey-finds-aligning-commercial-functions-as-sales-leaders-top-priority-for-2023.
171. *State of Sales*, Fifth Edition, 10.
172. *State of the Connected Customer*, Sixth edition, 8, 19.
173. Cuevas. 'The Transformation of Professional Selling: Implications for Leading the Modern Sales Organization.' 198–208.
174. James Allen, Frederick F Reichheld, Barney Hamilton and Rob Markey. 'Closing the Delivery Gap.' Bain & Company. 2005.

175. Mark Lindwall. 'Why Don't Buyers Want to Meet with Your Salespeople?' Forrester Research Inc. 29 September, 2014. Accessed 13 June, 2018. https://go.forrester.com/blogs/14-09-29-why_dont_buyers_want_to_meet_with_your_salespeople/.
176. Christina Torode. 'Vendor Contract Management Key to Cutting Costs Through Renegotiation.' *SearchCIO*. 27 January, 2010. http://searchcio.techtarget.com/news/1379759/Vendor-contract-management-key-to-cutting-costs-through-renegotiation.
177. 'The New B2B Buying Process.' Gartner.
178. Dixon and McKenna. *The Jolt Effect*, 4.
179. Hank Barnes and Todd Berkowitz. *Tech Go-to-Market: Complex Technology Buying Dynamics Mandate Account-Based Strategies for TSPs* (Stamford: Gartner, 2016), 8.
180. Toman, Adamson and Gomez. 'The New B2B Sales Imperative.'
181. Kelly Blum and Gloria Omale. 'Gartner Reveals New B2B Sales Approach to Win in Today's Information Age.' Gartner, 29 July, 2019. https://www.gartner.com/en/newsroom/press-releases/2019-07-29-gartner-reveals-new-b2b-sales-approach-to-win-in-toda.
182. 'Buyer Enablement: Simplify Your Buyers' Purchase Process and Empower Sellers to Deliver Value.' Gartner. Accessed 24 April, 2024. https://www.gartner.com/en/sales/insights/buyer-enablement.
183. Toman, Adamson and Gomez. 'The New B2B Sales Imperative.'
184. Toman, Adamson and Gomez. 'The New B2B Sales Imperative.'
185. *State of the Connected Customer*, Sixth edition, 15.
186. Ian Bruce and Zachary Stone. 'Are B2B Buyers Cowards?' Forrester Research Inc. 26 January, 2024. https://www.forrester.com/blogs/are-b2b-buyers-cowards/.
187. Megan Headley. '2023 B2B Buying Disconnect: The Self-Serve Economy Is Prove It or Lose It.' *TrustRadius for Vendors*, 13 June, 2023. https://solutions.trustradius.com/vendor-blog/2023-b2b-disconnect/.
188. Joe Kevens. '5 Vendor Takeaways from the 2023 B2B Buying Disconnect Report.' *TrustRadius for Vendors*, 1 August, 2023. https://solutions.trustradius.com/vendor-blog/5-vendor-takeaways-from-the-2023-b2b-buying-disconnect-report/.
189. Janhavi Devdutt. 'Your Company Is Too Risk-Averse.' *BusinessDay NG*, 9 April, 2020. https://businessday.ng/hbr/article/your-company-is-too-risk-averse/.
190. Kerry Cunningham. 'Your Buyer Is a Group, Not a Person. What Are You Doing about It?' Forrester Research Inc. 12 July, 2021. https://www.forrester.com/blogs/your-buyer-is-a-group-not-a-person-what-are-you-doing-about-it/.
191. 'The New B2B Buying Process.' Gartner.

192. Beth Wasko. 'How B2B Technology Buyers Need You to Market to Them.' Gartner, 12 October, 2020. https://www.gartner.com/smarterwithgartner/how-to-market-to-b2b-technology-buyers.
193. 'The New B2B Buying Process.' Gartner.
194. *State of the Connected Customer,* Sixth edition, 15.
195. Karl Schmidt, Brent Adamson and Anna Bird. 'Making the Consensus Sale.' *Harvard Business Review,* 1 March, 2015. https://hbr.org/2015/03/making-the-consensus-sale.
196. Siu Kit Yeung, Tijen Yay and Gilad Feldman. 'Action and Inaction in Moral Judgments and Decisions: Meta-Analysis of Omission Bias Omission-Commission Asymmetries.' *Personality and Social Psychology Bulletin* 48, no. 10 (9 September, 2021): 1499–1515. https://doi.org/10.1177/01461672211042315.
197. George Brontén. 'Why Salesforce CRM Sucks for Salespeople and How to Fix It.' LinkedIn, 8 March, 2018. https://www.linkedin.com/pulse/why-salesforce-crm-sucks-salespeople-how-fix-george-bront%C3%A9n/.
198. LoDolce and Brackenbury. 'Gartner Survey Finds Aligning Commercial Functions as Sales Leaders' Top Priority for 2023.'
199. *State of the Connected Customer,* Sixth edition, 15.
200. *The Growing Buyer-Seller Gap,* 5.
201. *The Growing Buyer-Seller Gap,* 7.
202. *The Growing Buyer-Seller Gap,* 8.
203. *The Growing Buyer-Seller Gap,* 9.
204. Dixon and McKenna. *The Jolt Effect,* xiv.
205. *State of Sales,* Fifth Edition, 7.
206. 'Revenue Recap 2022.' Bravado.
207. *Driving Seller Behavior Change* (Gartner, 2023), 3.
208. 'Revenue Recap 2022.' Bravado.
209. Hoar. *Death of a (B2B) Salesman,* 2.
210. Mark Ellwood. *How sales reps spend their time,* (Toronto, Ontario: Pace Productivity Inc., 2016).
211. William C Moncrief. 'Ten Key Activities of Industrial Salespeople.' *Industrial Marketing Management* 15, no. 4 (November 1986): 309–17. https://doi.org/10.1016/0019-8501(86)90023-4.
212. Moncrief and Marshall. 'The Evolution of the Seven Steps of Selling.' 13–22.
213. Petri Parvinen, Jaakko Aspara, Sami Kajalo and Joel Hietanen. 'Sales Activity Systematization and Performance: Differences between Product and Service Firms.' *Journal of Business & Industrial Marketing* 28, no. 6 (26 July, 2013): 494–505. https://doi.org/10.1108/jbim-04-2013-0101.
214. Arun Sharma and Jagdish N Sheth. 'A Framework of Technology Mediation in Consumer Selling: Implications for Firms and Sales Management.' *Journal of*

Personal Selling & Sales Management 30, no. 2 (March 2010): 121–29. https://doi.org/10.2753/pss0885-3134300203.

215. Régis Lemmens, Bill Donaldson and Javier Marcos. *From selling to co-creating: New trends, practices and tools to upgrade your sales force.* (Amsterdam: BIS Publishers, 2014).
216. Cruz et al. *Future of B2B sales*, 28.
217. 'Understanding the Financial Health of Your Subscription Business.' Digital image. LinkedIn SlideShare. 14 October, 2014. https://www.slideshare.net/totango/understanding-the-financial-health-of-your-subscription-business.
218. Nick Toman, Brent Adamson and Cristina Gomez. 'The New B2B Sales Imperative.' *Harvard Business Review*, 15 September, 2020. https://hbr.org/2017/03/the-new-sales-imperative.
219. 'Outside Sales Representative Salary in Australia in 2023.' Payscale. Accessed 4 April, 2024. https://www.payscale.com/research/AU/Job=Outside_Sales_Representative/Salary.
220. 'The World's Trusted Currency Authority.' XE. Accessed 4 April, 2024. http://www.xe.com/.
221. Scott Santucci et al. *Uncovering the Hidden Cost of Sales Support* (Forrester Research Inc. 2009).
222. Trailer, Dickie, Schenk, Petrik et al. *Drawing Back the Bow*, 22.
223. *Sales Development: Models, Metrics, and Compensation Research*, 20.
224. Trish Bertuzzi. '355 B2B Sales Orgs Spill the Beans in 2016 Metrics Report.' Sales Hacker. 15 April, 2016. https://www.saleshacker.com/355-b2b-sales-orgs-spill-beans-2016-metrics-report/.
225. Ji-a Min. 'How Much Does It Cost to Replace a Sales Rep? $114,957!' Ideal. 9 February, 2016. http://ideal.com/how-much-does-it-cost-to-replace-a-sales-rep-114957/.
226. Benson Smith and Tony Rutigliano. 'Creating a Successful Sales Culture.' Gallup.com, 9 May, 2022. https://news.gallup.com/businessjournal/328/creating-successful-sales-culture.aspx.
227. Will Barron. 'How to Recognize B2B Sales Burnout.' Salesman.com. Accessed 24 April, 2024. https://salesman.com/678-how-to-recognise-b2b-sales-burnout-with-tim-clarke/.
228. Brandon Rigoni and Jim Asplund. 'Strengths-Based Employee Development: The Business Results.' Gallup.com, 7 July, 2016. https://www.gallup.com/workplace/236297/strengths-based-employee-development-business-results.aspx.
229. 'The Benefits of Employee Engagement.' Gallup.com, 20 June, 2013. https://www.gallup.com/workplace/236927/employee-engagement-drives-growth.aspx.

230. 'What Are Customer Expectations, and How Have They Changed?' Salesforce. Accessed 24 April, 2024. https://www.salesforce.com/resources/articles/customer-expectations/.
231. Mimi An. 'Buyers Speak out: How Sales Needs to Evolve.' HubSpot Blog, 7 April, 2016. https://blog.hubspot.com/sales/buyers-speak-out-how-sales-needs-to-evolve.
232. *The LinkedIn State of Sales Report 2020: Global Edition* (LinkedIn, 2020), 13.
233. 'Revenue Recap 2022.' Bravado. Accessed 24 April, 2024. https://bravado.co/lp/revenue-recap-2022/complete.
234. Cruz et al. *Future of B2B sales*, 27.
235. *Sales Development: Models, Metrics, and Compensation Research*, 24.
236. *State of Sales*, Fifth Edition, 18.
237. *State of Sales*, Fifth Edition, 19.
238. Michael Kleinaltenkamp, Katharina Prohl-Schwenke and Laura Elgeti. *Customer Success Management: Helping Business Customers Achieve Their Goals*. (Cham: Springer, 2023) vii.
239. Customer Success Association, 31 March, 2024. https://www.customersuccessassociation.com/.
240. Ori Entis. 'Top 18 Customer Success Conferences to Attend in 2024.' Staircase AI | Customer Intelligence Platform, 16 November, 2023. https://staircase.ai/blog/top-18-customer-success-conferences-to-attend-in-2024/.
241. PricewaterhouseCoopers. 'Building Customer Loyalty and Retention—PWC Customer Loyalty Survey 2023.' PwC. 24 Accessed April, 2024. https://www.pwc.com/us/en/services/consulting/business-transformation/library/building-customer-loyalty-guide.html.
242. Kleinaltenkamp, Prohl-Schwenke and Elgeti. *Customer Success Management*, 2.
243. Alexander Osterwalder et al. *The Invincible Company* (Hoboken, NJ: Wiley, 2020) 232–33.
244. Chet Holmes. *The Ultimate Sales Machine: Turbocharge Your Business with Relentless Focus on 12 Key Strategies* (Penguin Portfolio, 2008).
245. Devish Shah et al. 'The Path to Customer Centricity.' *Journal of Service Research* 9 no. 2 (November 2006): 113–24. https://doi.org/10.1177/1094670506294666.
246. Hughes, Chapnick, Block and Ray. 'What Is Customer-Centricity, and Why Does It Matter?'
247. Schmidt-Subramanian, Maxie and Samuel Stern. 'How to Make the Case That CX Transformation Is Both Important and Urgent.' Forrester Research Inc. Accessed 10 May, 2024. https://www.forrester.com/blogs/make-the-case-that-cx-transformation-is-both-important-and-urgent/.
248. Johannes Habel et al. 'When do customers perceive customer centricity? The role of a firm's and salespeople's customer orientation.' *Journal of Personal*

Selling & Sales Management 40 no. 1 (January 2020): 25–42. doi:10.1080/08853134.2019.1631174.
249. Gallup. 'Customer Centricity.'
250. Janessa Lantz. 'New Ecommerce Data: Ecommerce Customer Loyalty Is Rare.' RJ Metrics. 29 May, 2015. https://web.archive.org/web/20150910123903/https://rjmetrics.com/about/press-releases/new-ecommerce-data-ecommerce-customer-loyalty-is-rare.
251. Sarabjit Singh Baveja, Sharad Rastogi, Chris Zook, Randall S Hancock and Julian Chu. 'The Value of Online Customer Loyalty.' *Bain & Company, Inc.*: 2. Accessed 10 May, 2024.
252. 'Loyalty Marketing Best Practices.' CRM Best Practices—Customer Relationship Management. Accessed 10 May, 2024. http://www.crmtrends.com/loyalty.html.
253. Paul W Harris, Neil Bendle, Phillip Pfeifer and David Reibstein. *Marketing Metrics*. Cambridge, MA: Marketing Science Institute, 2000.
254. *The ROI from Marketing to Existing Online Customers*. San Jose, CA: Adobe Systems Incorporated, 2012.
255. Amy Gallo. 'The Value of Keeping the Right Customers.' *Harvard Business Review*, 5 November, 2014. https://hbr.org/2014/10/the-value-of-keeping-the-right-customers.
256. Landon and Gebhardt. 'Report: How a Customer Centric Culture Ties to Happier Employees.'
257. Hughes, Chapnick, Block and Ray. 'What Is Customer-Centricity, and Why Does It Matter?'
258. *The Disconnected Customer: What digital customer experience leaders teach us about reconnecting with customers* (Capgemini, 2017), 9.
259. Shah et al. 'The Path to Customer Centricity.'
260. Wolfgang Ulaga. 'The Journey towards Customer Centricity and Service Growth in B2B: A Commentary and Research Directions.' AMS Review 8, no. 1–2 (23 May, 2018): 80–83. https://doi.org/10.1007/s13162-018-0119-x.
261. Louis Columbus. 'Customer Experiences Define Success in a Digital-First World.' *Forbes*, 18 June, 2019. https://www.forbes.com/sites/louiscolumbus/2019/06/18/customer-experiences-define-success-in-a-digital-first-world/?sh=13f3424ad484.
262. Brandon Vigliarolo. 'Report: Unused Enterprise Software Is Costing Businesses a Fortune.' TechRepublic, 3 April, 2023. https://www.techrepublic.com/article/report-unused-enterprise-software-is-costing-businesses-a-fortune/.
263. Ebru Gökalp and Veronica Martinez. 'Digital Transformation Maturity Assessment: Development of the Digital Transformation Capability Maturity

Model.' *International Journal of Production Research* 60, no. 20 (26 October, 2021): 6282–302. https://doi.org/10.1080/00207543.2021.1991020.

264. Holmes. *The Ultimate Sales Machine*, 69.
265. Jim Davis. 'Short Take: Blackberry Wireless Email Device Debuts.' CNET, 20 January, 1999. https://web.archive.org/web/20130522101747/http://news.cnet.com/short-take-blackberry-wireless-email-device-debuts/2110-1040_3-220388.html.
266. Siyam Adit. 'The Importance of Evolving Product Design: A Case Study of BlackBerry's Rise and Fall.' Medium, 30 April, 2023. https://bootcamp.uxdesign.cc/the-importance-of-evolving-product-design-a-case-study-of-blackberrys-rise-and-fall-5c21ceaf395a.
267. 'Blackberry (BB)—Market Capitalization.' CompaniesMarketCap.com. Accessed 30 March, 2024. https://companiesmarketcap.com/blackberry/marketcap/.
268. Jessi Hempel. 'Smartphone Wars.' CNNMoney, 17 August, 2009. https://money.cnn.com/2009/08/12/technology/blackberry_research_in_motion.fortune/index.htm.
269. Felix Richter. 'Infographic: The Terminal Decline of BlackBerry.' Statista Daily Data, 26 June, 2017. https://www.statista.com/chart/8180/blackberrys-smartphone-market-share/.
270. Adit. 'The Importance of Evolving Product Design.'
271. Sean Silcoff, Jacquie McNish and Steve Ladurantaye. 'How Blackberry Blew It: The Inside Story.' The Globe and Mail, 27 September, 2013. https://www.theglobeandmail.com/report-on-business/the-inside-story-of-why-blackberry-is-failing/article14563602/.
272. Silcoff, McNish and Ladurantaye. 'How Blackberry Blew It: The Inside Story.'
273. Juliette Garside. 'BlackBerry: How Business Went Sour.' *The Guardian*, 13 August, 2013. https://www.theguardian.com/technology/2013/aug/13/blackberry-how-business-went-sour.
274. 'BB's vs. Market Share Relative to Its Competitors, as of Q1 2024.' CSIMarket, 30 March, 2024. https://csimarket.com/stocks/competitionSEG2.php?code=BB.
275. 'Blackberry (BB)—Market Capitalization.' CompaniesMarketCap.com.
276. Gallo. 'The Value of Keeping the Right Customers.'
277. Shah et al. 'The Path to Customer Centricity.'
278. Ellwood. *How Sales Reps Spend Their Time*.
279. Gökalp and Martinez. 'Digital Transformation Maturity Assessment: Development of the Digital Transformation Capability Maturity Model.' 6282–302.
280. Steward, Narus, Roehm and Ritz. 'From Transactions to Journeys and Beyond: The Evolution of B2B Buying Process Modeling.' 288–300.

281. Paul Hague and Matthew Harrison. 'Market Segmentation in B2B Markets | B2B Segmentation.' B2B International. Accessed 8 April, 2024. https://www.b2binternational.com/publications/b2b-segmentation-research/.
282. Wasko. 'How B2B Technology Buyers Need You to Market to Them.'
283. 'Deep Sales: LinkedIn Sales Solutions.' LinkedIn. Accessed 30 May, 2024. https://business.linkedin.com/sales-solutions/deep-sales.
284. 'Australian Industry, 2021–22 Financial Year.' Australian Bureau of Statistics. Accessed 28 April, 2024. https://www.abs.gov.au/statistics/industry/industry-overview/australian-industry/latest-release.
285. Kelly Xie. 'Small Business Owners Shift Investment from Customer Acquisition to Customer Engagement—New Report by Manta and BIA/Kelsey.' BIA Advisory Services, 2 April, 2014. https://www.bia.com/small-business-owners-shift-investment-from-customer-acquisition-to-customer-engagement-new-report-by-manta-and-biakelsey/.
286. Hawkins. *The Future of the Sales Profession*, 78–98.
287. 'Outside Sales Representative Salary in Australia in 2023 | Payscale.' Payscale.
288. Shah et al. 'The Path to Customer Centricity.'
289. *State of the Connected Customer*, Sixth edition, 20.
290. Holmes. *The Ultimate Sales Machine.*
291. Aaron Ross and Marylou Tyler. *Predictable Revenue: Turn your business into a sales machine with the $100 million best practices of Salesforce.com.* (West Hollywood, CA: Pebblestorm Press, 2012).
292. Julie Schwartz. 'Like Fine Wine, ABM Improves with Age.' ITSMA, 18 August, 2017. https://web.archive.org/web/20200317001405/https://www.itsma.com/like-fine-wine-abm-improves-with-age/.
293. Ross and Tyler. *Predictable Revenue.*
294. Andris A Zoltners, P K Sinha and Sally E Lorimer. 'The Growing Power of inside Sales.' *Harvard Business Review*, 29 July, 2013. https://hbr.org/2013/07/the-growing-power-of-inside-sa.
295. Josiane Feigon. '10 Reasons Why Inside Sales Will Displace Field Sales Teams by 2015.' PointClear, 17 July, 2017. https://www.pointclear.com/bid/117119/10-Reasons-Why-Inside-Sales-Will-Displace-Field-Sales-Teams-by-2015.
296. *State of Sales Enablement 2022*, 4.
297. *State of Sales Enablement 2022*, 7.
298. *2017 CSO Insights Sales Enablement Optimization Study* (Littleton, CO: CSO Insights, 2017), 8.
299. *Sales Enablement Grows Up: The 2018 Sales Enablement Report* (Littleton, CO: CSO Insights, 2018), 36.
300. Greg Iacurci. '2022 Was the 'Real Year of the Great Resignation,' Says Economist.' CNBC, 1 February, 2023. https://www.cnbc.com/2023/02/01/why-2022-was-the-real-year-of-the-great-resignation.html.

301. *Sales Development: Models, Metrics, and Compensation Research*, 24.
302. Masahiko Aoki. *Information, incentives, and bargaining in the Japanese economy* (Cambridge: Cambridge University Press, 1996).
303. Louise Story. 'Facebook Is Marketing Your Brand Preferences (with Your Permission).' *The New York Times*, 7 November, 2007. https://www.nytimes.com/2007/11/07/technology/07iht-07adco.8230630.html.
304. 'The Most Powerful Ecosystem-Led Growth Platform.' Crossbeam, 23 April, 2024. https://www.crossbeam.com/.
305. Paul Petrone. 'Hidden Allies Defined—and How They Can Help You Win Deals.' LinkedIn, 16 April, 2024. https://www.linkedin.com/business/sales/blog/strategy/hidden-allies-in-sales-what-they-are-how-they-can-help-you-win-deals.
306. 'Jobs to Be Done.' Christensen Institute, 13 October, 2017. https://www.christenseninstitute.org/jobs-to-be-done/.
307. Gabriel Patrick. '10 Largest Tire Manufacturers.' Verified Market Research, 4 April, 2023. https://www.verifiedmarketresearch.com/blog/largest-tire-manufacturers/.
308. Emad. 'Michelin: Tires-as-a-Service.' Technology and Operations Management, 17 November, 2016. https://d3.harvard.edu/platform-rctom/submission/michelin-tires-as-a-service/.
309. Emad. 'Michelin: Tires-as-a-Service.'
310. 'Atlassian Announces Fourth Quarter and Fiscal Year 2023 Results.' Atlassian. 3 August, 2023. https://s28.q4cdn.com/541786762/files/doc_financials/2023/q4/TEAM-Q4-2023-Earnings-Release.pdf.
311. Wasko. 'How B2B Technology Buyers Need You to Market to Them.'
312. Harri Terho and Joona Keränen. 'Three Ways to Sell Value in B2B Markets.' MIT Sloan Management Review, 1 September, 2021. https://sloanreview.mit.edu/article/three-ways-to-sell-value-b2b-markets/.
313. Terho and Keränen. 'Three Ways to Sell Value in B2B Markets.'
314. Bob Tinker, Tae Hea Nahm and Fernando Pizarro. *Survival to Thrival: Building the enterprise startup* (Herndon, VA: Mascot Books, 2018): 42.
315. Tinker, Nahm and Pizarro. *Survival to Thrival*, 42.
316. 'Global Culture Survey 2021.' PricewaterhouseCoopers, 2021. https://www.pwc.com/gx/en/issues/upskilling/global-culture-survey-2021.html.
317. Carolyn Dewar and Reed Doucette. 'Culture: 4 Keys to Why It Matters.' McKinsey & Company, 27 March, 2018. https://www.mckinsey.com/capabilities/people-and-organizational-performance/our-insights/the-organization-blog/culture-4-keys-to-why-it-matters.

318. 'Core beliefs and culture: Chairman's survey findings.' Deloitte, 2012. https://www2.deloitte.com/content/dam/Deloitte/global/Documents/About-Deloitte/gx-core-beliefs-and-culture.pdf.
319. Shilpa Ahuja. 'More Than One-Third of Workers Would Pass on Perfect Job If Corporate Culture Was Not a Fit, Survey Finds.' RobertHalf, 27 November, 2018. https://press.roberthalf.com/2018-11-27-More-Than-One-Third-Of-Workers-Would-Pass-On-Perfect-Job-If-Corporate-Culture-Was-Not-A-Fit-Survey-Finds.
320. 'Culture over Cash? Glassdoor Multi-Country Survey Finds More than Half of Employees Prioritize Workplace Culture over Salary.' PR Newswire, 11 July, 2019. https://www.prnewswire.com/news-releases/culture-over-cash-glassdoor-multi-country-survey-finds-more-than-half-of-employees-prioritize-workplace-culture-over-salary-300883059.html.
321. Nate Dvorak and Ryan Pendell. 'Culture Wins by Attracting the Top 20% of Candidates.' Gallup.com, 20 March, 2024. https://www.gallup.com/workplace/237368/culture-wins-attracting-top-candidates.aspx.
322. Elizabeth Medina. *Job Satisfaction and Employee Turnover Intention: What Does Organizational Culture Have To Do With It?* (Columbia University, 2012). https://web.archive.org/web/20141208212237/http://qmss.columbia.edu/storage/Medina%20Elizabeth.pdf.
323. Dr Pragya Agarwal. 'How to Create a Positive Workplace Culture.' *Forbes*, 20 February, 2024. https://www.forbes.com/sites/pragyaagarwaleurope/2018/08/29/how-to-create-a-positive-work-place-culture/.
324. Allan Watkinson and Rohit Kar. 'Organizational Culture: What Leaders Need to Know.' Gallup.com, 18 October, 2023. https://www.gallup.com/workplace/471968/culture-transformation-leaders-need-know.aspx.
325. '2022 Annual Report.' Wells Fargo & Company, 2023, 30. https://www08.wellsfargomedia.com/assets/pdf/about/investor-relations/annual-reports/2022-annual-report.pdf.
326. Bethany McLean. 'How Wells Fargo's Cutthroat Corporate Culture Allegedly Drove Bankers to Fraud.' Vanity Fair, 31 May, 2017. http://www.vanityfair.com/news/2017/05/wells-fargo-corporate-culture-fraud.
327. McLean. 'How Wells Fargo's Cutthroat Corporate Culture Allegedly Drove Bankers to Fraud.'
328. McLean. 'How Wells Fargo's Cutthroat Corporate Culture Allegedly Drove Bankers to Fraud.'
329. McLean. 'How Wells Fargo's Cutthroat Corporate Culture Allegedly Drove Bankers to Fraud.'
330. Shah et al. 'The Path to Customer Centricity.'
331. Smith and Rutigliano. 'Creating a Successful Sales Culture.'

332. 'Loyalty Marketing Best Practices.' CRM Best Practices—Customer Relationship Management. Accessed May 10, 2024. http://www.crmtrends.com/loyalty.html.
333. Bryan Hochstein, Clay M Voorhees, Alexander B Pratt, Deva Rangarajan, Duane M Nagel and Vijay Mehrotra. 'Customer Success Management, Customer Health, and Retention in B2B Industries.' *International Journal of Research in Marketing* 40, no. 4 (December 2023): 912–32. https://doi.org/10.1016/j.ijresmar.2023.09.002.
334. Bryan Hochstein, Clay M Voorhees, Alexander B Pratt, Deva Rangarajan, Duane M Nagel and Vijay Mehrotra. 'Customer Success Management, Customer Health, and Retention in B2B Industries.'
335. Amanda Chordas. 'Forrester's Planning Assumptions Reveal Key Trends That Will Impact B2B Marketing, Sales, and Product Leaders in 2022.' Forrester Research Inc. 13 October, 2021. https://investor.forrester.com/news-releases/news-release-details/forresters-planning-assumptions-reveal-key-trends-will-impact.
336. *HubSpot Sales Trends Report* (HubSpot, 2024) 27.
337. Nitin Nohria, William Joyce and Bruce Roberson. 'What Really Works.' *Harvard Business Review*, July 2003. https://hbr.org/2003/07/what-really-works.
338. 'SalesTribe Podcast with Monday.Com.' Vimeo, 2022. https://vimeo.com/677073714.
339. E Scott Reckard. 'Wells Fargo's Pressure-Cooker Sales Culture Comes at a Cost.' *Los Angeles Times*, 21 December, 2013. https://www.latimes.com/business/la-fi-wells-fargo-sale-pressure-20131222-story.html.
340. McLean. 'How Wells Fargo's Cutthroat Corporate Culture Allegedly Drove Bankers to Fraud.'
341. Reckard. 'Wells Fargo's Pressure-Cooker Sales Culture Comes at a Cost.'
342. McLean. 'How Wells Fargo's Cutthroat Corporate Culture Allegedly Drove Bankers to Fraud.'
343. Matt Levine. 'Wells Fargo Opened a Couple Million Fake Accounts.' Bloomberg.com, 9 September, 2016. https://www.bloomberg.com/view/articles/2016-09-09/wells-fargo-opened-a-couple-million-fake-accounts.
344. Michael Harris and Bill Tayler. 'Don't Let Metrics Undermine Your Business.' *Harvard Business Review*, 27 October, 2019. https://hbr.org/2019/09/dont-let-metrics-undermine-your-business.
345. Chad Albrecht and Steve Marley. *The Future of Sales Compensation* (Evanston, IL: ZS Associates, 2016).
346. Ramon Elzinga. '4 Things We've Learned from Running a Zero Commission Sales Model.' LinkedIn. 2 August, 2017. https://www.linkedin.com/pulse/4-things-weve-learned-from-running-zero-commission-sales-elzinga/.

347. Michael J Boyle. 'How Did the Field of Accounting Evolve?' Investopedia, 27 April, 2024. https://www.investopedia.com/articles/08/accounting-history.asp.
348. Boyle. 'How Did the Field of Accounting Evolve?'
349. H David Sherman and S David Young. 'Where Financial Reporting Still Falls Short.' *Harvard Business Review*, August 2016. https://hbr.org/2016/07/where-financial-reporting-still-falls-short.
350. Robert S Kaplan and David P Norton. 'The Balanced Scorecard-Measures That Drive Performance.' *Harvard Business Review*, 1992. https://hbr.org/1992/01/the-balanced-scorecard-measures-that-drive-performance-2.
351. Kaplan and Norton. 'The Balanced Scorecard-Measures That Drive Performance.'
352. Kaplan and Norton. 'The Balanced Scorecard-Measures That Drive Performance.'
353. Kaplan and Norton. 'The Balanced Scorecard-Measures That Drive Performance.'
354. Wasko. 'How B2B Technology Buyers Need You to Market to Them.'
355. Dixon and McKenna. *The Jolt Effect*, xiv.
356. Bravado. 'Bravado on LinkedIn: #REVENUERECAP2023.'
357. *Sales Development: Models, Metrics, and Compensation Research*, 24.